Solutions Manual

for use with

Fundamentals of
Corporate Finance

Sixth Edition

Richard A. Brealey
London Business School

Stewart C. Myers
Massachusetts Institute of Technology

Alan J. Marcus
Boston College

Prepared By
Peter Crabb
Northwest Nazarene University

McGraw-Hill Irwin

Boston   Burr Ridge, IL   Dubuque, IA   New York   San Francisco   St. Louis
Bangkok   Bogotá   Caracas   Kuala Lumpur   Lisbon   London   Madrid   Mexico City
Milan   Montreal   New Delhi   Santiago   Seoul   Singapore   Sydney   Taipei   Toronto

Solutions Manual for use with
FUNDAMENTALS OF CORPORATE FINANCE
Richard A. Brealey, Stewart C. Myers, and Alan J. Marcus

Published by McGraw-Hill/Irwin, an imprint of The McGraw-Hill Companies, Inc., 1221 Avenue of the Americas, New York, NY 10020. Copyright © 2009, 2007, 2004, 2001, 1999, 1995 by The McGraw-Hill Companies, Inc. All rights reserved.

1 2 3 4 5 6 7 8 9 0 QPD/QPD 0 9 8

ISBN: 978-0-07-726596-0
MHID: 0-07-726596-3

www.mhhe.com

Table of Contents

Solutions to Chapter 1

Goals and Governance of the Firm

1. Investment decisions:

   - Should a new computer be purchased?
   - Should the firm develop a new drug?
   - Should the firm shut down an unprofitable factory?

   Financing decisions:

   - Should the firm borrow money from a bank or sell bonds?
   - Should the firm issue preferred stock or common stock?
   - Should the firm buy or lease a new machine that it is committed to acquiring?

2. A corporation is a distinct legal entity, separate from its owners (i.e., stockholders). The stockholders have limited liability for the debts and other obligations of the corporation. The liability of the individual stockholder is generally limited to the amount of the stockholder's investment in the shares of the corporation. Creation of a corporation is a legal process that requires the preparation of articles of incorporation. A distinctive feature of the typical large corporation is the separation between the ownership of the business and the management of the business. On the other hand, a sole proprietorship is not distinct from the individual who operates the business. Therefore, the sole proprietor (i.e., the individual) directly owns the business assets, manages the business, and is personally responsible for the debts of the sole proprietorship.

3. The key advantage of separating ownership and management in a large corporation is that it gives the corporation permanence. The corporation continues to exist if managers are replaced or if stockholders sell their ownership interests to other investors. The corporation's permanence is an essential characteristic in allowing corporations to obtain the large amounts of financing required by many business entities.

4. The individual stockholders of a corporation (i.e., the owners) are legally distinct from the corporation itself, which is a separate legal entity. Consequently, the stockholders are not personally liable for the debts of the corporation; the stockholders' liability for the debts of the corporation is limited to the investment each stockholder has made in the shares of the corporation.

5. *Double taxation* means that a corporation's income is taxed first at the corporate tax rate, and then, when the income is distributed to shareholders as dividends, the income is taxed again at the shareholder's personal tax rate.

6. a. A share of stock   financial

    b. A personal IOU   financial

    c. A trademark   real

    d. A truck   real

    e. Undeveloped land   real

    f. The balance in the firm's checking account   financial

    g. An experienced and hardworking sales force   real

    h. A bank loan agreement   financial

7. a, c, d.

8. A corporation might cut its labor force dramatically which could reduce immediate expenses and increase profits in the short term. Over the long term, however, the firm might not be able to serve its customers properly or it might alienate its remaining workers; if so, future profits will decrease, and the stock price, and the market value of the firm, will decrease in anticipation of these problems.

Similarly, a corporation can boost profits over the short term by using less costly materials even if this reduces the quality of the product. Once customers catch on, sales will decrease and profits will fall in the future. The stock price will fall.

The moral of these examples is that, because stock prices reflect present *and future* profitability, the corporation should not necessarily sacrifice future prospects for short-term gains.

9. Agency costs are caused by conflicts of interest between managers and shareholders, who are the owners of the firm. In most large corporations, the principals (i.e., the stockholders) hire the agents (i.e., managers) to act on behalf of the principals in making many of the major decisions affecting the corporation and its owners. However, it is unrealistic to believe that the agents' actions will always be consistent with the objectives that the stockholders would like to achieve. Managers may choose not to work hard enough, to over-compensate themselves, to engage in empire building, to over-consume perquisites, and so on.

Corporations use numerous arrangements in an attempt to ensure that managers' actions are consistent with stockholders' objectives. Agency costs can be mitigated by 'carrots,' linking the manager's compensation to the success of the firm, or by 'sticks,' creating an environment in which poorly performing managers can be removed.

10. Takeover defenses increase the target firm's agency problems. One of the mechanisms that stockholders rely on to mitigate agency problems is the threat that an underperforming company (with an underperforming management) will be taken over by another company. If management is protected against takeovers by takeover defenses, it is more likely that managers will act in their own best interest, rather than in the interests of the firm and its stockholders.

11. Both capital budgeting decisions and capital structure decisions are long-term financial decisions. However, capital budgeting decisions are long-term investment decisions, while capital structure decisions are long-term financing decisions. Capital structure decisions essentially involve selecting between equity financing and long-term debt financing.

12. A bank loan is not a 'real' asset that can be used to produce goods or services. Rather, a bank loan is a claim on cash flows generated by other activities, which makes it a financial asset.

13. Investment in research and development creates 'know-how.' This knowledge is then used to produce goods and services, which makes it a real asset.

14. The responsibilities of the treasurer include the following: supervise cash management, raising capital, and banking relationships.

    The controller's responsibilities include: supervise accounting, preparation of financial statements, and tax matters.

    The CFO of a large corporation supervises both the treasurer and the controller. The CFO is responsible for large-scale corporate planning and financial policy.

15. Limited liability is generally advantageous to large corporations. Large corporations would not be able to obtain financing from thousands or even millions of shareholders if those shareholders were not protected by the fact that the corporation is a distinct legal entity, conferring the benefit of limited liability on its shareholders. On the other hand, lenders do not view limited liability as advantageous to them. In some situations, lenders are not willing to lend to a corporation without personal guarantees from shareholders, promising repayment of a loan in the event that the corporation does not have the financial resources to repay the loan. Typically, these situations involve small corporations, with only a few shareholders; often these corporations can obtain debt financing only if the shareholders provide these personal guarantees.

16. The stock price reflects the value of both current and future dividends that the shareholders expect to receive. In contrast, profits reflect performance in the current year only. Profit maximizers may try to improve this year's profits at the expense of future profits. But stock price maximizers will take account of the entire stream of cash flows that the firm can generate. They are more apt to be forward looking.

17. a. This action might appear, superficially, to be a grant to *former* employees and thus not consistent with value maximization. However, such 'benevolent' actions might enhance the firm's reputation as a good place to work, might result in greater loyalty on the part of current employees, and might contribute to the firm's recruiting efforts. Therefore, from a broader perspective, the action may be value maximizing.

b. The reduction in dividends, in order to allow increased reinvestment, can be consistent with maximization of current market value. If the firm has attractive investment opportunities, and wants to save the expenses associated with issuing new shares to the public, then it could make sense to reduce the dividend in order to free up capital for the additional investments.

c. The corporate jet would have to generate benefits in excess of its costs in order to be considered stock-price enhancing. Such benefits might include time savings for executives, and greater convenience and flexibility in travel.

d. Although the drilling appears to be a bad bet, with a low probability of success, the project may be value maximizing if a successful outcome (although unlikely) is potentially sufficiently profitable. A one in five chance of success is acceptable if the payoff conditional on finding an oil field is ten times the costs of exploration.

18. a. Increased market share can be an inappropriate goal if it requires reducing prices to such an extent that the firm is harmed financially. Increasing market share *can* be part of a well-reasoned strategy, but one should always remember that market share is not a goal in itself. The owners of the firm want managers to maximize the value of their investment in the firm.

b. Minimizing costs can also conflict with the goal of value maximization. For example, suppose a firm receives a large order for a product. The firm should be willing to pay overtime wages and to incur other costs in order to fulfill the order, as long as it can sell the additional product at a price greater than those costs. Even though costs per unit of output increase, the firm still comes out ahead if it agrees to fill the order.

c. A policy of underpricing any competitor can lead the firm to sell goods at a price lower than the price that would maximize market value. Again, in some situations, this strategy might make sense, but it should not be the ultimate goal of the firm. It should be evaluated with respect to its effect on firm value.

d. Expanding profits is a poorly defined goal of the firm. The text gives three reasons:

(i) There may be a trade-off between accounting profits in one year versus accounting profits in another year. For example, writing off a bad investment may reduce this year's profits but increase profits in future years. Which year's profits should be maximized?

(ii) Investing more in the firm can increase profits, even if the increase in profits is insufficient to justify the additional investment. In this case the increased investment increases profits, but can reduce shareholder wealth.

(iii) Profits can be affected by accounting rules, so a decision that increases profits using one set of rules may reduce profits using another.

19. The contingency arrangement aligns the interests of the lawyer with those of the client. Neither makes any money unless the case is won. If a client is unsure about the skill or integrity of the lawyer, this arrangement can make sense. First, the lawyer has an incentive

to work hard. Second, if the lawyer turns out to be incompetent and loses the case, the client will not have to pay a bill. Third, the lawyer will not be tempted to accept a very weak case simply to generate bills. Fourth, there is no incentive for the lawyer to charge for hours not really worked. Once a client is more comfortable with the lawyer, and is less concerned with potential agency problems, a fee-for-service arrangement might make more sense.

20. The national chain has a great incentive to impose quality control on all of its outlets. If one store serves its customers poorly, that can result in lost future sales. The reputation of each restaurant in the chain depends on the quality in all the other stores. In contrast, if Joe's serves mostly passing travelers who are unlikely to show up again, unsatisfied customers pose a far lower cost. They are unlikely to be seen again anyway, so reputation is not a valuable asset.

    The important distinction is *not* that Joe has one outlet while the national chain has many. Instead, it is the likelihood of repeat relations with customers and the value of reputation. If Joe's were located in the center of town instead of on the highway, one would expect his clientele to be repeat customers from town. He would then have the same incentive to establish a good reputation as the chain.

21. Traders can earn huge bonuses when their trades are very profitable, but if the trades lose large sums, as in the case of Barings Bank, the trader's exposure is limited. This asymmetry can create an incentive to take big risks with the firm's (i.e., the shareholders') money. This is an agency problem.

22. a. A fixed salary means that compensation is (at least in the short run) independent of the firm's success.

    b. A salary linked to profits ties the employee's compensation to this measure of the success of the firm. However, profits are not a wholly reliable way to measure the success of the firm. The text points out that profits are subject to differing accounting rules, and reflect only the current year's situation rather than the long-run prospects of the firm.

    c. A salary that is paid partly in the form of the company's shares means that the manager earns the most when the shareholders' wealth is maximized. This is therefore most likely to align the interests of managers and shareholders.

23. Even if a shareholder could monitor and improve managers' performance, and thereby increase the value of the firm, the payoff would be small, since the ownership share in a large corporation is very small. For example, if you own $10,000 of GM stock and can increase the value of the firm by 5 percent, a very ambitious goal, you benefit by only: $0.05 \times \$10,000 = \$500$

    In contrast, a bank that has a multimillion-dollar loan outstanding to the firm has a large stake in making sure that the loan can be repaid. It is clearly worthwhile for the bank to spend considerable resources on monitoring the firm.

24. Clear and comprehensive financial reports provide essential information to the numerous shareholders of large corporations, allowing the shareholders to monitor the performance of the corporation and its board of directors and management. The debacles at WorldCom and Enron were directly related to a lack of clear and comprehensive financial reports.

25. While the answer to this question is largely a matter of opinion, and there are significant numbers of "commentators" on each side of the issue, the perspective of the authors is that the Enron and WorldCom debacles are a matter of a few "bad apples" rather than a symptom of systematic failure. The mechanisms discussed in the text (such as takeovers, compensation plans, and legal and regulatory requirements) for ameliorating agency problems generally contribute to effective corporate governance. On the other hand, commentators on both sides of the issue would likely welcome improvements in these mechanisms, such as those required by the Sarbanes-Oxley law.

26. Long-term relationships can encourage ethical behavior. If you know that you will engage in business with another party on a repeated basis, you will be less likely to take advantage of your business partner if an opportunity to do so arises. When people say "what goes around comes around," they recognize that the way they deal with their associates will influence the way their associates treat them. When relationships are short-lived, however, the temptation to be unfair is greater since there is less reason to fear reprisal, and less opportunity for fair dealing to be reciprocated.

27. As the text notes, the first step in doing well is doing good by your customers. Businesses cannot prosper for long if they do not provide to their customers the products and services they desire. In addition, reputation effects often make it in the firm's own interest to act ethically toward its business partners and employees since the firm's ability to make deals and to hire skilled labor depends on its reputation for dealing fairly.

    In some circumstances, when firms have incentives to act in a manner inconsistent with the public interest, taxes or fees can align private and public interests. For example, taxes or fees charged on pollution make it more costly for firms to pollute, thereby affecting the firm's decisions regarding activities that cause pollution. Other "incentives" used by governments to align private interests with public interests include: legislation to provide for worker safety and product, or consumer, safety, building code requirements enforced by local governments, and pollution and gasoline mileage requirements imposed on automobile manufacturers.

28. Some customers might consider this practice unethical. They might view the firm as gouging its customers during heat waves. On the other hand, the firm might try to convince customers that this practice allows it to charge *lower* prices in cooler periods, and that over long periods of time, prices even out. Whether customers and firms have an "implicit contract" to charge and pay stable prices is something of a cultural issue.

Solutions to Chapter 2

Financial Markets and Institutions

1. The story of Apple Computer provides three examples of financing sources: equity investments by the founders of the company, trade credit from suppliers and investments by venture capitalists. Other sources include reinvested earnings of the company and loans from banks and other financial institutions.

2. Yes. When the corporation retains cash and reinvests in the firm's operations, that cash is saved and invested on behalf of the firm's shareholders. The reinvested cash could have been paid out to the shareholders. By not taking the cash, these investors have reinvested their savings in the corporation. Individuals can also save and invest in a corporation by lending to, or buying shares in, a financial intermediary such as a bank or mutual fund that subsequently invests in the corporation.

3. Separation of ownership and control for public corporations means that the ultimate owners of the corporation are not its managers. These same managers will consider their own interest as well as shareholders when making decisions. This creates agency problems.

4. *Money markets*, where short-term debt instruments are bought and sold.

    Foreign-exchange markets. Most trading takes place in over-the-counter transactions between the major international banks.

    Commodities markets for agricultural commodities, fuels (including crude oil and natural gas) and metals (such as gold, silver and platinum).

    Derivatives markets, where options and other derivative instruments are traded.

5. Buy shares in a mutual fund. Mutual funds pool savings from many individual investors and then invest in a diversified portfolio of securities. Each individual investor then owns a proportionate share of the mutual fund's portfolio.

6. Defined contribution pension plans provide three key advantages as vehicles for retirement savings:

    - Professional management.
    - Diversification at low cost.
    - Pension plan contributions are tax-deductible, and taxes on the earnings in the fund are deferred until the fund's assets are distributed to retired employees.

7. Yes, an insurance company is a financial intermediary. Insurance companies sell policies and then invest part of the proceeds in corporate bonds and stocks and in direct loans to corporations. The returns from these investments help pay for losses incurred by policyholders.

8. The largest institutional investors in bonds are insurance companies. Other major institutional investors in bonds are pension funds, mutual funds, and banks and other savings institutions. The largest institutional investors in shares are pension funds, mutual funds, and insurance companies.

9. The major functions of financial markets and institutions in a modern financial system are:
    *   Channel savings to real investment: The savings of individual investors are made available for real investments by corporations and other business entities by way of financial markets and institutions.
    *   Transporting cash across time: Savers can save money now to be withdrawn and spent at a later time, while borrowers can borrow cash today, in effect spending today income to be earned in the future.
    *   Risk transfer and diversification: Insurance companies allow individuals and business firms to transfer risk to the insurance company, for a price. Financial institutions such as mutual funds allow an investor to reduce risk by diversification of the investor's holdings.
    *   Liquidity: Financial markets and institutions provide investors with the ability to exchange an asset for cash on short notice, with minimal loss of value. A deposit in a bank savings account earns interest, but can be withdrawn at almost any time. A share of stock in a publicly traded corporation can be sold at virtually any time.
    *   Payment mechanism: Financial institutions provide alternatives to cash payments, such as checks and credit cards.
    *   Information provided by financial markets: Financial markets reveal information about important economic and financial variables such as commodity prices, interest rates and company values (i.e., stock prices).

10. The market price of gold can be observed from transactions in commodity markets. For example, gold is traded on the Comex division of the New York Mercantile Exchange. Look up the price of gold and compare it to $1500/6 = $250 per ounce.

11. Financial markets provide extensive data that can be useful to financial managers. Examples include:
    *   Prices for agricultural commodities, metals and fuels.
    *   Interest rates for a wide array of loans and securities, including money market instruments, corporate and U.S. government bonds, and interest rates for loans and investments in foreign countries.
    *   Foreign exchange rates.
    *   Stock prices and overall market values for publicly listed corporations are determined by trading on the New York Stock Exchange, NASDAQ or stock markets in London, Frankfurt, Tokyo, etc.

12. When stockholders have access to modern financial markets and institutions, stockholders can readily avail themselves of the functions served by these markets and institutions: for example, transporting cash across time, risk transfer and diversification, liquidity, and access to payment mechanisms. Therefore, the objective of value maximization makes sense for stockholders because this is the only task stockholders require of corporate management. In addition, the financial markets provide the pricing mechanism and the information stockholders require in order to assess the performance of the firm's management in achieving this objective.

13. The opportunity cost of capital is the expected rate of return offered by the best alternative investment opportunity. When the firm makes capital investments on behalf of the owners of the firm (i.e., the shareholders), it must consider the shareholders' other investment opportunities. The firm should not invest unless the expected return on investment at least equals the expected return the shareholders could obtain on their own by investing in the financial markets.

   The opportunity cost of capital for a safe investment is the rate of return that shareholders could earn if they invested in risk-free securities, for example in U.S. Treasuries.

14. a. False. Financing could flow through an intermediary, for example.

    b. False. Investors can buy shares in a private corporation, for example.

    c. True. The largest source of financing for insurance companies is the sale of insurance policies. Insurance companies then invest a significant portion of the proceeds in corporate debt and equities.

    d. False. There is no centralized FOREX exchange. Foreign exchange trading takes place in the over-the-counter market.

    e. False. The opportunity cost of capital is the expected rate of return that shareholders can earn in the financial markets on investments with the same risk as the firm's capital investments.

    f. False. The cost of capital is an *opportunity* cost determined by expected rates of return in the financial markets. The opportunity cost of capital for risky investments is normally higher than the firm's borrowing rate.

15. Liquidity is important because investors want to be able to convert their investments into cash quickly and easily when it becomes necessary or desirable to do so. Should personal circumstances or investment considerations lead an investor to conclude that it is desirable to sell a particular investment, the investor prefers to be able to sell the investment quickly and at a price that does not require a significant discount from market value.

    Liquidity is also important to mutual funds. When the mutual fund's shareholders want to redeem their shares, the mutual fund is often forced to sell its securities. In order to maintain liquidity for its shareholders, the mutual fund requires liquid securities.

16. The key to the bank's ability to provide liquidity to depositors is the bank's ability to pool relatively small deposits from many investors into large, illiquid loans to corporate borrowers. A withdrawal by any one depositor can be satisfied from any of a number of sources, including new deposits, repayments of other loans made by the bank, bank reserves, and the bank's debt and equity financing.

17. a. Investor A buys shares in a mutual fund, which buys part of a new stock issue by a rapidly growing software company.

    b. Investor B buys shares issued by the Bank of New York, which lends money to a regional department store chain.

    c. Investor C buys part of a new stock issue by the Regional Life Insurance Company, which invests in corporate bonds issued by Neighborhood Refineries, Inc.

18. Commercial banks accept deposits and provide financing primarily for businesses. Investment banks do not accept deposits and do not loan money to businesses and individuals. Investment banks may make bridge loans as temporary financing for a takeover or acquisition. In addition, investment banks trade many different financial contracts, such as bonds and options, whiling providing investment advice and portfolio management for institutional and individual investors.

19. Mutual funds collect money from small investors and invest the money in corporate stocks or bonds, thus channeling savings from investors to corporations. For individuals, the advantages of mutual funds are diversification, professional investment management and record keeping.

20. In this situation, a "superior" rate of return is a rate of return that is greater than the rate of return investors could earn elsewhere in the financial markets from alternative investments with risk level equal to that of the "low-risk capital investment" described in the problem. Fritz (who is risk-averse) will applaud the investment because he can maintain the risk level he prefers while earning a "superior" return. Frieda (who is risk-tolerant) will applaud the investment because investors will be willing to pay more for the shares Frieda owns than they would have paid if the firm had not made this "low-risk capital investment." Frieda would be likely to sell her shares to a more risk-averse investor, and use the proceeds of her sale to invest in shares of a company with a very high rate of return, and commensurate high level of risk.

21. The opportunity cost of capital is not the rate at which Quince can borrow from the bank. The opportunity cost of capital is the rate of return available from investments in the financial markets at the same level of risk as Quince's average-risk investments. Therefore, the opportunity cost of capital is also the minimum acceptable rate of return for a firm's capital investments. The rate of return on the "average-risk investment project" must be compared to the firm's cost of capital in order to determine whether to "move ahead" with the project.

22. The opportunity cost of capital for this investment is the rate of return that investors can earn in the financial markets from safe investments, such as U.S. Treasury securities and top-quality (AAA) corporate debt issues. The highest quality investments in Table 2-2 paid 4.84% per year. The investment under consideration is guaranteed, so the opportunity cost of capital should be somewhat less than 4.84%. Furthermore, a better estimate of the opportunity cost of capital would rely on interest rates on U.S. Treasuries with the same maturity as the proposed investment, i.e., one-year Treasury bills.

23. a. Since the government guarantees the payoff for the investment, the opportunity cost of capital is the rate of return on U.S. Treasuries with one year to maturity (i.e., one-year Treasury bills).

    b. Since the average rate of return from an investment in carbon is expected to be about 20 percent, this is the opportunity cost of capital for the investment under consideration by Pollution Busters, Inc. Purchase of the additional sequesters is not a worthwhile capital investment because the expected rate of return is 15 percent (i.e., a $15,000 gain on a $100,000 investment), less than the opportunity cost of capital.

Solutions to Chapter 3

Accounting and Finance

1.

Assets		Liabilities & Shareholders' Equity	
Cash	$ 10,000	Accounts payable	$ 17,000
Accounts receivable	22,000	Long-term debt	170,000
Inventory	200,000	Shareholders' equity	145,000
Store & property	100,000		
		Total liabilities & Shareholders' equity	
Total assets	$332,000		$332,000

2. The balance sheet shows the position of the firm at one point in time. It shows the amounts of assets and liabilities at that particular time. In this sense it is like a snap shot. The income statement shows the effect of business activities over the entire year. Since it captures events over an extended period, it is more like a video. The statement of cash flow is like the income statement in that it summarizes activity over the full year, so it too is like a video.

3. Accounting revenues and expenses can differ from cash flows because some items included in the computation of revenues and expenses do not entail immediate cash flows. For example, sales made on credit are considered revenue even though cash is not collected until the customer makes a payment. Also, depreciation expense reduces net income, but does not entail a cash outflow. Conversely, some cash flows are not included in revenues or expenses. For example, collection of accounts receivable results in a cash inflow but is not revenue. Purchases of inventory require cash outlays, but are treated as investments in working capital, not as expenses.

4. Working capital ought to be increasing. The firm will be building up stocks of inventory as it ramps up production. In addition, as sales increase, accounts receivable will increase rapidly. While accounts payable will probably also increase, the increase in accounts receivable will tend to dominate since sales prices exceed input costs.

5. a. Taxes = $(0.10 \times \$8,025) + 0.15 \times (\$20,000 - \$8,025) = \$2,599$

   Average tax rate = $\$2,599/\$20,000 = 0.12995 = 12.995\%$

   Marginal tax rate = 15%

   b. Taxes = $(0.10 \times \$8,025) + 0.15 \times (\$32,550 - \$8,025) + 0.25 \times (\$50,000 - \$32,550)$
   $= \$8844$

   Average tax rate = $\$8,844/\$50,000 = 0.17688 = 17.688\%$

   Marginal tax rate = 25%

c. Taxes = $(0.10 \times \$8{,}025) + 0.15 \times (\$32{,}550 - \$8{,}025) + 0.25 \times (\$78{,}850 - \$32{,}550)$
    $+ 0.28 \times (\$164{,}550 - \$78{,}750) + 0.33 \times (\$300{,}000 - \$164{,}550) = \$84{,}751$

Average tax rate = $\$84{,}751/\$300{,}000 = 0.2825 = 28.25\%$

Marginal tax rate = 33%

d. Taxes = $(0.10 \times \$8{,}025) + 0.15 \times (\$32{,}550 - \$8{,}025) + 0.25 \times (\$78{,}850 - \$32{,}550)$
    $+ 0.28 \times (\$164{,}550 - \$78{,}750) + 0.33 \times (\$357{,}700 - \$164{,}550)$
    $+ 0.35 \times (\$3{,}000{,}000 - \$357{,}700) = \$1{,}009{,}556$

Average tax rate = $\$1{,}009{,}556/\$3{,}000{,}000 = 0.3365 = 33.65\%$

Marginal tax rate = 35%

6. Taxes = $(0.15 \times \$50{,}000) + 0.25 \times (\$75{,}000 - \$50{,}000) + 0.34 \times (\$100{,}000 - \$75{,}000)$
    $= \$22{,}250$

Average tax rate = $\$22{,}250/\$100{,}000 = 0.2225 = 22.25\%$

Marginal tax rate = 34%

7. Taxes = $(0.10 \times \$16{,}050) + 0.15 \times (\$65{,}100 - \$16{,}050) + 0.25 \times (\$95{,}000 - \$65{,}100)$
    $= \$16{,}437.50$

Average tax rate = $\$16{,}437.50/\$95{,}000 = 0.1730 = 17.30\%$

Marginal tax rate = 25%

8. a. Cash will increase as one current asset (inventory) is exchanged for another (cash).

    b. Cash will increase. The machine will bring in cash when it is sold, but the lease payments will be made over several years.

    c. The firm will use cash to buy back the shares from existing shareholders. Cash balance will decrease.

9. Net income = Increase in retained earnings + dividends

$\$900{,}000 = (\$3{,}700{,}000 - \$3{,}400{,}000) + \text{dividends} \Rightarrow \text{dividends} = \$600{,}000$

10. Taxes on your salary = $(0.10 \times \$8{,}025) + 0.15 \times (\$32{,}550 - \$8{,}025)$
    $+ 0.25 \times (\$70{,}000 - \$32{,}550) = \$13{,}844$

Taxes on corporate income = $0.15 \times \$30{,}000 = \$4{,}500$

Total taxes = $\$13{,}844 + \$4{,}500 = \$18{,}344$

If you rearrange income so that your salary and the firm's profit are both $50,000 then:

Taxes on your salary = $(0.10 \times \$8{,}025) + 0.15 \times (\$32{,}550 - \$8{,}025)$

$$+ 0.25 \times (\$50{,}000 - \$32{,}550) = \$8{,}844$$

Taxes on corporate income = $0.15 \times \$50{,}000 = \$7{,}500$

Total taxes = $\$8{,}844 + \$7{,}500 = \$16{,}344$

Total taxes are reduced by $\$18{,}344 - \$16{,}344 = \$2{,}000$

11. a. Book value equals the $200,000 the founder of the firm has contributed in tangible assets. Market value equals the value of his patent plus the value of the production plant: $50,000,000 + $200,000 = $50,200,000

   b. Price per share = $50.2 million/2 million shares = $25.10

   Book value per share = $200,000/2 million shares = $0.10

12.
Sales	$ 10,000
Cost of goods sold	6,500
General & administrative expenses	1,000
Depreciation expense	1,000
EBIT	1,500
Interest expense	500
Taxable income	1,000
Taxes (35%)	350
Net income	$ 650

Cash flow from operations = net income + depreciation expense = $1,650

13. Cash flow from operations can be positive even if net income is negative. For example, if depreciation expenses are large, then negative net income might correspond to positive cash flow because depreciation is treated as an expense in calculating net income, but does not represent a cash outflow.

   Conversely, if net income is positive, but a large portion of sales are made on credit, cash flow can be negative since the sales are revenue but do not yet generate cash. Look back to Table 3-3, and you will see that increases in accounts receivable reduce cash provided by operations.

14. The calculations are presented in the following table. Sales occur in quarters 2 and 3, so this is when the cost of goods sold is recognized. Therefore, net income is zero in quarters 1 and 4. In quarter 1, the production of the kits is treated as an investment in inventories. The level of inventories then falls as goods are sold in quarters 2 and 3. Accounts receivable in quarters 2 and 3 equal the sales in those quarters since it takes one quarter for receivables

to be collected. Notice that cash flow in quarter 1 equals the cost of producing the kits, and in quarters 3 and 4, cash flow equals cash received for the kits previously sold.

a.	Quarter 1	Quarter 2	Quarter 3	Quarter 4
Sales	$ 0	$ 550	$ 600	$ 0
Cost of goods sold	0	500	500	0
Net income	$ 0	$ 50	$ 100	$ 0

b.,c.				
Inventories	$1,000	$ 500	$ 0	$ 0
Accounts receivable	0	550	600	0
Net working capital	$1,000	$1,050	$ 600	$ 0
Cash flow	−$1,000	$ 0	$ 550	$ 600

Cash flow = net income − change in net working capital

15. Cash flow = Profits − Δ Accounts receivable   − 10,000
                        + Δ Accounts payable   + 5,000
                        − Δ Inventory   −(−2,000)

Cash flow = Profits − 10,000 + 5,000 − (−2,000) = Profits − 3,000

Therefore, cash flow is $3,000 less than profits. This corresponds to the increase of $3,000 in net working capital.

16. a. If the firm paid income taxes of $2,000, and the average tax rate was 20%, then taxable income must have been: $2,000/0.20 = $10,000

Therefore: Net income = taxable income − taxes = $8,000

b.

Revenues	???
− Cost of goods sold	8,000
− Administrative expenses	3,000
− Depreciation expense	1,000
− Interest expense	1,000
Taxable income	$10,000 [from part (a)]

We conclude that revenues were $23,000.

c.

Revenues	$23,000
− Cost of goods sold	8,000
− Administrative expenses	3,000
− Depreciation expense	1,000
EBIT	$11,000

17. a.
Sales	$ 14.00 million
– Cost of goods sold	8.00
– Interest expense	1.00
– Depreciation expense	2.00
Taxable income	3.00
– Taxes (35%)	1.05
Net income	$ 1.95 million

Cash flow = Net income + Depreciation expense = $3.95 million

b. If depreciation expense were increased by $1 million, net income would be *reduced* by $0.65 million. Cash flow (= net income + depreciation) would be *increased* by: –$0.65 million + $1 million = $0.35 million

Cash flow increases because depreciation expense is not a cash outflow, but increasing the depreciation expense for tax purposes reduces taxes paid by $0.35 million.

c. The impact on stock price is likely to be positive. Cash available to the firm would increase. The reduction in net income would be recognized as resulting entirely from accounting changes, not as a consequence of any changes in the underlying profitability of the firm.

d. If interest expense were $1 million higher, both net income and cash flow would decrease by $0.65 million, i.e., by the $1 million increase in expenses less the $0.35 million reduction in taxes. This differs from part (b) because, in contrast to depreciation, interest expense represents an actual cash outlay.

18.
	April	May	June
Sales	$ 0	$150,000	$ 0
Cost of goods sold	0	100,000	0
ΔAccounts receivable	0	150,000	−150,000
ΔInventory	100,000	−100,000	0
Cash flow*	−100,000	0	150,000
Net income**	$ 0	$ 50,000	$ 0

*Cash flow = Sales − COGS − ΔA/R −ΔInventory
** Net income = Sales − COGS

19.

Assets	2008	2009	*Liabilities and* *Owners' equity*	2008	2009
Current assets	310	420	Current liabilities	210	240
Net fixed assets	1,200	1,420	Long-term debt	830	920
Total assets	1,510	1,840	Total liabilities	1,040	1,160
			Owners' equity	470	680

a. Owners' equity = Total assets − Total liabilities (as shown in the balance sheet above).

b. If the firm issued no stock, the increase in owners' equity must be due entirely to retained earnings. Since owners' equity increased by $210, and dividends were $100, net income must have been $310.

c. Since net fixed assets increased by $220, and the firm purchased $300 of new fixed assets, the depreciation charge must have been $80.

d. Net working capital increased by $80, from ($310 − $210) = $100 in 2008 to ($420 − $240) = $180 in 2009.

e. Since long-term debt increased by $90, and the firm issued $200 of new long-term debt, $110 of outstanding debt must have been paid off.

20. a. Shareholders' equity = Total assets − total liabilities

   2008: Shareholders' equity = $890 − $650 = $240

   2009: Shareholders' equity = $1,040 − $810 = $230

b. Net working capital = current assets − current liabilities

   2008: Net working capital = $90 − $50 = $40

   2009: Net working capital = $140 − $60 = $80

c. Taxable income = $1,950 − $1,030 − $350 − $240 = $330

   Taxes paid = 0.35 × $330 = $115.50

   Net income = $214.50

d.
Net income	$214.50
Decrease (increase) in current assets	(50.00)
Increase in current liabilities	10.00
Cash provided by operations	$174.50

e. Gross investment = Increase in net fixed assets + depreciation

   = $100 + $350 = $450

f. Current liabilities increased by $10. Therefore, current liabilities other than accounts payable must have increased by $45.

21.

Assets	2008	2009	Liabilities and Shareholders' equity	2008	2009
Cash & marketable securities	$ 800	$ 300	Accounts payable	$ 300	$ 350
Inventories	300	350	Notes payable	1,000	600
Accounts receivable	400	450	Long-term debt	2,000	2,400
Net fixed assets	5,000	5,800	Total liabilities	3,300	3,350
Total assets	$ 6,500	$ 6,900	Shareholders' equity	3,200	3,550
			Total liabilities plus Shareholders' equity	$6,500	$6,900

22. Net working capital (2008) = ($800 + $300 + $400) – ($300 + $1,000) = $200

Net working capital (2009) = ($300 + $350 + $450) – ($350 + $600) = $150

Net working capital decreased by $50.

23.

	2008	2009
Revenue	$ 4,000	$ 4,100
Cost of goods sold	1,600	1,700
Administrative expenses	500	550
Depreciation expense	500	520
Interest expense	150	150
Taxable income	1,250	1,180
Federal & state income taxes	400	420
Net income	$ 850	$ 760

Increase in retained earnings in 2009 = Net income – dividends = $760 – $410 = $350

In 2009, shareholders' equity increased by the amount of the increase in retained earnings.

24. Earnings per share in 2008 = $850,000/500,000 shares = $1.70

Earnings per share in 2009 = $760,000/500,000 shares = $1.52

25. Average tax bracket in 2008 = taxes/taxable income = $400/$1250 = 0.320 = 32.0%

Average tax bracket in 2009 = $420/$1180 = 0.356 = 35.6%

In order to determine the firm's marginal tax bracket, one would need information regarding tax rates applicable for both federal and state income taxes.

26. Net fixed assets increased by $800,000 during 2009, while depreciation expense in 2009 was $520,000. Therefore, gross investment in plant and equipment was $1,320,000.

27. **Cash provided by operations**

Net income	$ 760
Noncash expenses	
Depreciation expense	520
Changes in working capital	
Decrease (increase) in accounts receivable	(50)
Decrease (increase) in inventories	(50)
Increase (decrease) in accounts payable	50
Total change in working capital	(50)
Cash provided by operations	$1,230

Cash flows from investments

Cash provided by (used for) disposal of	(1,320)
(additions to) property, plant & equipment	
Cash provided by (used for) investments	(1,320)

Cash provided by (used for) financing activities

Additions to (reductions in) notes payable	(400)
Additions to (reductions in) long-term debt	400
Dividends paid	(410)
Cash provided by (used for) financing activities	(410)
Net increase (decrease) in cash and cash equivalents	($ 500)

28.

Market value balance sheet, 2009
(Figures in thousands of dollars)

Assets			Liabilities & Shareholders' Equity		
Cash	$	300	Accounts payable	$	350
Inventories		350	Notes payable		600
Accounts receivable		450	Long-term debt		2,400
Employee skills		2,900	Total liabilities		3,350
Net fixed assets		6,000	Shareholders' equity*		6,650
			Total liabilities &		
Total assets		$10,000	Shareholders' equity		$10,000

* Shareholders' equity = Total assets – total liabilities

Price per share = $6,650,000/500,000 shares = $13.30

29. a.

Income	Taxes Due	Average Tax Rate
10000	1,099	10.99%
20000	2,599	12.99%
40000	6,344	15.86%
80000	16,378	20.47%
100000	21,978	21.98%
150000	35,978	23.99%
200000	51,751	25.88%
250000	68,251	27.30%
300000	84,751	28.25%
350000	101,251	28.93%
450000	136,097	30.24%
550000	171,097	31.11%
650000	206,097	31.71%
750000	241,097	32.15%
1000000	328,597	32.86%
2000000	678,597	33.93%
4000000	1,378,597	34.46%
6000000	2,078,597	34.64%
8000000	2,778,597	34.73%
10000000	3,478,597	34.79%

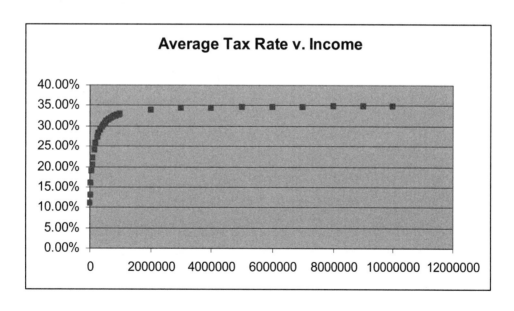

b. As shown in the table and graph above, the difference between average tax rates and the top marginal tax rate of 35% becomes very small as income becomes large.

c. For corporations the marginal tax rate is 35%. When analyzing very large firms we are content simply treating the corporate tax rate as 35% since average taxes are likely to be equal. Very large firms are unlikely to have incomes in the lower brackets.

30. To minimize taxes, you should not have income in one tax category (that is, personal versus corporate) if you can move the income into the other category at a lower tax rate. First, suppose that your total income is $79,700. Then you could allocate $50,000 to corporate income, the maximum amount that would be taxed at 15%, and $29,700 to personal income, the maximum amount that would be taxed at 15%. Additional corporate income, up to an additional ($75,000 – $50,000) = $25,000, would be taxed at 25%, and additional individual income, up to an additional ($71,950 – $29,700) = $42,250, would also be taxed at 25%. Therefore, you are indifferent as to whether the remaining ($100,000 – $79,700) = $20,300 in income is allocated to corporate income or individual income or a combination of the two.

Solutions to Chapter 4

Measuring Corporate Performance

1. a. $\text{Long-term debt ratio} = \dfrac{7,018}{7,018 + 9,724} = 0.42$

   b. $\text{Total debt ratio} = \dfrac{4,794 + 7,018 + 6,178}{27,714} = 0.65$

   c. $\text{Times interest earned} = \dfrac{2,566}{685} = 3.75$

   d. $\text{Cash coverage ratio} = \dfrac{2,566 + 2,518}{685} = 7.42$

   e. $\text{Current ratio} = \dfrac{3,525}{4,794} = 0.74$

   f. $\text{Quick ratio} = \dfrac{89 + 2,382}{4,794} = 0.52$

   g. $\text{Operating profit margin} = \dfrac{1,311 + 685}{13,193} = 0.151 = 15.1\%$

   h. $\text{Inventory turnover} = \dfrac{4,060}{(187 + 238)/2} = 19.11$

   i. $\text{Days sales in inventory} = \dfrac{(187 + 238)/2}{4,060/365} = 19.10 \text{ days}$

   j. $\text{Average collection period} = \dfrac{(2,382 + 2,490)/2}{13,193/365} = 67.39 \text{ days}$

   k. $\text{Return on equity} = \dfrac{1,311}{(9,724 + 9,121)/2} = 0.139 = 13.9\%$

   l. $\text{Return on assets} = \dfrac{1,311 + 685}{(27,714 + 27,503)/2} = 0.072 = 7.2\%$

   m. $\text{Payout ratio} = \dfrac{856}{1,311} = 0.65$

2. Gross investment during the year

      = Increase in net property, plant, equipment + depreciation

      = ($19,973 − $19,915) + $2,518 = $2,576

3. Market-to-book ratio = $17.2 billion/$9.724 billion = 1.77

   Earnings per share = $1,311 million/205 million = $6.40

   Price-earnings ratio = $17.2 billion/$1.311 billion = 13.1

4. a. EVA = net income − (cost of equity x equity)

      = 5,642 − (.10 x 14,251) = $4,217

   EVA fell since the cost of equity is higher.

  b. Accounting profits are unaffected by changes in the cost of equity.

  c. Economic Value Added is a better measure of company performance because accounting profits do not include all costs; specifically, the cost of equity capital.

5. a. MVA = market value of shares − book value of equity

      = $97,334 − 15,368 = $81,966

   MVA fell as the market value of the shares dropped 5%

  b. No, the expected return on all shares has risen.

  c. Yes, the cost of equity capital has increased for Pepsi.

6. a. Sustainable growth = (1 − payout ratio) × ROE

      = (1 − 0.57) × 0.396 = 0.1703, or 17.03%

   Pepsi's sustainable growth rate will fall with the lower plowback ratio.

  b. Sustainable growth = (1 − 0.67) × 0.095 = 0.0637, or 6.37%

      The sustainable growth will fall below its cost of equity due to the payout of earnings.

7. $\text{ROA} = \dfrac{\text{Net income} + \text{interest}}{\text{Average total assets}} = \dfrac{1{,}311 + 685}{27{,}608.5} = 0.0723 = 7.23\%$

$\text{Asset turnover} = \dfrac{\text{Sales}}{\text{Average total assets}} = \dfrac{13{,}193}{27{,}608.5} = 0.4779 = 47.79\%$

$\text{Operating profit margin} = \dfrac{\text{Net income} + \text{interest}}{\text{Sales}} = \dfrac{1{,}311 + 685}{13{,}193} = 0.1513 = 15.13\%$

$\text{Asset turnover} \times \text{Operating profit margin} = 0.4779 \times 0.1513 = 0.0723 = \text{ROA}$

8. a. $\text{ROE} = \dfrac{1{,}311}{(9{,}724 + 9{,}121)/2} = \dfrac{1{,}311}{9{,}422.50} = 0.1391 = 13.91\%$

   b. $\dfrac{\text{Assets}}{\text{Equity}} \times \dfrac{\text{Sales}}{\text{Assets}} \times \dfrac{\text{Net income} + \text{interest}}{\text{Sales}} \times \dfrac{\text{Net income}}{\text{Net income} + \text{interest}}$

   $= \dfrac{27{,}608.5}{9{,}422.5} \times \dfrac{13{,}193}{27{,}608.5} \times \dfrac{1{,}311 + 685}{13{,}193} \times \dfrac{1{,}311}{1{,}311 + 685} = 0.1391 = 13.91\%$

   (Notice that we have used average assets and average equity in this solution.)

9. a. The consulting firm has relatively few assets. The major 'asset' is the know-how of its employees. The consulting firm has the higher asset turnover ratio.

   b. The Catalog Shopping Network generates far more sales relative to assets since it does not have to sell goods from stores with high expenses and probably can maintain relatively lower inventories. The Catalog Shopping Network has the higher asset turnover ratio.

   c. The supermarket has a far higher ratio of sales to assets. The supermarket itself is a simple building and the store sells a high volume of goods with relatively low mark-ups (profit margins). Standard Supermarkets has the higher asset turnover.

10. ROE = net income / equity, or

    net income = ROE × equity

    EVA = net income – (cost of equity × equity), substituting

    EVA = (ROE × equity) – (cost of equity × equity), or

    EVA = equity × (ROE – cost of equity)

    Thus, EVA is positive if ROE exceeds the cost of equity

11. a. $\text{Debt-equity ratio} = \dfrac{\text{Long-term debt}}{\text{Equity}}$

b. $\text{Return on equity} = \dfrac{\text{Net income}}{\text{Average equity}}$

c. $\text{Profit margin} = \dfrac{\text{Net income} + \text{interest}}{\text{Sales}}$

d. $\text{Inventory turnover} = \dfrac{\text{Cost of goods sold}}{\text{Average inventory}}$

e. $\text{Current ratio} = \dfrac{\text{Current assets}}{\text{Current liabilities}}$

f. $\text{Average collection period} = \dfrac{\text{Average receivables}}{\text{Average daily sales}}$

g. $\text{Quick ratio} = \dfrac{\text{Cash} + \text{marketable securities} + \text{receivables}}{\text{Current liabilities}}$

12. If Pepsi borrows $300 million and invests the funds in marketable securities, both current assets and current liabilities will increase.

a. Liquidity ratios

$$\text{Current ratio} = \frac{8,639 + 300}{6,752 + 300} = 1.27$$

$$\text{Quick ratio} = \frac{1,280 + 2,999 + 300}{6,752 + 300} = 0.649$$

$$\text{Cash ratio} = \frac{1,280 + 300}{6,752 + 300} = 0.224$$

The transaction would result in a slight decrease in the current ratio and an increase in the quick ratio and the cash ratio, so that the company might *appear* to be more liquid. However, a financial analyst would be very unlikely to conclude that the company is *actually* more liquid after engaging in such a transaction.

b. Leverage ratios

The long-term debt ratio and the debt-equity ratio would be unaffected since current liabilities are not included in these ratios. The total debt ratio will increase slightly, however:

$$\frac{\text{Total liabilities}}{\text{Total assets}} = \frac{14,415 + 300}{27,987 + 300} = 0.5202$$

The very slight increase in the total debt ratio (from 0.5151 to 0.5202) indicates that the company would *appear* to be *very slightly* more leveraged. However, a financial analyst would conclude that the company is *actually* no more leveraged than prior to the transaction.

13. a. Current ratio will be unaffected. Inventories are replaced with either cash or accounts receivable, but total current assets are unchanged.

b. Current ratio will be unaffected. Accounts due are replaced with the bank loan, but total current liabilities are unchanged.

c. Current ratio will be unaffected. Receivables are replaced with cash, but total current assets are unchanged.

d. Current ratio will be unaffected. Inventories replace cash, but total current assets are unchanged.

14. The current ratio will be unaffected. Inventories replace cash, but total current assets are unchanged. The quick ratio falls, however, since inventories are not included in the most liquid assets.

15. Average collection period equals average receivables divided by average daily sales:

$$\text{Average collection period} = \frac{6,333}{9,800/365} = 236 \text{ days}$$

16. $$\text{Days' sales in inventories} = \frac{400}{73,000/365} = 2 \text{ days}$$

17. Annual cost of goods sold = $10,000 \times 365/30 = \$121,667$

$$\text{Inventory turnover} = \frac{121,667}{10,000} = 12.167 \text{ times per year}$$

18. a. Interest expense = $0.08 \times \$10$ million = $\$800,000$

Times interest earned = $\$1,000,000/\$800,000 = 1.25$

b. $$\text{Cash coverage ratio} = \frac{1,000,000 + 200,000}{800,000} = 1.5$$

c. $$\text{Fixed payment coverage} = \frac{1,000,000 + 200,000}{800,000 + 300,000} = 1.09$$

19. a. ROA = Asset turnover × Operating profit margin = $3 \times 0.05 = 0.15 = 15\%$

    b. If debt/equity = 1, then debt = equity, so total assets are twice equity.

    $$ROE = \frac{Assets}{Equity} \times ROA \times Debt\ burden = \frac{2}{1} \times 0.15 \times \frac{20{,}000 - 8{,}000 - 8{,}000}{20{,}000 - 8{,}000} = 0.10 = 10\%$$

20. Total sales = $\$3{,}000 \times 365/20 = \$54{,}750$

    Asset turnover ratio = $\$54{,}750/\$75{,}000 = 0.73$

    ROA = Asset turnover × Operating profit margin = $0.73 \times 0.05 = 0.0365 = 3.65\%$

21. Debt-equity ratio $\dfrac{\text{Long-term debt}}{\text{Equity}}$

    $$0.4 = \frac{\text{Long-term debt}}{\$1{,}000{,}000} \Rightarrow \text{Long-term debt} = 0.4 \times \$1{,}000{,}000 = \$400{,}000$$

    $\dfrac{\text{Current assets}}{\text{Current liabilities}} = 2.0$ and Current assets = $\$200{,}000$

    Therefore, Current liabilities = $\$200{,}000/2 = \$100{,}000 = $ Notes payable

    Total liabilities = $\$500{,}000$

    Total assets = total liabilities + equity = $\$500{,}000 + \$1{,}000{,}000 = \$1{,}500{,}000$

    Total debt ratio = $\$500{,}000/\$1{,}500{,}000 = 0.33$

22. $\dfrac{\text{Book Debt}}{\text{Book Equity}} = 0.5$

    $\dfrac{\text{Market Equity}}{\text{Book Equity}} = 2$

    $\dfrac{\text{Book Debt}}{\text{Market Equity}} = \dfrac{0.5}{2} = 0.25$

23. EBIT = Revenues – COGS – Depreciation

    $= \$3{,}000{,}000 - \$2{,}500{,}000 - \$200{,}000 = \$300{,}000$

    Interest = 8% of face value = $\$80{,}000$

    Times interest earned = $\$300{,}000/\$80{,}000 = 3.75$

24. The firm has less debt relative to equity than the industry average but its ratio of (EBIT plus depreciation) to interest expense is lower. Perhaps the firm has a lower ROA than its competitors, and is therefore generating less EBIT per dollar of assets. Perhaps the firm pays a higher interest rate on its debt. Or perhaps its depreciation charges are lower because it uses less capital or older capital.

25. A decline in market interest rates will increase the value of the fixed-rate debt and thus increase the market-value debt-equity ratio. By this measure, leverage will increase. The decline in interest rates will also reduce the firm's interest payments on the floating rate debt, which will increase the times-interest-earned ratio. By this measure, leverage will decrease. The impact of the lower rates on 'leverage' is thus ambiguous. The firm has higher indebtedness relative to assets, but greater ability to cover its cash flow obligations.

26. a. The shipping company, which has more tangible assets, will tend to have the higher debt-equity ratio. (See Chapter 15, Sections 15.3 and 15.4, for a discussion of the reasons that firms holding tangible assets with active secondary markets tend to maintain higher debt-equity ratios.)

    b. United Foods is in a more mature industry and probably has fewer favorable opportunities for reinvesting income. We would expect United Foods to have the higher payout ratio.

    c. The paper mill will have higher sales per dollar of assets. It is less capital intensive (that is, has less capital per dollar of sales) than the integrated firm.

    d. The discount outlet sells many of its goods for cash. The power company bills monthly and usually gives customers a month to pay bills and therefore will have the longer collection period.

    e. Fledging Electronics will have the higher price-earnings multiple, reflecting its greater growth prospects. (Recall from Chapter 6, Section 6.5, that the P/E ratio is an indicator of the firm's growth prospects.)

27. Leverage ratios are of interest to banks or other investors lending money to the firm. They want to be assured that the firm is not borrowing more than it can reasonably be expected to repay.

    Liquidity ratios are also of interest to creditors who prefer that a firm's current assets are well in excess of its current liabilities. Liquidity ratios are especially important to those who lend to the firm for short periods, for example, by extending trade credit. If a firm buys goods on credit, the seller wants to know that, when the bill comes due, the firm will have enough cash on hand to pay it.

    Efficiency ratios might be of interest to stock market analysts who want to know how well the firm is being run. These ratios are also of great concern to the firm's own management, which needs to know if it is running as tight a ship as its competitors.

28. **Income Statement**

	Millions of dollars
Net sales	$199.93
Cost of goods sold	120.00
Selling, general & administrative expenses	10.00
Depreciation	20.00
EBIT	49.93
Interest expense	6.27
Income before tax	43.66
Tax	30.13
Net income	$ 13.53

Balance Sheet

	Millions of dollars	
	This year	Last year
Assets		
Cash and marketable securities	$ 11	$ 20
Receivables	44	34
Inventories	22	26
Total current assets	77	80
Net property, plant, equipment	38	25
Total assets	$ 115	$ 105
Liabilities & Shareholders' Equity		
Accounts payable	$ 25	$ 20
Notes payable	30	35
Total current liabilities	55	55
Long-term debt	24	20
Shareholders' equity	36	30
Total liabilities & Shareholders' equity	$ 115	$ 105

Solution Procedure:

1. Total current liabilities = 25 + 30 = 55
2. Total current assets = $55 \times 1.4 = 77$
3. Cash = $55 \times 0.2 = 11$
4. Accounts receivable + cash = $55 \times 1.0 = 55$
5. Accounts receivable = 55 – cash = 55 – 11 = 44
6. Inventories = 77 – 11 – 44 = 22
7. Total assets = Total liabilities and Shareholders' equity = 115
8. Net Property, plant, equipment = 115 – 77 = 38
9. Cost of goods sold = Inventory turnover $\times$ Avg. inventory = $5.0 \times (22 + 26)/2 = 120$
10. Sales = (365/Collection period) $\times$ Average receivables
    $= (365/71.2) \times [(44 + 34)/2] = 199.93$

11. EBIT = 199.93 − 120 − 10 − 20 = 49.93
12. Net income + interest = EBIT − tax = ROA × Average total assets
$$= 0.18 \times (115 + 105)/2 = 19.8$$
13. Tax = 49.93 − 19.8 = 30.13
14. LT Debt + equity = 115 − Current liabilities = 115 − 55 = 60
15. LT debt = LT debt ratio × 60 = 0.4 × 60 = 24
16. Shareholders' equity = 60 − 24 = 36
17. Net income = ROE × Average equity = 0.41 × [(36+30)/2] = 13.53
18. Income before tax = 30.13 + 13.53 = 43.66
19. Interest expense = EBIT − Income before taxes = 49.93 − 43.66 = 6.27

29. a. See table and graph below

Industry	Oper. Profit Margin	Asset Turnover
Oil	8.5%	1.47
Food	10.2%	0.88
Textiles	9.2%	1.04
Paper	8.5%	0.81
Chemicals	9.5%	0.95
Pharmaceuticals	19.8%	0.60
Metals	10.5%	1.16
Machinery	10.6%	0.94
Computers	8.6%	0.88
Semiconductors	9.6%	0.93
Telecoms	11.5%	0.46
Utilities	13.2%	0.40
Retailers	3.8%	2.26
Software	12.4%	0.63

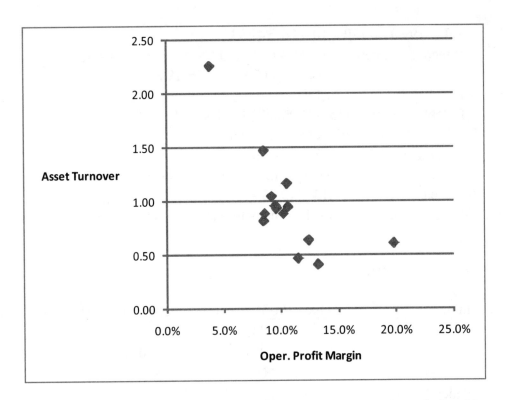

Asset turnover declines as operating profit margin rises. This relationship makes sense as firms with low profit margins need to generate more volume. That is, if margins are low, each dollar
of total assets must work harder to produce the same amount of total profit.

b.   See table and graph below

Industry	Cash Ratio	Quick Ratio
Oil	0.33	0.98
Food	0.21	0.83
Textiles	0.4	1.49
Paper	0.14	1.17
Chemicals	0.27	1.51
Pharmaceuticals	0.8	0.87
Metals	0.27	1.18
Machinery	0.21	1.9
Computers	0.8	1.05
Semiconductors	1.33	1.02
Telecoms	0.15	0.79
Utilities	0.15	0.64
Retailers	0.26	0.34
Software	0.76	1.06

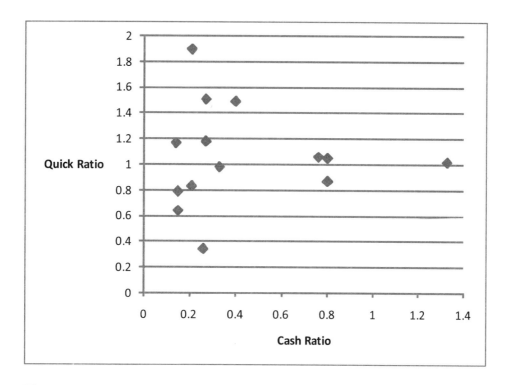

These two measures of liquidity do not appear to move together. You cannot conclude that once you know one of these ratios there is little to be gained by calculating the other.

Solution to Minicase for Chapter 4

You will find an Excel spreadsheet solution for this minicase at the Online Learning Center (www.mhhe.com/bmm6e).

Problems for HH are apparent in the areas of debt and assets. Leverage ratios improved between 2003 and 2007, but debt (both long-term and short-term) has increased significantly in 2008. Liquidity ratios began to deteriorate in 2007, at the same time that the number of employees increased substantially. Further deterioration in liquidity ratios occurred in 2008, when inventories more than doubled and current liabilities increased by more than 85%. At the same time, sales remained virtually unchanged from 2007.

Solutions to Chapter 5

The Time Value of Money

1. a. $\$100/(1.08)^{10} = \$46.32$

    b. $\$100/(1.08)^{20} = \$21.45$

    c. $\$100/(1.04)^{10} = \$67.56$

    d. $\$100/(1.04)^{20} = \$45.64$

2. a. $\$100 \times (1.08)^{10} = \$215.89$

    b. $\$100 \times (1.08)^{20} = \$466.10$

    c. $\$100 \times (1.04)^{10} = \$148.02$

    d. $\$100 \times (1.04)^{20} = \$219.11$

3. $\$100 \times (1.04)^{113} = \$8,409.45$

   $\$100 \times (1.08)^{113} = \$598,252.29$

4. With simple interest, you earn 4% of $1,000 or $40 each year. There is no interest on interest. After 10 years, you earn total interest of $400, and your account accumulates to $1,400. With compound interest, your account grows to: $\$1,000 \times (1.04)^{10} = \$1480.24$ Therefore $80.24 is interest on interest.

5. $PV = \$700/(1.05)^5 = \$548.47$

6.

	Present Value	Years	Future Value	Interest Rate
a.	$400	11	$684	$\left[\dfrac{684}{400}\right]^{(1/11)} - 1 = 5.00\%$
b.	$183	4	$249	$\left[\dfrac{249}{183}\right]^{(1/4)} - 1 = 8.00\%$
c.	$300	7	$300	$\left[\dfrac{300}{300}\right]^{(1/7)} - 1 = 0\%$

To find the interest rate, we rearrange the basic future value equation as follows:

$$FV = PV \times (1 + r)^t \Rightarrow r = \left[\frac{FV}{PV}\right]^{(1/t)} - 1$$

7. You should compare the present values of the two annuities.

a. $PV = \$1,000 \times \left[\dfrac{1}{0.05} - \dfrac{1}{0.05 \times (1.05)^{10}}\right] = \$7,721.73$

$PV = \$800 \times \left[\dfrac{1}{0.05} - \dfrac{1}{0.05 \times (1.05)^{15}}\right] = \$8,303.73$

b. $PV = \$1,000 \times \left[\dfrac{1}{0.20} - \dfrac{1}{0.20 \times (1.20)^{10}}\right] = \$4,192.47$

$PV = \$800 \times \left[\dfrac{1}{0.20} - \dfrac{1}{0.20 \times (1.20)^{15}}\right] = \$3,740.38$

c. When the interest rate is low, as in part (a), the longer (i.e., 15-year) but smaller annuity is more valuable because the impact of discounting on the present value of future payments is less significant.

8. $\$100 \times (1 + r)^3 = \$115.76 \Rightarrow r = 5.00\%$

$\$200 \times (1 + r)^4 = \$262.16 \Rightarrow r = 7.00\%$

$\$100 \times (1 + r)^5 = \$110.41 \Rightarrow r = 2.00\%$

9. $PV = (\$200/1.06) + (\$400/1.06^2) + (\$300/1.06^3) = \$188.68 + \$356.00 + \$251.89 = \$796.57$

10. In these problems, you can either solve the equation provided directly, or you can use your financial calculator, setting: PV = (–)400, FV = 1000, PMT = 0, i as specified by the problem. Then compute n on the calculator.

a. $\$400 \times (1.04)^t = \$1,000 \Rightarrow t = 23.36$ periods

b. $\$400 \times (1.08)^t = \$1,000 \Rightarrow t = 11.91$ periods

c. $\$400 \times (1.16)^t = \$1,000 \Rightarrow t = 6.17$ periods

11.

	APR	Compounding period	Effective annual rate
a.	12%	1 month (m = 12/yr)	$1.01^{12} - 1 = 0.1268 = 12.68\%$
b.	8%	3 months (m = 4/yr)	$1.02^4 - 1 = 0.0824 = 8.24\%$
c.	10%	6 months (m = 2/yr)	$1.05^2 - 1 = 0.1025 = 10.25\%$

12.

	Effective Rate	Compounding period	Per period rate	APR
a.	10.00%	1 month (m = 12/yr)	$1.10^{(1/12)} - 1 = 0.0080$	$0.096 = 9.6\%$
b.	6.09%	6 months (m = 2/yr)	$1.0609^{(1/2)} - 1 = 0.0300$	$0.060 = 6.0\%$
c.	8.24%	3 months (m = 4/yr)	$1.0824^{(1/4)} - 1 = 0.0200$	$0.080 = 8.0\%$

13. Solve the following for t: $1.08^t = 2 \Rightarrow t = 11.9$ years

On a financial calculator, enter: PV = (–)1, FV = 2, PMT = 0, i = 6 and then compute n.

14. Semiannual compounding means that the 8.6 percent loan really carries interest of 4.3 percent per half year. Similarly, the 8.4 percent loan has a *monthly* rate of 0.7 percent.

APR	Compounding period	Effective annual rate
8.6%	6 months (m = 2/yr)	$1.043^2 - 1 = 0.0878 = 8.78\%$
8.4%	1 month (m = 12/yr)	$1.007^{12} - 1 = 0.0873 = 8.73\%$

Choose the 8.4 percent loan for its slightly lower effective rate.

15. APR = 1% × 52 = 52%

EAR = $(1.01)^{52} - 1 = 0.6777 = 67.77\%$

16. Since we are assuming that it is currently 2007, 107 years have passed since 1900.

    a. $\$1,000 \times (1.05)^{107} = \$185,035.50$

    b. $PV \times (1.05)^{107} = \$1,000,000 \Rightarrow PV = \$5,404.37$

17. $\$1,000 \times 1.04 = \$1,040.00 \Rightarrow$ interest $= \$40$

    $\$1,040 \times 1.04 = \$1,081.60 \Rightarrow$ interest $= \$1,081.60 - \$1,040 = \$41.60$

    After 9 years, your account has grown to: $\$1,000 \times (1.04)^9 = \$1,423.31$

    After 10 years, your account has grown to: $\$1,000 \times (1.04)^{10} = \$1,480.24$

    Interest earned in tenth year $= \$1,480.24 - \$1,423.31 = \$56.93$

18. If you earned simple interest (without compounding), then the total growth in your account after 25 years would be: 4% per year $\times$ 25 years = 100%
    Therefore, your money would double. With compound interest, your money would grow faster than it would with simple interest, and therefore would require less than 25 years to double.

19. We solve the following equation for r:

    $$422.41 \times (1 + r)^{10} = 1000 \Rightarrow r = 9.00\%$$

    [On a financial calculator, enter: PV = (–)422.41, FV = 1000, n = 10, PMT = 0, and compute the interest rate.]

20. The PV for the quarterback is the present value of a 5-year, $3 million annuity:

    $3 million $\times$ annuity factor(10%, 5 years)

    $$= \$3 \text{ million} \times \left[\frac{1}{0.10} - \frac{1}{0.10(1.10)^5} \right] = \$11.37 \text{ million}$$

    The receiver gets $4 million now plus a 5-year, $2 million annuity. The present value of the annuity is:

    $$\$2 \text{ million} \times \left[\frac{1}{0.10} - \frac{1}{0.10(1.10)^5} \right] = \$7.58 \text{ million}$$

    With the $4 million immediate payment, the receiver's contract is worth:

    $4 million + $7.58 million = $11.58 million

    The receiver's contract is worth more than the quarterback's even though the receiver's *undiscounted* total payments are less than the quarterback's.

21. Rate of growth for apples: $\$0.93 \times (1 + r)^{10} = \$1.18 \Rightarrow r = 2.41\%$

Rate of growth for oranges: $\$0.96 \times (1 + r)^{10} = \$1.50 \Rightarrow r = 4.56\%$

Price of apples in 2024: $\$1.18 \times (1.0241)^{20} = \$1.90$

Price of oranges in 2024: $\$1.50 \times (1.0456)^{20} = \$3.66$

22. If the payment is denoted C, then:

$$C \times \left[\frac{1}{(0.10/12)} - \frac{1}{(0.10/12) \times [1 + (0.10/12)]^{48}} \right] = \$8,000 \Rightarrow C = PMT = \$202.90$$

The monthly interest rate is: $0.10/12 = 0.008333 = 0.8333$ percent

Therefore, the effective annual interest rate on the loan is:

$(1.008333)^{12} - 1 = 0.1047 = 10.47$ percent

23. a. $PV = 100 \times$ annuity factor(6%, 3 periods) $= 100 \times \left[\frac{1}{0.06} - \frac{1}{0.06(1.06)^3} \right] = \$267.30$

b. If the payment stream is deferred by an additional year, then each payment is discounted by an additional factor of 1.06. Therefore, the present value is reduced by a factor of 1.06 to: $\$267.30/1.06 = \$252.17$

24. a. This is an annuity problem; use trial-and-error to solve for r in the following equation:

$$\$600 \times \left[\frac{1}{r} - \frac{1}{r \times (1 + r)^{240}} \right] = \$80,000 \Rightarrow r = 0.548\%$$

Using a financial calculator, enter: PV = (−)80,000, n = 20 × 12 = 240 months FV = 0, PMT = 600, compute i. To compute EAR:

$EAR = (1 + 0.00548)^{12} - 1 = 0.0678 = 6.78\%$

b. Compute the payment by solving for C in the following equation:

$$C \times \left[\frac{1}{0.005} - \frac{1}{0.005 \times (1.005)^{240}} \right] = \$80,000 \Rightarrow C = PMT = \$573.14$$

Using a financial calculator, enter: n = 240, i = 0.5%, FV = 0, PV = (−)80,000 and compute PMT = \$573.14

25. a. Your monthly payments of $400 can support a loan of: $15,189.58
    This is computed as follows:

    $$PV = \$400 \times \left[\frac{1}{0.01} - \frac{1}{0.01 \times (1.01)^{48}} \right] = \$15,189.58$$

    Using a financial calculator, enter: n = 48, i = 12%/12 = 1%, FV = 0, PMT = 400 and compute PV = $15,189.58

    With a down payment of $2,000, you can pay at most $17,189.58 for the car.

    b. In this case, n increases from 48 to 60. You can take out a loan of $17,982.02 based on this payment schedule. This is computed as follows:

    $$PV = \$400 \times \left[\frac{1}{0.01} - \frac{1}{0.01 \times (1.01)^{60}} \right] = \$17,982.02$$

    Thus, you can pay $19,982.02 for the car.

26. a. With PV = $9,000 and FV = $10,000, the annual interest rate is determined by solving the following equation for r:

    $$\$9,000 \times (1 + r) = \$10,000 \Rightarrow r = 11.11\%$$

    b. The present value is: $10,000 \times (1 - d)$

    The future value to be paid back is $10,000.

    Therefore, the annual interest rate is determined as follows:

    $$PV \times (1 + r) = FV$$

    $$[\$10,000 \times (1 - d)] \times (1 + r) = \$10,000$$

    $$1 + r = \frac{1}{1-d} \Rightarrow r = \frac{1}{1-d} - 1 = \frac{d}{1-d} > d$$

    c. The discount is calculated as a fraction of the future value of the loan. In fact, the proper way to compute the interest rate is as a fraction of the funds borrowed. Since PV is less than FV, the interest payment is a smaller fraction of the future value of the loan than it is of the present value. Thus, the true interest rate exceeds the stated discount factor of the loan.

27. a. If we assume cash flows come at the end of each period (ordinary annuity) when in fact they actually come at the beginning (annuity due), we discount each cash flow by one period too many. Therefore we can obtain the PV of an annuity due by multiplying the PV of an ordinary annuity by $(1 + r)$.

    b. Similarly, the FV of an annuity due equals the FV of an ordinary annuity times $(1 + r)$. Because each cash flow comes at the beginning of the period, it has an extra period to earn interest compared to an ordinary annuity.

28. Use trial-and-error to solve the following equation for r:

$$\$240 \times \left[\frac{1}{r} - \frac{1}{r \times (1+r)^{48}} \right] = \$8,000 \Rightarrow r = 1.599\%$$

Using a financial calculator, enter: PV = (–)8000; n = 48; PMT = 240; FV = 0, then compute r = 1.599% per month.

$$APR = 1.599\,\% \times 12 = 19.188\%$$

The effective annual rate is: $(1.01599)^{12} - 1 = 0.2097 = 20.97\%$

29. The annual payment over a four-year period that has a present value of $8,000 is computed by solving the following equation for C:

$$C \times \left[\frac{1}{0.2097} - \frac{1}{0.2097 \times (1.2097)^4} \right] = \$8,000 \Rightarrow C = PMT = \$3,147.29$$

[Using a financial calculator, enter: PV = (–)8000, n = 4, FV = 0, i = 20.97, and compute PMT.] With monthly payments, you would pay only $240 \times 12 = \$2,880$ per year. This value is lower because the monthly payments come before year-end, and therefore have a higher PV.

30. Leasing the truck means that the firm must make a series of payments in the form of an annuity. Calculate the present value as follows:

$$PV = \$8,000 \times \left[\frac{1}{0.07} - \frac{1}{0.07 \times (1.07)^6} \right] = \$38,132.32$$

Using a financial calculator, enter: PMT = 8,000, n = 6, i = 7%, FV = 0, and compute PV = $38,132.32

Since $38,132.32 < $40,000 (the cost of buying a truck), it is less expensive to lease than to buy.

31. PV of an annuity due = PV of ordinary annuity $\times (1 + r)$

(See problem 27 for a discussion of the value of an ordinary annuity versus an annuity due.) Therefore, with immediate payment, the value of the lease payments increases from $38,132.32 (as shown in the previous problem) to:

$$\$38,132.32 \times 1.07 = \$40,801.58$$

Since this is greater than $40,000 (the cost of buying a truck), we conclude that, if the first payment on the lease is due immediately, it is less expensive to buy the truck than to lease it.

32. Compare the present value of the payments. Assume the product sells for $100.

Installment plan:

$$PV = \$25 + [\$25 \times \text{annuity factor}(5\%, 3 \text{ years})]$$

$$PV = \$25 + \$25 \times \left[\frac{1}{0.05} - \frac{1}{0.05 \times (1.05)^3} \right] = \$93.08$$

Pay in full: Payment net of discount = $90

Choose the second payment plan for its lower present value of payments.

33. Installment plan:

$$PV = \$25 \times \text{annuity factor}(5\%, 4 \text{ years})$$

$$PV = \$25 \times \left[\frac{1}{0.05} - \frac{1}{0.05 \times (1.05)^4} \right] = \$88.65$$

Now the installment plan offers the lower present value of payments.

34. a. Solve for C in the following equation:

$$C \times \text{annuity factor}(12\%, 5 \text{ years}) = \$1,000$$

$$C \times \left[\frac{1}{0.12} - \frac{1}{0.12 \times (1.12)^5} \right] = \$1,000$$

$$C \times 3.6048 = \$1,000 \Rightarrow C = PMT = \$277.41$$

b. If the first payment is made immediately instead of in a year, the annuity factor will be greater by a factor of 1.12. Therefore:

$$C \times (3.6048 \times 1.12) = \$1,000 \Rightarrow C = PMT = \$247.69$$

35. This problem can be approached in two steps. First, find the present value of the $10,000, 10-year annuity as of year 3, when the first payment is exactly one year away (and is therefore an ordinary annuity). Then discount the value back to today.

(1) $PV_3 = \$10,000 \times \left[\dfrac{1}{0.05} - \dfrac{1}{0.05 \times (1.05)^{10}} \right] = \$77,217.35$

[Using a financial calculator, enter: PMT = 10,000; FV = 0; n = 10; i = 5%, and compute PV_3 = $77,217.35]

(2) $PV_0 = \dfrac{PV_3}{(1+r)^3} = \dfrac{\$77,217.35}{1.05^3} = \$66,703.25$

36. The monthly payment is based on a $100,000 loan:

$C \times \left[\dfrac{1}{0.01} - \dfrac{1}{0.01 \times (1.01)^{360}} \right] = \$100,000 \Rightarrow C = PMT = \$1,028.61$

The net amount received is $98,000. Therefore:

$\$1,028.61 \times \left[\dfrac{1}{r} - \dfrac{1}{r \times (1+r)^{360}} \right] = \$98,000 \Rightarrow r = 1.023\% \text{ per month}$

The effective rate is: $(1.01023)^{12} - 1 = 0.1299 = 12.99\%$

37. The payment on the mortgage is computed as follows:

$C \times \left[\dfrac{1}{(0.06/12)} - \dfrac{1}{(0.06/12) \times [1 + (0.06/12)]^{360}} \right] = \$100,000 \Rightarrow C = PMT = \$599.55$

After 12 years, 216 months remain on the loan, so the loan balance is:

$\$599.55 \times \left[\dfrac{1}{(0.06/12)} - \dfrac{1}{(0.06/12) \times [1 + (0.06/12)]^{216}} \right] = \$79,079.37$

38. a. $C \times \left[\dfrac{1}{0.08} - \dfrac{1}{0.08 \times (1.08)^4} \right] = \$1,000 \Rightarrow C = PMT = \$301.92$

Using a financial calculator, enter: PV = (–)1,000, FV = 0, i = 8%, n = 4, and compute PMT = $301.92

b.

Time	Loan balance	Year-end interest due	Year-end payment	Amortization of loan
0	$1,000.00	$80.00	$301.92	$221.92
1	$ 778.08	$62.25	$301.92	$239.67
2	$ 538.41	$43.07	$301.92	$258.85
3	$ 279.56	$22.36	$301.92	$279.56
4	$ 0.00	$ 0.00	--	--

c. $PV = \$301.92 \times \left[\dfrac{1}{0.08} - \dfrac{1}{0.08 \times (1.08)^3} \right] = \$778.08$

Therefore, the loan balance is $778.08 after one year.

39. The loan repayment is an annuity with present value equal to $4,248.68. Payments are made monthly, and the monthly interest rate is 1%. We need to equate this expression to the amount borrowed ($4,248.68) and solve for the number of months (t).

$$\$200 \times \left[\frac{1}{0.01} - \frac{1}{0.01 \times (1.01)^t} \right] = \$4,248.68 \Rightarrow t = 24 \text{ months, or 2 years}$$

Using a financial calculator, enter: PV = (–)4248.68, FV = 0, i = 1%, PMT = 200, and compute n = 24.

The effective annual rate on the loan is: $(1.01)^{12} - 1 = 0.1268 = 12.68\%$

40. The present value of the $2 million, 20-year annuity, discounted at 8%, is:

$$PV = \$2 \text{ million} \times \left[\frac{1}{0.08} - \frac{1}{0.08 \times (1.08)^{20}} \right] = \$19.64 \text{ million}$$

If the payment comes immediately, the present value increases by a factor of 1.08 to $21.21 million.

41. The real rate is zero. With a zero real rate, we simply divide her savings by the years of retirement: $450,000/30 = $15,000 per year

42. r = 0.5% per month

$1,000 \times (1.005)^{12} = \$1,061.68$

$1,000 \times (1.005)^{18} = \$1,093.93$

43. You are repaying the loan with payments in the form of an annuity. The present value of those payments must equal $100,000. Therefore:

$$\$804.62 \times \left[\frac{1}{r} - \frac{1}{r \times (1+r)^{360}} \right] = \$100,000 \Rightarrow r = 0.750\% \text{ per month}$$

[Using a financial calculator, enter: PV = (–)100,000, FV = 0, n = 360, PMT = 804.62, and compute the interest rate.]

The effective annual rate is: $(1.00750)^{12} - 1 = 0.0938 = 9.38\%$

The lender is more likely to quote the APR ($0.750\% \times 12 = 9\%$), which is lower.

44. $\text{EAR} = e^{0.06} - 1 = 1.0618 - 1 = 0.0618 = 6.18\%$

45. The present value of the payments for option (a) is $22,000.
The present value of the payments for option (b) is:

$$\text{PV} = \$500 \times \left[\frac{1}{0.01} - \frac{1}{0.01 \times (1.01)^{48}} \right] = \$18,986.98$$

Option (b) is the better deal.

46. $\$100 \times e^{0.10 \times 8} = \$222.55$

$\$100 \times e^{0.08 \times 10} = \$222.55$

47 Your savings goal is FV = $30,000. You currently have in the bank PV = $20,000. Solve the following equation for t:

$$(\$20,000 \times 1.005^{t}) + \$100 \times \left[\frac{1.005^{t} - 1}{0.005} \right] = \$30,000 \Rightarrow t = 44.74 \text{ months}$$

Using a financial calculator, enter FV = 30000, PV = (–)20000, PMT = (–)100 and r = 0.5%. Solve for n to find n = 44.74 months.

48. The present value of your payments to the bank equals:

$$\text{PV} = \$100 \times \left[\frac{1}{0.06} - \frac{1}{0.06 \times (1.06)^{10}} \right] = \$736.01$$

The present value of your receipts is the value of a $100 perpetuity deferred for 10 years:

$$\frac{100}{0.06} \times \frac{1}{(1.06)^{10}} = \$930.66$$

This is a good deal if you can earn 6% on your other investments.

49. If you live forever, you will receive a $100 perpetuity that has present value equal to: $100/r

Therefore: $100/r = $2500 \Rightarrow r = 4$ percent

50. $r = \$10,000/\$125,000 = 0.08 = 8$ percent

51. a. The present value of the ultimate sales price is: $4 million/$(1.08)^5 = \$2.722$ million

  b. The present value of the sales price is less than the cost of the property, so this would not be an attractive opportunity.

  c. The present value of the total cash flows from the property is now:

$$PV = [\$0.2 \text{ million} \times \text{annuity factor}(8\%, 5 \text{ years})] + \$4 \text{ million}/(1.08)^5$$

$$= \$0.2 \text{ million} \times \left[\frac{1}{0.08} - \frac{1}{0.08 \times (1.08)^5} \right] + \frac{\$4 \text{ million}}{(1.08)^5}$$

$$= \$0.799 \text{ million} + \$2.722 \text{ million} = \$3.521 \text{ million}$$

Therefore, the property is an attractive investment if you can buy it for $3 million.

52. PV of cash flows = ($120,000/1.12) + ($180,000/1.12^2) + ($300,000/1.12^3) = \$464,171.83

This exceeds the cost of the factory, so the investment is attractive.

53. a. The present value of the future payoff is: $2,000/(1.06)^{10} = \$1,116.79

This is a good deal: present value exceeds the initial investment.

  b. The present value is now equal to: $2,000/(1.10)^{10} = \$771.09

This is now less than the initial investment. Therefore, this is a bad deal.

54. Suppose the purchase price is $1. If you pay today, you get the discount and pay only $0.97. If you wait a month, you pay $1. Thus, you can view the deferred payment as saving a cash flow of $0.97 today, but paying $1 in a month. Therefore, the monthly rate is:

$0.03/0.97 = 0.0309 = 3.09\%$

The effective annual rate is: $(1.0309)^{12} - 1 = 0.4408 = 44.08\%$

55. You borrow $1,000 and repay the loan by making 12 monthly payments of $100. Solve for r in the following equation:

$$\$100 \times \left[\frac{1}{r} - \frac{1}{r \times (1+r)^{12}} \right] = \$1,000 \Rightarrow r = 2.923\% \text{ per month}$$

[Using a financial calculator, enter: PV = (−)1,000, FV = 0, n = 12, PMT = 100, and compute r = 2.923%]

Therefore, the APR is: $2.923\% \times 12 = 35.076\%$

The effective annual rate is: $(1.02923)^{12} - 1 = 0.41302 = 41.302\%$

If you borrowed $1,000 today and paid back $1,200 one year from today, the true rate would be 20%. You should have known that the true rate must be greater than 20% because the twelve $100 payments are made before the end of the year, thus increasing the true rate above 20%.

56. You will have to pay back the original $1,000 plus $(3 \times 20\%) = 60\%$ of the loan amount, or $1600 over the three years. This implies monthly payments of:

$$\$1,600/36 = \$44.44$$

The monthly interest rate is obtained by solving:

$$\$44.44 \times \left[\frac{1}{r} - \frac{1}{r \times (1+r)^{36}} \right] = \$1,000 \Rightarrow r = 2.799\% \text{ per month}$$

Using a financial calculator, enter: PV = (−)1,000, FV = 0, n = 36, PMT = 44.44, and compute r = 2.799%

Therefore, the APR is: $2.799\% \times 12 = 33.588\%$

The effective annual rate is: $(1.02799)^{12} - 1 = 0.39273 = 39.273\%$

57. For every $1,000 borrowed, the present value is: $[\$1,000 \times (1 - d)]$

The future value to be paid back is $1,000. Therefore, the annual interest rate is determined as follows:

$$PV \times (1 + r) = FV$$

$$[\$1,000 \times (1 - d)] \times (1 + r) = \$1,000$$

$$1 + r = \frac{1}{1-d} \Rightarrow r = \frac{1}{1-d} - 1 = \frac{d}{1-d} > d$$

If d = 20%, then the effective annual interest rate is: $(0.2/0.8) = 0.25 = 25\%$

58. After one year, each dollar invested at First National will grow to:

$$\$1 \times (1.031)^2 = \$1.06296$$

After one year, each dollar invested at Second National will grow to:

$$\$1 \times (1.005)^{12} = \$1.06168$$

First National pays the higher effective annual rate.

59. Since the $20 initiation fee is taken out of the proceeds of the loan, the amount actually borrowed is: $1,000 − $20 = $980

The monthly rate is found by solving the following equation for r:

$$\$90 \times \left[\frac{1}{r} - \frac{1}{r \times (1+r)^{12}} \right] = \$980 \Rightarrow r = 1.527\% \text{ per month}$$

The effective rate is: $(1.01527)^{12} - 1 = 0.1994 = 19.94\%$

60. The future value of the payments into your savings fund must accumulate to $500,000. We choose the payment (C) so that:

$$C \times \text{future value of an annuity} = \$500,000$$

$$C \times \left[\frac{1.06^{40} - 1}{0.06} \right] = \$500,000 \Rightarrow C = PMT = \$3,230.77$$

Using a financial calculator, enter: n = 40; i = 6; PV = 0; FV = 500,000, compute PMT = $3,230.77

61. If you invest the $100,000 received in year 10 until your retirement in year 40, it will grow to: $100,000 \times (1.06)^{30} = \$574,349.12$

Therefore, you do not need any additional savings; investing the $100,000 produces a future value that exceeds your $500,000 requirement.

62. By the time you retire you will need:

$$PV = \$40,000 \times \left[\frac{1}{0.06} - \frac{1}{0.06 \times (1.06)^{20}} \right] = \$458,796.85$$

The future value of the payments into your savings fund must accumulate to: $458,796.85
We choose the payment (C) so that:

C × future value of an annuity = $458,796.85

$$C \times \left[\frac{1.06^{40} - 1}{0.06} \right] = \$458,796.85 \Rightarrow C = PMT = \$2,964.53$$

Using a financial calculator, enter: n = 40; i = 6; PV = 0; FV = 458,796.85 and compute PMT = $2,964.53

63.　a.　After 30 years, the couple will have accumulated the future value of a $3,000 annuity, plus the future value of the $10,000 gift. The sum of the savings from these sources is:

$$\$3,000 \times \left[\frac{1.08^{30} - 1}{0.08} \right] + (\$10,000 \times 1.08^{25})$$

$$= \$339,849.63 + \$68,484.75 = \$408,334.38$$

　　b.　If they wish to accumulate $800,000 by retirement, they have to save an *additional* amount *per year* to provide additional accumulations of: $391,665.62
This requires additional annual savings of:

$$C \times \left[\frac{1.08^{30} - 1}{0.08} \right] = \$391,665.62 \Rightarrow C = PMT = \$3,457.40$$

[Using a financial calculator, enter: i = 8; n = 30; PV = 0; FV = 391,665.62 and compute PMT.]

64.　a.　The *present value* of the planned consumption stream *as of the retirement date* will be:

$$PV = \$30,000 \times \left[\frac{1}{0.08} - \frac{1}{0.08 \times (1.08)^{25}} \right] = \$320,243.29$$

Therefore, they need to have accumulated this amount of savings by the time they retire. So, their savings plan must provide a *future value* of: $320,243.29
With 50 years to save at 8%, the savings annuity must be:

$$C \times \left[\frac{1.08^{50} - 1}{0.08} \right] = \$320,243.29 \Rightarrow C = PMT = \$558.14$$

Another way to think about this is to recognize that the present value of the savings stream must equal the present value of the consumption stream. The PV of consumption as of today is: $320,243.29/(1.08)^{50} = \$6,827.98$

Therefore, we set the *present* value of savings equal to this value, and solve for the required savings stream.

b. The couple needs to accumulate additional savings with a present value of:

$$\$60,000/(1.08)^{20} = \$12,872.89$$

The total PV of savings is now: $\$12,872.89 + \$6,827.98 = \$19,700.87$

Now we solve for the required savings stream as follows:

$$C \times \left[\frac{1}{0.08} - \frac{1}{0.08 \times (1.08)^{50}} \right] = \$19,700.87 \Rightarrow C = PMT = \$1,610.41$$

Using a financial calculator, enter: n = 50; i = 8; PV = (–)19,700.87; FV = 0; and then compute PMT = $1,610.41

65. $60,000/6.9 = $8,696. Her real income increased from $6,000 to $8,696.

66. (1 + nominal interest rate) = (1 + real interest rate) × (1 + inflation rate)

   a. $1.03 \times 1.0 = 1.03 \Rightarrow$ nominal interest rate = 3.00%

   b. $1.03 \times 1.04 = 1.0712 \Rightarrow$ nominal interest rate = 7.12%

   c. $1.03 \times 1.06 = 1.0918 \Rightarrow$ nominal interest rate = 9.18%

67. real interest rate $= \dfrac{1 + \text{nominal interest rate}}{1 + \text{inflation rate}} - 1$

   a. $(1.06/1) - 1 = 0.0600 = 6.00\%$

   b. $(1.06/1.03) - 1 = 0.0291 = 2.91\%$

   c. $(1.06/1.06) - 1 = 0.0\%$

68. a. $PV = \$100/(1.08)^3 = \$79.38$

   b. real value $= \$100/(1.03)^3 = \$91.51$

   c. real interest rate $= \dfrac{1 + \text{nominal interest rate}}{1 + \text{inflation rate}} - 1 = 0.04854 = 4.854\%$

   d. $PV = \$91.51/(1.04854)^3 = \$79.38$

69. a. The real interest rate is: $(1.06/1.02) - 1 = 3.92\%$

   Therefore, the present value is:

$$PV = \$100,000 \times \left[\frac{1}{0.0392} - \frac{1}{0.0392 \times (1.0392)^5} \right] = \$446,184.51$$

   b. If cash flow is level in nominal terms, use the 6% nominal interest rate to discount. The annuity factor is now 4.21236 and the cash flow stream is worth only $421,236.

70. a. $1 million will have a real value of: $1 million/$(1.03)^{50} = \$228,107$

   b. At a real rate of 2%, this can support a real annuity of:

$$C \times \left[\frac{1}{0.02} - \frac{1}{0.02 \times (1.02)^{20}} \right] = \$228,107 \Rightarrow C = PMT = \$13,950$$

   [To solve this on a financial calculator, enter: n = 20, i = 2, PV = 228,107, FV = 0, and then compute PMT.]

71. According to the Rule of 72, at an interest rate of 6%, it will take 72/6 = 12 years for your money to double. For it to quadruple, your money must double, and then double again. This will take approximately 24 years.

   Using a financial calculator, enter: i = 6, PV = (–)1, FV = , and then compute n = 23.79 years.

   The real interest rate is: (1.06/1.04) – 1 = 0.0192 = 1.92%

   Purchasing power increases by: $(1.0192)^{24} - 1 = 0.5784 = 57.84\%$

72. $(1+1.11)^{12} - 1 = 7786.37 = 778,637\%\%$

   Prices increased by 778,637 percent per year.

73. Using the perpetuity formula, the 4% perpetuity will sell for: £4/0.06 = £66.67

   The 2½% perpetuity will sell for: £2.50/0.06 = £41.67

74. a. $PV = \$30,000 \times \left[\frac{1}{0.10} - \frac{1}{0.10 \times (1.10)^{15}} \right] = \$228,182.39$

   b. The present value of the retirement goal is:

   $\$228,182.39/(1.10)^{30} = \$13,076.80$

   The present value of your 30-year savings stream must equal this present value. Therefore, we need to find the payment for which:

$$C \times \left[\frac{1}{0.10} - \frac{1}{0.10 \times (1.10)^{30}} \right] = \$13,076.80 \Rightarrow C = PMT = \$1,387.18$$

   You must save $1,387.18 per year.

   c. $1.00 \times (1.04)^{30} = \$3.24$

d. We repeat part (a) using the real interest rate: $(1.10/1.04) - 1 = 0.0577$ or 5.77%

The retirement goal in real terms is:

$$PV = \$30,000 \times \left[\frac{1}{0.0577} - \frac{1}{0.0577 \times (1.0577)^{15}} \right] = \$295,796.61$$

e. The future value of your 30-year savings stream must equal: $295,796.61
Therefore, we solve for payment (PMT) in the following equation:

$$C \times \left[\frac{1.0577^{30} - 1}{0.0577} \right] = \$295,796.61 \Rightarrow C = PMT = \$3,895.66$$

Therefore, we find that you must save $3,895.66 per year in real terms. This value is much higher than the result found in part (b) because the rate at which purchasing power grows is less than the nominal interest rate, 10%.

f. If the *real* amount saved is $3,895.66 and prices rise at 4 percent per year, then the amount saved at the end of one year, in nominal terms, will be:

$3,895.66 \times 1.04 = \$4,051.49$

The thirtieth year will require nominal savings of:

$3,895.66 \times (1.04)^{30} = \$12,635.17$

75. a. We redo problem 64, but now we use the real interest rate, which is:

$(1.08/1.04) - 1 = 0.0385 = 3.85\%$

We note that the $30,000 expenditure stream now must be interpreted as a real annuity, which will rise along with the general level of prices at the inflation rate of 4%.

We find that the PV of the required real savings stream *as of the retirement date* is:

$$PV = \$30,000 \times \left[\frac{1}{0.0385} - \frac{1}{0.0385 \times (1.0385)^{25}} \right] = \$476,182.14$$

[Using a financial calculator, enter: n = 25; i = 3.85; FV = 0; PMT = 30,000 and compute PV.]

This requires a savings stream with a real future value of $476,182.14, which means that the real savings stream must be: $3,266.82

$$C \times \left[\frac{1.0385^{50} - 1}{0.0385} \right] = \$476,182.14 \Rightarrow C = PMT = \$3,266.82$$

[Using a financial calculator, enter: n = 50; i = 3.85; FV = (−)476,182.14; and then compute PMT.]

b. Nominal savings in year one will be: $3,266.82 \times 1.04 = \$3,397.49$

c. Nominal savings in the last year will be: $3,266.82 \times (1.04)^{50} = \$23,216.26$

d. Nominal expenditures in the first year of retirement will be:

$$\$30,000 \times (1.04)^{51} = \$221,728.52$$

Nominal expenditures in the last year of retirement will be:

$$\$30,000 \times (1.04)^{75} = \$568,357.64$$

76. The interest rate per three months is: 6%/4 = 1.5%

Therefore, the value of the perpetuity is: $100/0.015 = $6,666.67

77. $FV = PV \times (1 + r_0) \times (1 + r_1) = \$1 \times 1.08 \times 1.10 = \$1.188$

$$PV = \frac{FV}{(1+r_0) \times (1+r_1)} = \frac{\$1}{1.08 \times 1.10} = \$0.8418$$

78. You earned compound interest of 6% for 8 years and 4% for 13 years. Your $1,000 has grown to:

$$\$1,000 \times (1.06)^8 \times (1.04)^{13} = \$2,653.87$$

79. a. First, calculate the present value of all lifetime expenditures

General living expenses of $50,000 per year for 50 years:

$$\$50,000 \times \left[\frac{1}{0.05} - \frac{1}{0.05 \times (1.05)^{50}} \right] = \$912,796$$

Apartment rental of $16,000 for 8 years

$$\$16,000 \times \left[\frac{1}{0.05} - \frac{1}{0.05 \times (1.05)^8} \right] = \$103,411$$

Home purchase of $250,000 in 9 years

$$PV = \$250,000/(1.05)^9 = \$161,152$$

Five automobile purchases of $30,000 in each of years 0, 10, 20, 30, 40, and 50.

$$PV = \$30,000/(1.05)^0 = \$30,000$$
$$PV = \$30,000/(1.05)^{10} = \$18,417$$
$$PV = \$30,000/(1.05)^{20} = \$11,307$$
$$PV = \$30,000/(1.05)^{30} = \$6,941$$
$$PV = \$30,000/(1.05)^{40} = \$4,261$$
$$PV = \$30,000/(1.05)^{50} = \$2,616$$

College education of $150,000 in 25 years

$$PV = \$150,000/(1.05)^{25} = \$44,295$$

College education of $150,000 in 30 years

$$PV = \$150,000/(1.05)^{30} = \$34,707$$

Retirement Portfolio of $436,177 in 50 years ($436,177 = PV of a 20 year annuity paying $35,000).

$$\$35,000 \times \left[\frac{1}{0.05} - \frac{1}{0.05 \times (1.05)^{20}} \right] = \$436,177$$

$$PV = \$436,177/(1.05)^{50} = \$38,036$$

Summing the present value of all lifetime expenditures gives
$1,367,939 = 912,796 + 103,411 + 161,152 + 30,000 + 18,417 + 11,307 + 6,941 + 4,261 + 2,616 + 44,295 + 34,707 + 38,036.

To find the average salary necessary to support this lifetime consumption plan we solve for the 50 year payment with the same present value:

$$C \times \left[\frac{1}{0.05} - \frac{1}{0.05 \times (1.05)^{50}} \right] = \$1,367,939 \Rightarrow C = PMT = \$74,931$$

b. In part a we have discounted real cash flows using a nominal interest rate. Here we repeat the process using a real interest rate of 1.94% (0.0194 = 1.05/1.03 – 1).

General living expenses of $50,000 per year for 50 years:

$$\$50,000 \times \left[\frac{1}{0.0194} - \frac{1}{0.00194 \times (1.0194)^{50}} \right] = \$1,591,184$$

Apartment rental of $16,000 for 8 years

$$\$16,000 \times \left[\frac{1}{0.0194} - \frac{1}{0.00194 \times (1.0194)^{8}} \right] = \$117,511$$

Home purchase of $250,000 in 9 years

$$PV = \$250,000/(1.00194)^{9} = \$210,300$$

Five automobile purchases of $30,000 in each of years 0, 10, 20, 30, 40, and 50.

$$PV = \$30,000/(1.0194)^0 = \$30,000$$
$$PV = \$30,000/(1.0194)^{10} = \$24,756$$
$$PV = \$30,000/(1.0194)^{20} = \$20,428$$
$$PV = \$30,000/(1.0194)^{30} = \$16,857$$
$$PV = \$30,000/(1.0194)^{40} = \$13,910$$
$$PV = \$30,000/(1.0194)^{50} = \$11,479$$

College education of $150,000 in 25 years

$$PV = \$150,000/(1.0194)^{25} = \$92,785$$

College education of $150,000 in 30 years

$$PV = \$150,000/(1.0194)^{30} = \$84,285$$

Retirement Portfolio of $575,530 in 50 years ($575,530 = PV of a 20 year annuity paying $35,000).

$$\$35,000 \times \left[\frac{1}{0.0194} - \frac{1}{0.0194 \times (1.0194)^{20}} \right] = \$575,530$$

$$PV = \$575,530/(1.00194)^{50} = \$220,210$$

Summing the present value of all lifetime expenditures gives
$2,433,705 = 1,591,184 + 117,511 + 210,300 + 30,000 + 24,756 + 20,428 + 16,857 + 13,910 + 11,479 + 92,785 + 84,285 + 220,210.

To find the average salary necessary to support this lifetime consumption plan we solve for the 50 year payment with the same present value:

$$C \times \left[\frac{1}{0.0194} - \frac{1}{0.0194 \times (1.0194)^{50}} \right] = \$2,433,705 \Rightarrow C = PMT = \$76,475$$

This average real salary is equivalent to the salary from part a, $74,931, growing to $135,334 in just 20 years ($74,931 \times (1 + 0.03)^{20} = \$135,334).

With these expected lifetime expenditures a 2010 graduate must "save" on average $76,475 each year; a challenge, given that the required annual savings will grow along with other prices each year.

80. a. Using Table 5-4, the annuity factor is 11.4699. The annual payment on the loan is therefore $100,000/11.4699 = \$8,718.47$.

b.

Year	Beginning-of-Year Balance	Year-End Interest Due on Balance	Year-End Payment	Amortization of Loan	End-of-Year Balance
1	100,000.00	6,000	8,718.46	2,718.46	97,281.54
2	97,281.54	5,837	8,718.46	2,881.56	94,399.98
3	94,399.98	5,664	8,718.46	3,054.46	91,345.52
4	91,345.52	5,481	8,718.46	3,237.72	88,107.80
5	88,107.80	5,286	8,718.46	3,431.99	84,675.81
6	84,675.81	5,081	8,718.46	3,637.91	81,037.91
7	81,037.91	4,862	8,718.46	3,856.18	77,181.72
8	77,181.72	4,631	8,718.46	4,087.55	73,094.17
9	73,094.17	4,386	8,718.46	4,332.81	68,761.37
10	68,761.37	4,126	8,718.46	4,592.77	64,168.59
11	64,168.59	3,850	8,718.46	4,868.34	59,300.25
12	59,300.25	3,558	8,718.46	5,160.44	54,139.81
13	54,139.81	3,248	8,718.46	5,470.07	48,669.75
14	48,669.75	2,920	8,718.46	5,798.27	42,871.47
15	42,871.47	2,572	8,718.46	6,146.17	36,725.31
16	36,725.31	2,204	8,718.46	6,514.94	30,210.37
17	30,210.37	1,813	8,718.46	6,905.83	23,304.54
18	23,304.54	1,398	8,718.46	7,320.18	15,984.35
19	15,984.35	959	8,718.46	7,759.39	8,224.96
20	8,224.96	493	8,718.46	8,224.96	0.00

c. The initial loan payment is 6,000 of 8,718.46, or 69%. Amortization is 31%. The last loan payment is 493 of 8,718.46, or 6%. After 10 years $35,831.41 has been paid off, or 36% of the loan.

d. If the inflation rate is 2% the real interest rate on the loan is approximately 4%. The real value of the first payment is $\$8,718.46/(1+.04)^1$, or $8,383.13. The real value of the last payment is $\$8,718.46/(1+.04)^{20}$, or $3,978.99.

e. If the inflation rate is 8% and the real interest rate is unchanged the nominal interest rate is approximately, 12%.

Year	Beginning-of-Year Balance	Year-End Interest Due on Balance	Year-End Payment	Amortization of Loan	End-of-Year Balance
1	100,000.00	12,000	13,387.88	1,387.88	98,612.12
2	98,612.12	11,833	13,387.88	1,554.42	97,057.70
3	97,057.70	11,647	13,387.88	1,740.95	95,316.74
4	95,316.74	11,438	13,387.88	1,949.87	93,366.88
5	93,366.88	11,204	13,387.88	2,183.85	91,183.02
6	91,183.02	10,942	13,387.88	2,445.92	88,737.11
7	88,737.11	10,648	13,387.88	2,739.43	85,997.68
8	85,997.68	10,320	13,387.88	3,068.16	82,929.53
9	82,929.53	9,952	13,387.88	3,436.33	79,493.19
10	79,493.19	9,539	13,387.88	3,848.70	75,644.50
11	75,644.50	9,077	13,387.88	4,310.54	71,333.96
12	71,333.96	8,560	13,387.88	4,827.80	66,506.16
13	66,506.16	7,981	13,387.88	5,407.14	61,099.02
14	61,099.02	7,332	13,387.88	6,056.00	55,043.02
15	55,043.02	6,605	13,387.88	6,782.72	48,260.30
16	48,260.30	5,791	13,387.88	7,596.64	40,663.66
17	40,663.66	4,880	13,387.88	8,508.24	32,155.42
18	32,155.42	3,859	13,387.88	9,529.23	22,626.20
19	22,626.20	2,715	13,387.88	10,672.73	11,953.46
20	11,953.46	1,434	13,387.88	11,953.46	0.00

The real value of the first payment is $13,387.88/(1+.04)^1$, or \$12,872.96. The real value of the last payment is $13,387.88/(1+.04)^{20}$, or \$6,110.05.

f. High inflation hurts the real estate market by increasing the real costs of the homeownership.

Solution to Minicase for Chapter 5

How much can Mr. Road spend each year? First let's see what happens if we ignore inflation.

1. Account for Social Security income of $750 per month, or $9,000 annually.

2. Account for the income from the savings account. Because Mr. Road does not want to run down the balance of this account, he can spend only the interest income:

   $0.05 \times \$12,000 = \$600$ annually

3. Compute the annual consumption available from his investment account. We find the 20-year annuity with present value equal to the value in the account:

   Present Value = annual payment × 20-year annuity factor at 9% interest rate:

   $$PV = \text{annual payment} \times \left[\frac{1}{0.09} - \frac{1}{0.09 \times (1.09)^{20}} \right]$$

   $\$180,000 = \text{annual payment} \times 9.129 \Rightarrow \text{Annual payment} = \$180,000/9.129 = \$19,717$

   Notice that the investment account provides annual income of $19,717, which is more than the annual interest from the account. This is because Mr. Road plans to run the account down to zero by the end of his life.

So Mr. Road can spend: $19,717 + $600 + $9,000 = $29,317 per year
This is comfortably above his current living expenses, which are $2,000 per month or $24,000 annually.

The problem of course is inflation. We have mixed up real and nominal flows. The Social Security payments are tied to the consumer price index and therefore are level in *real* terms. But the annuity of $19,717 per year from the investment account and the $600 interest from the savings account are fixed in *nominal* terms, and therefore the purchasing power of these flows will steadily decline.

For example, let's look out 15 years. At 4 percent inflation, prices will increase by a factor of $(1.04)^{15} = 1.80$. Income in 15 years will therefore be as follows:

Income Source	Nominal Income	Real Income
Social security (indexed to CPI, fixed in real terms at $9,000)	$ 16,200	$ 9,000
Savings account	600	333
Investment account (fixed nominal annuity)	19,717	10,954
Total income	$ 36,517	$20,287

Once we recognize inflation, we see that, in fifteen years, income from the investment account will buy only a bit more than one-half of the goods it buys today.

Obviously Mr. Road needs to spend less today and put more aside for the future. Rather than spending a constant *nominal* amount out of his savings, he would probably be better off spending a constant *real* amount.

Since we are interested in level real expenditures, we must use the real interest rate to calculate the 20-year annuity that can be provided by the $180,000. The real interest rate is:

real interest rate = (1.09/1.04) − 1 = 1.048 − 1 = 4.8%

We therefore calculate the real sum that can be spent out of savings as follows:

$$C \times \left[\frac{1}{0.048} - \frac{1}{0.048 \times (1.048)^{20}} \right] = \$180,000 \Rightarrow C = PMT = \$14,200$$

[Using a financial calculator, enter: n = 20; i = 4.8; PV = (−)180,000; and then compute PMT = $14,200]

Thus Mr. Road's investment account can generate real income of $14,200 per year. The real value of Social Security is fixed at $9,000. Finally, if we assume that Mr. Road wishes to maintain the *real* value of his savings account at $12,000, then he will have to increase the balance of the account in line with inflation, that is, by 4% each year. Since the nominal interest rate on the account is 5%, only the first 1% of interest earnings on the account, or $120 real dollars, is available for spending each year. The other 4% of earnings must be re-invested. So total real income is: $14,200 + $9,000 + $120 = $23,320

To keep pace with inflation Mr. Road will have to spend 4 percent more of his savings each year. After one year of inflation, he will spend: 1.04 × $23,320 = $24,253

After two years he will spend: $(1.04)^2 \times \$23,320 = \$25,223$

The picture fifteen years out looks like this:

Income Source	Nominal Income	Real Income
Social security	$16,200	$ 9,000
Net income from savings account(i.e., net of reinvested interest)	216	120
Investment account (fixed *real* annuity)	25,560	14,200
Total income	$41,976	$23,320

Mr. Road's income and expenditure will nearly double in 15 years but his real income and expenditure are unchanged at $23,320.

This may be bad news for Mr. Road since his living expenses are $24,000. Do you advise him to prune his living expenses? Perhaps he should put part of his nest egg in junk bonds which offer higher *promised* interest rates, or into the stock market, which has generated higher returns on average than investment in bonds. These higher returns might support a higher real annuity—but is Mr. Road prepared to bear the extra risks?

Should Mr. Road consume more today and risk having to sell his house if his savings are run down late in life? These issues make the planning problem even more difficult. It is clear, however, that one cannot plan for retirement without considering inflation.

Solutions to Chapter 6

Valuing Bonds

1. a. Coupon rate = 6%, which remains unchanged. The coupon payments are fixed at $60 per year.

   b. When the market yield increases, the bond price will fall. The cash flows are discounted at a higher rate.

   c. At a lower price, the bond's yield to maturity will be higher. The higher yield to maturity for the bond is commensurate with the higher yields available in the rest of the bond market.

   d. Current yield = coupon rate/bond price
      As coupon rate remains the same and the bond price decreases, the current yield increases.

2. When the bond is selling at a discount, $970 in this case, the yield to maturity is greater than 8%. We know that if the yield to maturity were 8%, the bond would sell at par. At a price below par, the yield to maturity exceeds the coupon rate.

   Current yield = coupon payment/bond price = $80/$970

   Therefore, current yield is also greater than 8%.

3. Coupon payment = 0.08 × $1,000 = $80

   Current yield = $80/bond price = 0.07

   Therefore: bond price = $80/0.07 = $1,142.86

4. Coupon rate = $80/$1,000 = 0.080 = 8.0%

   Current yield = $80/$950 = 0.0842 = 8.42%

   To compute the yield to maturity, use trial and error to solve for r in the following equation:

   $$\$950 = \$80 \times \left[\frac{1}{r} - \frac{1}{r \times (1+r)^6} \right] + \frac{\$1,000}{(1+r)^6} \Rightarrow r = 9.119\%$$

   Using a financial calculator, compute the yield to maturity by entering:
   n = 6; PV = (–)950; FV = 1000; PMT = 80, compute i = 9.119%

   Verify the solution as follows:

   $$PV = \$80 \times \left[\frac{1}{0.09119} - \frac{1}{0.09119(1.09119)^6} \right] + \frac{\$1,000}{1.09119^6} = \$949.98$$

   (difference due to rounding)

5. In order for the bond to sell at par, the coupon rate must equal the yield to maturity. Since Circular bonds yield 9.119%, this must be the coupon rate.

6. a. Current yield = coupon/price = $80/$1,100 = 0.0727 = 7.27%

   b. To compute the yield to maturity, use trial and error to solve for r in the following equation:

   $$\$1,100 = \$80 \times \left[\frac{1}{r} - \frac{1}{r \times (1+r)^{10}}\right] + \frac{\$1,000}{(1+r)^{10}} \Rightarrow r = 6.602\%$$

   Using a financial calculator, compute the yield to maturity by entering:
   n = 10; PV = (−)1100; FV = 1000; PMT = 80, compute i = 6.602%

   Verify the solution as follows:

   $$PV = \$80 \times \left[\frac{1}{0.06602} - \frac{1}{0.06602(1.06602)^{10}}\right] + \frac{\$1,000}{1.06602^{10}} = \$1,100.02$$

   (difference due to rounding)

7. When the bond is selling at face value, its yield to maturity equals its coupon rate. This firm's bonds are selling at a yield to maturity of 9.25%. So the coupon rate on the new bonds must be 9.25% if they are to sell at face value.

8. The bond pays a coupon of 7.125% which means annual interest is $71.25. The bond is selling for: 130 5/32 = $1,301.5625. Therefore, the current yield is: $71.25/$1301.5625 = 5.47%

   The current yield exceeds the yield-to-maturity on the bond because the bond is selling at a premium. At maturity the holder of the bond will receive only the $1,000 face value, reducing the total return on investment.

9. Bond 1

   Year 1: $PV = \$80 \times \left[\frac{1}{0.10} - \frac{1}{0.10(1.10)^{10}}\right] + \frac{\$1,000}{1.10^{10}} = \$877.11$

   Year 2: $PV = \$80 \times \left[\frac{1}{0.10} - \frac{1}{0.10(1.10)^{9}}\right] + \frac{\$1,000}{1.10^{9}} = \$884.82$

   Using a financial calculator:

   Year 1: PMT = 80, FV = 1000, i = 10%, n = 10; compute PV_0 = $877.11

   Year 2: PMT = 80, FV = 1000, i = 10%, n = 9; compute PV_1 = $884.82

$$\text{Rate of return} = \frac{\$80 + (\$884.82 - \$877.11)}{\$877.11} = 0.100 = 10.0\%$$

Bond 2

$$\text{Year 1: PV} = \$120 \times \left[\frac{1}{0.10} - \frac{1}{0.10(1.10)^{10}} \right] + \frac{\$1,000}{1.10^{10}} = \$1,122.89$$

$$\text{Year 2: PV} = \$120 \times \left[\frac{1}{0.10} - \frac{1}{0.10(1.10)^{9}} \right] + \frac{\$1,000}{1.10^{9}} = \$1,115.18$$

Using a financial calculator:

Year 1: PMT = 120, FV = 1000, i = 10%, n = 10; compute PV_0 = $1,122.89

Year 2: PMT = 120, FV = 1000, i = 10%, n = 9; compute PV_1 = $1,115.18

$$\text{Rate of Return} = \frac{\$120 + (\$1,115.18 - \$1,122.89)}{\$1,122.89} = 0.100 = 10.0\%$$

Both bonds provide the same rate of return.

10. a. If yield to maturity = 8%, price will be $1,000.

b. Rate of return =

$$\frac{\text{coupon income} + \text{price change}}{\text{investment}} = \frac{\$80 + (\$1,000 - \$1,100)}{\$1,100} = -0.0182 = -1.82\%$$

c. $\text{Real return} = \dfrac{1 + \text{nominal interest rate}}{1 + \text{ inflation rate}} - 1 = \dfrac{0.9818}{1.03} - 1 = -0.0468 = -4.68\%$

11. a. With a par value of $1,000 and a coupon rate of 8%, the bondholder receives $80 per year.

b. $\text{PV} = \$80 \times \left[\dfrac{1}{0.07} - \dfrac{1}{0.07 \times (1.07)^{9}} \right] + \dfrac{\$1,000}{(1.07)^{9}} = \$1,065.15$

c. If the yield to maturity is 6%, the bond will sell for:

$$\text{PV} = \$80 \times \left[\frac{1}{0.06} - \frac{1}{0.06 \times (1.06)^{9}} \right] + \frac{\$1,000}{(1.06)^{9}} = \$1,136.03$$

12. a. To compute the yield to maturity, use trial and error to solve for r in the following equation:

$$\$900 = \$80 \times \left[\frac{1}{r} - \frac{1}{r \times (1+r)^{30}} \right] + \frac{\$1,000}{(1+r)^{30}} \Rightarrow r = 8.971\%$$

Using a financial calculator, compute the yield to maturity by entering:
n = 30; PV = (–)900; FV = 1000; PMT = 80, compute i = 8.971%

Verify the solution as follows:

$$PV = \$80 \times \left[\frac{1}{0.08971} - \frac{1}{0.08971(1.08971)^{30}} \right] + \frac{\$1,000}{1.08971^{30}} = \$899.99$$

(difference due to rounding)

b. Since the bond is selling for face value, the yield to maturity = 8.000%

c. To compute the yield to maturity, use trial and error to solve for r in the following equation:

$$\$1,100 = \$80 \times \left[\frac{1}{r} - \frac{1}{r \times (1+r)^{30}} \right] + \frac{\$1,000}{(1+r)^{30}} \Rightarrow r = 7.180\%$$

Using a financial calculator, compute the yield to maturity by entering:
n = 30; PV = (–)1100; FV = 1000; PMT = 80, compute i = 7.180%

Verify the solution as follows:

$$PV = \$80 \times \left[\frac{1}{0.07180} - \frac{1}{0.07180(1.07180)^{30}} \right] + \frac{\$1,000}{1.07180^{30}} = \$1,099.94$$

(difference due to rounding)

13. a. To compute the yield to maturity, use trial and error to solve for r in the following equation:

$$\$900 = \$40 \times \left[\frac{1}{r} - \frac{1}{r \times (1+r)^{60}} \right] + \frac{\$1,000}{(1+r)^{60}} \Rightarrow r = 4.483\%$$

Using a financial calculator, compute the yield to maturity by entering:
n = 60; PV = (–)900; FV = 1000; PMT = 40, compute i = 4.483%

Verify the solution as follows:

$$PV = \$40 \times \left[\frac{1}{0.04483} - \frac{1}{0.04483(1.04483)^{60}} \right] + \frac{\$1,000}{1.04483^{60}} = \$900.02$$

(difference due to rounding)

Therefore, the annualized bond equivalent yield to maturity is:

4.483% × 2 = 8.966%

b. Since the bond is selling for face value, the semi-annual yield = 4%

Therefore, the annualized bond equivalent yield to maturity is: $4\% \times 2 = 8\%$

c. To compute the yield to maturity, use trial and error to solve for r in the following equation:

$$\$1{,}100 = \$40 \times \left[\frac{1}{r} - \frac{1}{r \times (1+r)^{60}} \right] + \frac{\$1{,}000}{(1+r)^{60}} \Rightarrow r = 3.592\%$$

Using a financial calculator, compute the yield to maturity by entering:
n = 60; PV = (−)1100; FV = 1000; PMT = 40, compute i = 3.592%
Verify the solution as follows:

$$PV = \$40 \times \left[\frac{1}{0.03592} - \frac{1}{0.03592(1.03592)^{60}} \right] + \frac{\$1{,}000}{1.03592^{60}} = \$1{,}099.92$$

(difference due to rounding)

Therefore, the annualized bond equivalent yield to maturity is:

$3.592\% \times 2 = 7.184\%$

14. In each case, we solve the following equation for the missing variable:

Price = $\$1{,}000/(1 + y)^{\text{maturity}}$

Price	Maturity (Years)	Yield to Maturity
$300.00	30.00	4.095%
$300.00	15.64	8.000%
$385.54	10.00	10.000%

15. PV of perpetuity = coupon payment/rate of return.

PV = C/r = $60/0.06 = $1,000.00

If the required rate of return is 10%, the bond sells for:

PV = C/r = $60/0.10 = $600.00

16. Current yield = 0.098375 so bond price can be solved from the following:

$90/Price = 0.098375 $\Rightarrow$ Price = $914.87

To compute the remaining maturity, solve for t in the following equation:

$$\$914.87 = \$90 \times \left[\frac{1}{0.10} - \frac{1}{0.10 \times (1.10)^{t}} \right] + \frac{\$1{,}000}{(1.10)^{t}} \Rightarrow t = 20.0$$

Using a financial calculator, compute the remaining maturity by entering:
PV = (−)914.87; FV = 1000; PMT = 90, i = 10 and compute n = 20.0 years.

17. Solve the following equation for PMT:

$$\$1{,}065.15 = PMT \times \left[\frac{1}{0.07} - \frac{1}{0.07 \times (1.07)^9} \right] + \frac{\$1{,}000}{(1.07)^9} \Rightarrow PMT = \$80.00$$

Using a financial calculator, compute the annual payment by entering:
n = 9; PV = (–)1065.15; FV = 1000; i = 7, compute PMT = $80.00

Since the annual payment is $80, the coupon rate is 8%.

18. a. The coupon rate must be 7% because the bonds were issued at face value with a yield to maturity of 7%. Now, the price is:

$$PV = \$70 \times \left[\frac{1}{0.15} - \frac{1}{0.15(1.15)^8} \right] + \frac{\$1{,}000}{1.15^8} = \$641.01$$

b. The investors pay $641.01 for the bond. They expect to receive the promised coupons plus $800 at maturity. We calculate the yield to maturity based on these expectations by solving the following equation for r:

$$\$641.01 = \$70 \times \left[\frac{1}{r} - \frac{1}{r \times (1+r)^8} \right] + \frac{\$800}{(1+r)^8} \Rightarrow r = 12.87\%$$

Using a financial calculator, enter: n = 8; PV = (–)641.01; FV = 800; PMT = 70, and then compute i = 12.87%

19. a. At a price of $1,100 and remaining maturity of 9 years, find the bond's yield to maturity by solving for r in the following equation:

$$\$1{,}100 = \$80 \times \left[\frac{1}{r} - \frac{1}{r \times (1+r)^9} \right] + \frac{\$1{,}000}{(1+r)^9} \Rightarrow r = 6.50\%$$

Using a financial calculator, enter: n = 9; PV = (–)1100; FV = 1000; PMT = 80, and then compute i = 6.50%

b. Rate of return $= \dfrac{\$80 + (\$1{,}100 - \$980)}{\$980} = 20.41\%$

20. $$PV_0 = \$80 \times \left[\frac{1}{0.09} - \frac{1}{0.09(1.09)^{20}} \right] + \frac{\$1{,}000}{1.09^{20}} = \$908.71$$

$$PV_1 = \$80 \times \left[\frac{1}{0.10} - \frac{1}{0.10(1.10)^{19}} \right] + \frac{\$1{,}000}{1.10^{19}} = \$832.70$$

Rate of return $= \dfrac{\$80 + (\$832.70 - \$908.71)}{\$908.71} = 0.0044 = 0.44\%$

21. a, b.

Price of each bond at different yields to maturity

	Maturity of bond		
Yield	4 years	8 years	30 years
7%	$1,033.87	$1,059.71	$1,124.09
8%	$1,000.00	$1,000.00	$1,000.00
9%	$ 967.60	$ 944.65	$ 897.26

   c. The table shows that prices of longer-term bonds are more sensitive to changes in interest rates.

22. The price of the bond at the end of the year depends on the interest rate at that time. With one year until maturity, the bond price will be: $1,080/(1 + r)

   a. Price = $1,080/1.06 = $1,018.87

   Rate of Return = [$80 + ($1,018.87 − $1,000)]/$1,000 = 0.0989 = 9.89%

   b. Price = $1,080/1.08 = $1,000.00

   Rate of Return = [$80 + ($1,000 − $1,000)]/$1,000 = 0.0800 = 8.00%

   c. Price = $1,080/1.10 = $981.82

   Rate of Return = [$80 + ($981.82 − $1,000)]/$1000 = 0.0618 = 6.18%

23. The original price of the bond is computed as follows:

$$PV = \$40 \times \left[\frac{1}{0.07} - \frac{1}{0.07(1.07)^{30}} \right] + \frac{\$1,000}{1.07^{30}} = \$627.73$$

After one year, the maturity of the bond will be 29 years and its price will be:

$$PV = \$40 \times \left[\frac{1}{0.08} - \frac{1}{0.08(1.08)^{29}} \right] + \frac{\$1,000}{1.08^{29}} = \$553.66$$

The capital loss on the bond is $74.07. The rate of return is therefore:

   ($40 − $74.07)/$627.73 = −0.0543 = −5.43%

24. The bond's yield to maturity will increase from 7.5% to 7.8% when the perceived default risk increases. The bond price will fall:

$$\text{Initial Price} = PV = \$70 \times \left[\frac{1}{0.075} - \frac{1}{0.075(1.075)^{10}} \right] + \frac{\$1,000}{1.075^{10}} = \$965.68$$

$$\text{New Price} = PV = \$70 \times \left[\frac{1}{0.078} - \frac{1}{0.078(1.078)^{10}} \right] + \frac{\$1,000}{1.078^{10}} = \$945.83$$

25. The nominal rate of return is 6%.

   The real rate of return is: $[1.06/(1 + \text{inflation})] - 1$

   a. $1.06/1.02 - 1 = 0.0392 = 3.92\%$

   b. $1.06/1.04 - 1 = 0.0192 = 1.92\%$

   c. $1.06/1.06 - 1 = 0.00 = 0\%$

   d. $1.06/1.08 - 1 = -0.0185 = -1.85\%$

26. The principal value of the bond will increase by the inflation rate, and since the coupon is 4% of the principal, the coupon will also increase along with the general level of prices. The total cash flow provided by the bond will be:

   $$1000 \times (1 + \text{inflation rate}) + \text{coupon rate} \times 1000 \times (1 + \text{inflation rate}).$$

   Since the bond is purchased for face value, or $1,000, total dollar nominal return is therefore the *increase* in the principal due to the inflation indexing, plus coupon income:

   $$\text{Income} = [\$1,000 \times \text{inflation rate}] + [\text{coupon rate} \times \$1,000 \times (1 + \text{inflation rate})]$$

   Finally: nominal rate of return = income/$1,000

   a. Nominal rate of return $= \dfrac{\$20 + (\$40 \times 1.02)}{\$1,000} = 0.0608 = 6.08\%$

   Real rate of return $= \dfrac{1.0608}{1.02} - 1 = 0.0400 = 4.00\%$

   b. Nominal rate of return $= \dfrac{\$40 + (\$40 \times 1.04)}{\$1,000} = 0.0816 = 8.16\%$

   Real rate of return $= \dfrac{1.0816}{1.04} - 1 = 0.0400 = 4.00\%$

   c. Nominal rate of return $= \dfrac{\$60 + (\$40 \times 1.06)}{\$1,000} = 0.1024 = 10.24\%$

   Real rate of return $= \dfrac{1.1024}{1.06} - 1 = 0.0400 = 4.00\%$

   d. Nominal rate of return $= \dfrac{\$80 + (\$40 \times 1.08)}{\$1,000} = 0.1232 = 12.32\%$

   Real rate of return $= \dfrac{1.1232}{1.08} - 1 = 0.0400 = 4.00\%$

27.	First year cash flow	Second year cash flow
a.	$40 \times 1.02 = \$40.80$	$\$1,040 \times 1.02^2 = \$1,082.016$
b.	$40 \times 1.04 = \$41.60$	$\$1,040 \times 1.04^2 = \$1,124.864$
c.	$40 \times 1.06 = \$42.40$	$\$1,040 \times 1.06^2 = \$1,168.544$
d.	$40 \times 1.08 = \$43.20$	$\$1,040 \times 1.08^2 = \$1,213.056$

28. The coupon bond will fall from an initial price of $1,000 (when yield to maturity − 8%) to a new price of $897.26 when yield to maturity immediately rises to 9%. This is a 10.27% decline in the bond price.

$$\text{The initial price of the zero-coupon bond is: } \frac{\$1,000}{1.08^{30}} = \$99.38$$

$$\text{The new price of the zero-coupon bond is: } \frac{\$1,000}{1.09^{30}} = \$75.37$$

This is a price decline of 24.16%, far greater than that of the coupon bond.

The price of the coupon bond is much less sensitive to the change in yield. It seems to act like a shorter maturity bond. This makes sense: there are many coupon payments for the 8% bond, most of which come years before the bond's maturity date. Each payment may be considered to have its own "maturity date" which suggests that the *effective* maturity of the bond should be measured as some sort of average of the maturities of *all* the cash flows paid out by the bond. The zero-coupon bond, by contrast, makes only one payment at the final maturity date.

29. a, b.

Yield	Price A	Price B	%diff(8%) A	%diff(8%) B
2%	144.93	324.67	165%	124%
3%	119.68	277.14	119%	91%
4%	100.00	239.00	83%	65%
5%	84.55	208.15	54%	43%
6%	72.33	183.00	32%	26%
7%	62.59	162.35	14%	12%
8%	54.76	145.24	0%	0%
9%	48.41	130.95	−12%	−10%
10%	43.22	118.92	−21%	−18%
11%	38.93	108.72	−29%	−25%
12%	35.36	99.99	−35%	−31%
13%	32.35	92.48	−41%	−36%
14%	29.80	85.95	−46%	−41%
15%	27.62	80.25	−50%	−45%

c.

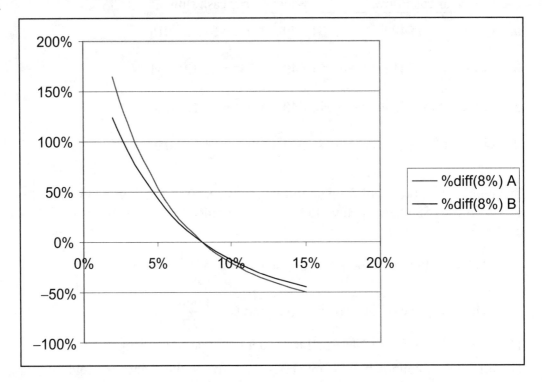

The price of bond A is more sensitive to interest rate changes as reflected in the steeper curve.

d. Bond A has a higher effective maturity (higher duration). A bond that pays a high coupon rate has a lower effective maturity since a greater proportion of the total return to the investment is received before maturity. A bond that pays a lower coupon rate has a longer average time to each payment.

30. a, b.

Year	YTM	Cash Flow from Bond	PV of Cash Flow
1	4.0%	100	96.15384615
2	5.0%	100	90.70294785
3	5.5%	100	85.16136642
4	5.5%	100	80.72167433
5	5.5%	100	76.51343538
6	6.0%	100	70.49605404
7	6.0%	100	66.50571136
8	6.0%	100	62.74123713
9	6.0%	100	59.18984635
10	6.0%	1100	614.2342546

Bond Price (PV) = 1302.420374
YTM (RATE) =   5.91%

c. The yield to maturity on the zero-coupon bond is higher. The zero-coupon has a higher effective maturity (higher duration) in that a greater proportion of the cash flow is received at the maturity. The zero-coupon bond is therefore more sensitive to changes in interest rates which are expected to rise based on this upward sloping yield curve.

Solutions to Chapter 7

Valuing Stocks

1. No, this does not invalidate the dividend discount model. The dividend discount model allows for the fact that firms may not *currently* pay dividends. As the market matures, and Amazon's growth opportunities moderate, investors may justifiably believe that Amazon will enjoy high future earnings and will then pay dividends. The stock price today can still reflect the present value of the expected per share stream of dividends.

2. Dividend yield = Dividend/Price = DIV_1/P_0

    $0.08 = 2.40/P_0 \Rightarrow P_0 = \$30$

3. The preferred stock pays a level perpetuity of dividends. The expected dividend next year is the same as this year's dividend ($8).

    a. $\$8.00/0.12 = \$66.67$

    b. $\$8.00/0.12 = \$66.67$

    c. Dividend yield = $\$8/\$66.67 = 0.12 = 12\%$

        Capital gains yield = 0

        Expected rate of return = 12%

4. $r = DIV_1/P_0 + g = 8\% + 5\% = 13\%$

5. The value of a share of common stock equals the present value of dividends received out to the investment horizon, plus the present value of the forecast stock price at the horizon. But the stock price at the horizon date depends on expectations of dividends from that date forward. So, even if an investor plans to hold a stock for only a year or two, the price ultimately received from another investor depends on dividends to be paid after the date of purchase. Therefore, the stock's present value is the same for investors with different time horizons.

6. a. $P_0 = DIV_1/(r - g)$

        $\$30 = \$3/(r - 0.04) \Rightarrow r = 0.14 = 14\%$

    b. $P_0 = \$3/(0.165 - 0.04) = \$24$

7. The annual dividend is: $\$2 \times 4 = \$8$

    $DIV_1/P_0 = 0.048 \Rightarrow \$8/P_0 = 0.048 \Rightarrow P_0 = \$8/0.048 = \$166.67$

8. weak, semistrong, strong, fundamental, technical

9. The statement is correct. The search for information and insightful analysis makes investor assessments of stock values as reliable as possible. Since the rewards accrue to the investors who uncover relevant information *before* it is reflected in stock prices, competition among these investors means that there is always an active search for mispriced stocks.

10. The two broad areas of investors' behavioral biases are in their attitudes towards risk and their assessments of probabilities. Investors appear to be less averse to losses following substantial gains than they are to losses that follow other losses. Consequently, the early gains of the "dot-com bubble" may have led investors to increase their investments in dot-com stocks, leading to the tremendous gains leading up to March 2000.

In addition, psychologists believe that investors make two mistakes in their assessment of stock market probabilities. First, when assessing the future of stock market performance, investors attach too much importance to the recent past, largely ignoring events of the more distant past. Second, investors suffer from overconfidence, believing that they are better stock pickers than they are in reality. These two biases reinforced the bubble prior to March 2000: overconfident investors attached too much importance to their experiences during the preceding five years.

11. a. $DIV_1 = \$1 \times 1.04 = \$1.04$

   $DIV_2 = \$1 \times 1.04^2 = \$1.0816$

   $DIV_3 = \$1 \times 1.04^3 = \$1.1249$

   b. $P_0 = \dfrac{DIV_1}{r-g} = \dfrac{\$1.04}{0.12-0.04} = \$13.00$

   c. $P_3 = \dfrac{DIV_4}{r-g} = \dfrac{\$1.1249 \times 1.04}{0.12-0.04} = \$14.6237$

   d. Your payments will be:

	Year 1	Year 2	Year 3
DIV	$1.04	$1.0816	$ 1.1249
Selling Price			14.6237
Total Cash Flow	$1.04	$1.0816	$15.7486
PV of Cash Flow	$0.9286	$0.8622	$11.2095

   Sum of PV = $13.00, the same as the answer to part (b).

12. $g = \text{return on equity} \times \text{plowback ratio} = 0.15 \times 0.40 = 0.06 = 6.0\%$

$$40 = \frac{4}{r - 0.06} \Rightarrow r = \frac{4}{40} + 0.06 = 0.16 = 16.0\%$$

13. a. $P_0 = \dfrac{DIV_1}{r - g} = \dfrac{\$3 \times 1.05}{0.15 - 0.05} = \$31.50$

   b. $P_0 = \dfrac{\$3 \times 1.05}{0.12 - 0.05} = \$45$

   The lower discount rate makes the present value of future dividends higher.

14. $\$50 = \dfrac{\$5}{0.14 - g} \Rightarrow g = 0.14 - \dfrac{\$5}{\$50} = 0.04 = 4.0\%$

15. a. $r = DIV_1/P_0 + g = [(\$1.64 \times 1.03)/27] + 0.03 = 0.0926 = 9.26\%$

   b. If $r = 0.10$, then: $0.10 = [(\$1.64 \times 1.03)/27] + g \Rightarrow g = 0.0374 = 3.74\%$

   c. $g = \text{return on equity} \times \text{plowback ratio}$

   $5\% = \text{return on equity} \times 0.4 \Rightarrow \text{return on equity} = 0.125 = 12.5\%$

16. $P_0 = DIV_1/(r - g) = \$2/(0.12 - 0.06) = \$33.33$

17. a. $P_0 = DIV_1/(r - g) = \$3/[0.15 - (-0.10)] = \$3/0.25 = \$12$

   b. $P_1 = DIV_2/(r - g) = \$3(1 - 0.10)/0.25 = \$10.80$

   c. expected rate of return =

$$\frac{DIV_1 + \text{Capital gain}}{P_0} = \frac{\$3 + (\$10.80 - \$12)}{\$12} = 0.150 = 15.0\%$$

   d. 'Bad companies' may be declining, but if the stock price already reflects this fact, the investor can still earn a fair rate of return, as shown in part (c).

18. a. (i) reinvest 0% of earnings: $g = 0$ and $DIV_1 = \$6$

$$P_0 = \frac{DIV_1}{r-g} = \frac{\$6}{0.15-0} = \$40.00$$

(ii) reinvest 40%: $g = 15\% \times 0.40 = 6\%$ and $DIV_1 = \$6 \times (1 - 0.40) = \$3.60$

$$P_0 = \frac{DIV_1}{r-g} = \frac{\$3.60}{0.15-0.06} = \$40.00$$

(iii) reinvest 60%: $g = 15\% \times 0.60 = 9\%$ and $DIV_1 = \$6 \times (1 - 0.60) = \$2.40$

$$P_0 = \frac{DIV_1}{r-g} = \frac{\$2.40}{0.15-0.09} = \$40.00$$

b. (i) reinvest 0%: $P_0 = \dfrac{\$6}{0.15-0} = \$40.00 \Rightarrow PVGO = \$0$

(ii) reinvest 40%: $P_0 = \dfrac{\$3.60}{0.15-(0.2\times0.40)} = \$51.43 \Rightarrow$

$$PVGO = \$51.43 - \$40.00 = \$11.43$$

(iii) reinvest 60%: $P_0 = \dfrac{\$2.40}{0.15-(0.2\times0.60)} = \$80.00 \Rightarrow$

$$PVGO = \$80.00 - \$40.00 = \$40.00$$

c. In part (a), the return on reinvested earnings is equal to the discount rate. Therefore, the NPV of the firm's new projects is zero, and PVGO is zero in all cases, regardless of the reinvestment rate. While higher reinvestment results in higher growth rates, it does not result in a higher value of growth opportunities. This example illustrates that there is a difference between growth and growth opportunities.

In part (b), the return on reinvested earnings is greater than the discount rate. Therefore, the NPV of the firm's new projects is positive, and PVGO is positive. In this case, PVGO is higher when the reinvestment rate is higher because the firm is taking greater advantage of its opportunities to invest in positive NPV projects.

19. a. $P_0 = \dfrac{\$1.00}{1.10} + \dfrac{\$1.25}{(1.10)^2} + \dfrac{\$1.50 + \$20}{(1.10)^3} = \$18.10$

b. $DIV_1/P_0 = \$1/\$18.10 = 0.0552 = 5.52\%$

20.

	Stock A	Stock B
a. Payout ratio	$1/$2 = 0.50	$1/$1.50 = 0.67
b. g = ROE × plowback ratio	15% × 0.5 = 7.5%	10% × 0.333 = 3.33%
c. $Price = \dfrac{DIV_1}{r-g}$	$\dfrac{\$1}{0.15-0.075} = \$13.33$	$\dfrac{\$1}{0.15-0.0333} = \$8.57$

21. a. g = ROE × plowback ratio = 20% × 0.30 = 6%

   b. $E = \$3, r = 0.12 \Rightarrow P_0 = \dfrac{\$3 \times (1-0.30)}{0.12-0.06} = \$35.00$

   c. No-growth value = E/r = $3/0.12 = $25.00

   PVGO = P_0 – No-growth value = $35 – $25 = $10

   d. P/E = $35/$3 = 11.667

   e. If all earnings were paid as dividends, price would equal the no-growth value ($25) and P/E would be: $25/$3 = 8.333

   f. High P/E ratios reflect expectations of high PVGO.

22. a. $\dfrac{\$2.40}{0.12-0.04} = \$30.00$

   b. No-growth value = E/r = $3.10/0.12 = $25.83

   PVGO = P_0 – No-growth value = $30 – $25.83 = $4.17

23. a. Earnings = DIV_1 = $4

   Growth rate = g = 0

   $P_0 = \dfrac{\$4}{0.12-0} = \$33.33$

   P/E = $33.33/$4 = 8.33

   b. If r = 0.10 $\Rightarrow P_0 = \dfrac{\$4}{0.10} = \$40.00 \Rightarrow$ P/E increases to: $40/$4 = 10

24. a. Plowback ratio $= 0 \Rightarrow DIV_1 = \$4$ and $g = 0$

Therefore: $P_0 = \dfrac{\$4}{0.10 - 0} = \$40.00 \Rightarrow$ P/E ratio $= \$40/\$4 = 10$

b. Plowback ratio $= 0.40 \Rightarrow DIV_1 = \$4(1 - 0.40) = \$2.40$ and $g = 10\% \times 0.40 = 4\%$

Therefore: $P_0 = \dfrac{\$2.40}{0.10 - 0.04} = \$40.00 \Rightarrow$ P/E ratio $= \$40/\$4 = 10$

c. Plowback ratio $= 0.80 \Rightarrow DIV_1 = \$4(1 - 0.80) = \$0.80$ and $g = 10\% \times 0.80 = 8\%$

Therefore: $P_0 = \dfrac{\$0.80}{0.10 - 0.08} = \$40.00 \Rightarrow$ P/E ratio $= \$40/\$4 = 10$

Regardless of the plowback ratio, the stock price = $40 because all projects offer return on equity equal to the opportunity cost of capital.

25. a. $P_0 = DIV_1/(r - g) = \$5/(0.10 - 0.06) = \$125$

b. If Trendline followed a zero-plowback strategy, it could pay a perpetual dividend of $8. Its value would be: $8/0.10 = $80. Therefore, the value of assets in place is $80. The remainder of its value must be due to growth opportunities, so that:

        PVGO = $125 − $80 = $45

26. a. $g = 20\% \times 0.30 = 6\%$

$P_0 = \$4(1 - 0.30)/(0.12 - 0.06) = \$46.67$

P/E = $46.67/$4 = 11.667

b. If the plowback ratio is reduced to $0.20 \Rightarrow g = 20\% \times 0.20 = 4\%$

$P_0 = \$4(1 - 0.20)/(0.12 - 0.04) = \$40$

P/E = $40/$4 = 10

P/E falls because the firm's value of growth opportunities is now lower: It takes less advantage of its attractive investment opportunities.

c. If the plowback ratio $= 0 \Rightarrow g = 0$ and $DIV_1 = \$4$

$P_0 = \$4/0.12 = \$33.33$ and E/P $= \$4/\$33.33 = 0.12 = 12.0\%$

27. a. $DIV_1 = \$2.00$ $PV = \$2/1.10 = \$1.818$

$DIV_2 = \$2(1.20) = \$2.40$ $PV = \$2.40/1.10^2 = \$1.983$

$DIV_3 = \$2(1.20)^2 = \$2.88$ $PV = \$2.88/1.10^3 = \$2.164$

b. This could not continue indefinitely. If it did, the stock would be worth an infinite amount.

28. a. Book value = $200 million

Earnings = $200 million $\times$ 0.24 = $48 million

Dividends = Earnings $\times$ (1 – plowback ratio) = $48 million $\times$ (1 – 0.5) = $24 million

g = return on equity $\times$ plowback ratio = $0.24 \times 0.50 = 0.12 = 12.0\%$

$$\text{Market value} = \frac{\$24\,\text{million}}{0.15 - 0.12} = \$800\,\text{million}$$

Market-to-book ratio = $800/$200 = 4

b. Now g falls to $(0.10 \times 0.50) = 0.05$, earnings decline to $20 million, and dividends decline to $10 million.

$$\text{Market value} = \frac{\$10\,\text{million}}{0.15 - 0.05} = \$100\,\text{million}$$

Market-to-book ratio = ½

This result makes sense because the firm now earns less than the required rate of return on its investments. The project is worth less than it costs.

29. $$P_0 = \frac{\$2}{1.12} + \frac{\$2.50}{(1.12)^2} + \frac{\$18}{(1.12)^3} = \$16.59$$

30. a. $DIV_1 = \$2 \times 1.20 = \$2.40$

b. $DIV_1 = \$2.40$ $DIV_2 = \$2.88$ $DIV_3 = \$3.456$

$$P_3 = \frac{\$3.456 \times 1.04}{0.15 - 0.04} = \$32.675$$

$$P_0 = \frac{\$2.40}{1.15} + \frac{\$2.88}{(1.15)^2} + \frac{\$3.456 + \$32.675}{(1.15)^3} = \$28.021$$

31. a. $P_0 = \dfrac{\$2.88}{1.15} + \dfrac{\$3.456 + \$32.675}{(1.15)^2} = \$29.825$

Capital gain $= P_1 - P_0 = \$29.825 - \$28.021 = \$1.804$

b. $r = \dfrac{\$2.40 + \$1.804}{\$28.021} = 0.1500 = 15.00\%$

32. a. An individual *can* do crazy things and not affect the efficiency of financial markets. An irrational person can give assets away for free or offer to pay twice the market value. However, when the person's supply of assets or money runs out, the price will adjust back to its prior level (assuming that there is no new, relevant information released by these actions). If you are lucky enough to trade with such a person you *will* receive a positive gain at that investor's expense. You had better not count on this happening very often though. Fortunately, an efficient market protects irrational investors in cases less extreme than the above. Even if they trade in the market in an 'irrational' manner, they can be assured of getting a fair price since the price reflects all information.

b. Yes, and how many people have dropped a bundle? Or more to the point, how many people have made a bundle only to lose it later? People can be lucky and some people can be very lucky; efficient markets do not preclude this possibility.

c. Investor psychology is a slippery concept, more often than not used to explain price movements that the individual invoking it cannot personally explain. Even if it exists, is there any way to make money from it? If investor psychology drives up the price one day, will it do so the next day also? Or will the price drop to a 'true' level? Almost no one can tell you beforehand what 'investor psychology' will do. Theories based on it have no content.

33. Investments in financial markets, such as stocks or bonds, are available to all participants in the marketplace. As a result, the prices of these investments are bid up to 'fair' levels, that is, prices which reflect the present value of expected cash flows. If the investment weren't zero-NPV, investors would buy or sell the asset and thereby put pressure on its price until the investment becomes a zero-NPV prospect.

In contrast, investments in product markets are made by firms with various forms of protection from full competition. Such protection comes from specialized knowledge, name recognition and customer loyalty, and patent protection. In these cases, a project may be positive NPV for one firm with the know-how to make it work, but not positive NPV for other firms. Or a project may be positive NPV, but only available to one firm because it owns a name brand or patent. In these cases, competitors are kept out of the market, and the costs of the firm's investment opportunities are not bid to levels at which NPV is reduced to zero.

34. There are several thousand mutual funds in the United States. With so many professional managers, it is no surprise that some managers will demonstrate brilliant performance over various periods of time. As an analogy, consider a contest in which 10,000 people flip a coin 20 times. It would not surprise you if *someone* managed to flip heads 18 out of 20 times. But it would be surprising if he could repeat that performance. Similarly, while many investors have shown excellent performance over relatively short time horizons, and have received favorable publicity for their work, far fewer have demonstrated consistency over long periods.

35. If the firm is stable and well run, its price will reflect this information, and the stock may not be a bargain. There is a difference between a 'good company' and a 'good stock.' The best buys in the stock market are not necessarily the best firms; instead, you want to identify firms that are *better* than anyone else realizes. When the market catches up to your assessment and prices adjust, you will profit.

36. Remember the first lesson of market efficiency: The market has no memory. Just because long-term interest rates are high relative to past levels does not mean they won't go higher still. Unless you have special information indicating that long-term rates are *too* high, issuing long-term bonds should be a zero-NPV transaction. Issuing short-term debt or common stock should also be a zero-NPV transaction.

37. The stock price will decrease. The original price reflects an anticipation of a 25% increase in earnings. The actual increase is a *disappointment* compared to original expectations.

38. It seems that behavioral finance might explain anomalies such as the earnings announcement puzzle and the new-issue puzzle. For example, we expect that the announcement of unexpectedly good earnings would initially generate a positive reaction. However, the fact that the announced higher earnings figure is 'unexpected' indicates that perhaps investors had been accustomed to lower earnings in the recent past, so that investors under-react initially, out of excessive concern about the risk of loss and also giving too much weight to the lower earnings of the recent past. However, the initial increase in price, coupled with investors' attitudes towards risk and their tendency to be overconfident, would produce additional stock price increases in the future.

39. $$\$50 = \frac{\$2.50}{0.15 - g} \Rightarrow g = 0.15 - \frac{\$2.50}{\$50} = 0.10 = 10.0\%$$

$g = 0.10 =$ return on equity $\times$ plowback ratio = return on equity $\times$ 0.60 $\Rightarrow$

return on equity $= 0.10/0.60 = 0.1667 = 16.67\%$

40. a. $P_0 = \dfrac{DIV_1}{1+r} + \dfrac{DIV_2 + P_2}{(1+r)^2}$

   $DIV_1 = \$2$

   $DIV_2 = \$4$

   $P_2 = \dfrac{DIV_2 \times (1+g)}{r-g} = \dfrac{\$4 \times 1.05}{0.12 - 0.05} = \$60.00$

   $P_0 = \dfrac{\$2}{1.12} + \dfrac{\$4 + \$60}{(1.12)^2} = \$52.806$

   b. Next year: $P_1 = \dfrac{DIV_2}{0.12 - 0.05} = \dfrac{\$4}{0.07} = \$57.143$

   c. $r = \dfrac{DIV_1 + (P_1 - P_0)}{P_0} = \dfrac{\$2 + (\$57.143 - \$52.806)}{\$52.806} = 0.1200 = 12.00\%$

   $r = \dfrac{\$2}{\$52.806} + \dfrac{\$57.143 - \$52.806}{\$52.806} = 0.1200$

41. $DIV_1 = \$1$

   $DIV_2 = \$2$

   $DIV_3 = \$3$

   $g = 0.06 \Rightarrow P_3 = (\$3 \times 1.06)/(0.14 - 0.06) = \$39.75$

   $P_0 = \dfrac{\$1}{1.14} + \dfrac{\$2}{(1.14)^2} + \dfrac{\$3 + \$39.75}{(1.14)^3} = \$31.27$

42. a. $DIV_1 = \$4$ and $g = 4\%$

   Expected return $= (DIV_1/P_0) + g = (\$4/\$100) + 4\% = 8\%$

   b. $DIV_1 = $ Earnings $\times (1 - $ plowback ratio$)$

   Therefore: Earnings $= DIV_1/(1 - $ plowback ratio$) = \$4/(1 - 0.4) = \$6.6667$

   If the discount rate is 8% (the expected return on the stock), then the no-growth value of the stock is: $\$6.6667/0.08 = \$83.33$

   Therefore: PVGO $= \$100 - \$83.33 = \$16.67$

c. For the first 5 years: $g = 10\% \times 0.8 = 8\%$

Thereafter: $g = 10\% \times 0.4 = 4\%$

Year	1	2	3	4	5	6
Earnings	$6.67	$7.20	$7.78	$8.40	$9.07	$9.80
plowback	0.80	0.80	0.80	0.80	0.80	0.40
DIV	$1.33	$1.44	$1.56	$1.68	$1.81	$5.88
g	0.08	0.08	0.08	0.08	0.08	0.04

After year 6, the plowback ratio falls to 0.40 and the growth rate falls to 4 percent. [We assume $g = 8\%$ in year 5 (i.e., from $t = 5$ to $t = 6$) because the plowback ratio in year 5 is still high at $b = 0.80$. Notice the large jump in the dividends when the plowback ratio falls.] By year 6, the firm enters a steady-growth phase, and the constant-growth dividend discount model can be used to value the stock.

The stock price in year 6 will be:

$$P_6 = \frac{D_6 \times (1+g)}{k-g} = \frac{\$5.88 \times 1.04}{0.08 - 0.04} = \$152.88$$

$$P_0 = \frac{\$1.33}{1.08} + \frac{\$1.44}{(1.08)^2} + \frac{\$1.56}{(1.08)^3} + \frac{\$1.68}{(1.08)^4} + \frac{\$1.81}{(1.08)^5} + \frac{\$5.88 + \$152.88}{(1.08)^6} = \$106.22$$

43. a. $DIV_1 = 1.00 \times 1.20 = \$1.20$

   $DIV_2 = 1.00 \times (1.20)^2 = \$1.44$

   $DIV_3 = 1.00 \times (1.20)^3 = \$1.728$

   $DIV_4 = 1.00 \times (1.20)^4 = \$2.0736$

b. $P_4 = DIV_5/(r-g) = [DIV_4 \times (1+g)]/(r-g)$

   $= (\$2.0736 \times 1.05)/(0.10 - 0.05) = \$43.5456$

c. $P_0 = \frac{\$1.20}{1.10} + \frac{\$1.44}{(1.10)^2} + \frac{\$1.728}{(1.10)^3} + \frac{\$2.0736 + \$43.5456}{(1.10)^4} = \$34.738$

d. $DIV_1/P_0 = \$1.20/\$34.738 = 0.0345 = 3.45\%$

e. Next year the price will be:

$$P_1 = \frac{\$1.44}{1.10} + \frac{\$1.728}{(1.10)^2} + \frac{\$2.0736 + \$43.5456}{(1.10)^3} = \$37.012$$

f. $r = \frac{DIV_1 + \text{Capital Gain}}{P_0} = \frac{\$1.20 + (\$37.012 - \$34.738)}{\$34.738} = 0.1000 = 10.00\%$

The expected return equals the discount rate (as it should if the stock is fairly priced).

44. a,b. $P_4 = DIV_5/(r - g) = [DIV_4 \times (1 + g)]/(r - g)$
$= (\$2.0736 \times 1.06)/(0.10 - 0.06) = \$54.95$

$$P_0 = \frac{\$1.20}{1.10} + \frac{\$1.44}{(1.10)^2} + \frac{\$1.728}{(1.10)^3} + \frac{\$2.0736 + \$54.95}{(1.10)^4} = \$42.53$$

Sustainable Growth Rate	Intrinsic Value (PV)	% change in PV
5.00%	34.74	
6.00%	42.53	22.42%
6.50%	48.09	13.08%
7.00%	55.51	15.43%
7.50%	65.90	18.71%
8.00%	81.48	23.64%
8.50%	107.44	31.87%
9.00%	159.37	48.33%

c. The percentage change in the value of the firm increases at a faster rate with each 1 percent increase in the assumed final growth rate, g. The intrinsic value is more sensitivity to changes in g as the sustainable growth rate approaches the discount rate. The dividend growth model is less reliable as the sustainable growth rate approaches the discount rate.

45. Two important points in the discussion of the yield curve (in Section 6.5) are: first, the yield curve is usually upward sloping (i.e., yields tend to be higher for longer maturity bonds) and, second, an upward sloping yield curve often indicates that future interest rates are expected to increase. The relatively unusual case of a downward sloping yield curve often indicates that future interest rates are expected to decrease.

Solution to Minicase for Chapter 7

The goal is to value the company under both investment plans and to choose the better investment plan.

The discount rate is the 11% that investors believe they can earn on similar-risk investments, not the 15% return on book equity. Return on equity is useful, however, for computing the growth rate of dividends under the rapid growth scenario. Starting in 2013, in the rapid growth scenario, two-thirds of earnings will be paid out as dividends, and one-third will be reinvested. Therefore, the sustainable growth rate as of 2013 is:

return on equity × plowback ratio = 15% × 1/3 = 5%

Valuation based on past growth scenario:

The firm has been growing at 5% per year. Dividends are proportional to book value and have grown at 5% annually. Dividends paid in the most recent year (2012) were $7.7 million and are projected to be $8 million next year, in 2013. The value of the firm is therefore:

$$\text{Value}_{2010} = \frac{\text{DIV}_{2011}}{r - g} = \frac{\$8 \text{ million}}{0.11 - 0.05} = \$133.33 \text{ million}$$

The value per share is: $133.33 million/400,000 = $333.33

Therefore, it is clear that Mr. Breezeway was correct in advising his relative not to sell for book value of $200 per share.

Valuation based on rapid growth scenario

If the firm reinvests all income for the next five years (until 2017), dividends paid in that year will reach $14 million, far greater than in the constant growth scenario. However, shareholders will have to give up dividend payments until 2017 in order to achieve this rapid growth. The value of the firm in 2017 will be:

$$\text{Value}_{2015} = \frac{\text{DIV}_{2016}}{r - g} = \frac{\$14.7 \text{ million}}{0.11 - 0.05} = \$245 \text{ million}$$

The value of the firm as of the year 2012 is the present value of this amount plus the present value of the dividend to be paid in 2017, which is projected to be $14 million. (Remember, there will be no dividend flows in the years leading up to 2017.)

$$\text{Value}_{2010} = \frac{14 + 245}{1.11^5} = \$153.70 \text{ million}$$

Value per share is: $153.70 million/400,000 = $384.25

Thus, it appears that the rapid growth plan is in fact preferable. If the firm follows this plan, it will be able to go public — that is, sell its shares to the public — at a higher price.

Solutions to Chapter 8

Net Present Value and Other Investment Criteria

1. $NPV_A = -\$200 + [\$80 \times$ annuity factor(11%, 4 periods)]

$$= -\$200 + \$80 \times \left[\frac{1}{0.11} - \frac{1}{0.11 \times (1.11)^4} \right] = \$48.20$$

$NPV_B = -\$200 + [\$100 \times$ annuity factor(11%, 3 periods)]

$$= -\$200 + \$100 \times \left[\frac{1}{0.11} - \frac{1}{0.11 \times (1.11)^3} \right] = \$44.37$$

Both projects are worth pursuing.

2. Choose Project A, the project with the higher NPV.

3. $NPV_A = -\$200 + [\$80 \times$ annuity factor(16%, 4 periods)]

$$= -\$200 + \$80 \times \left[\frac{1}{0.16} - \frac{1}{0.16 \times (1.16)^4} \right] = \$23.85$$

$NPV_B = -\$200 + [\$100 \times$ annuity factor(16%, 3 periods)]

$$= -\$200 + \$100 \times \left[\frac{1}{0.16} - \frac{1}{0.16 \times (1.16)^3} \right] = \$24.59$$

Therefore, you should now choose project B.

4. IRR_A = Discount rate (r) which is the solution to the following equation:

$$\$80 \times \left[\frac{1}{r} - \frac{1}{r \times (1+r)^4} \right] = \$200 \Rightarrow r = IRR_A = 21.86\%$$

IRR_B = Discount rate (r) which is the solution to the following equation:

$$\$100 \times \left[\frac{1}{r} - \frac{1}{r \times (1+r)^3} \right] = \$200 \Rightarrow r = IRR_B = 23.38\%$$

5. No. Even though project B has the higher IRR, its NPV is lower than that of project A when the discount rate is lower (as in Problem 1) and higher when the discount rate is higher (as in Problem 3). This example shows that the project with the higher IRR is not necessarily better. The IRR of each project is fixed, but as the discount rate increases, project B becomes *relatively* more attractive compared to project A. This is because B's cash flows come earlier, so the present value of these cash flows decreases less rapidly when the discount rate increases.

6. The profitability indexes are as follows:

   Project A: $48.20/$200 = 0.2410

   Project B: $44.37/$200 = 0.2219

   In this case, *with equal initial investments*, both the profitability index and NPV give projects the same ranking. This is an unusual case, however, since it is rare for the initial investments to be equal.

7. Project A has a payback period of: $200/$80 = 2.5 years

   Project B has a payback period of 2 years.

8. No. Despite its longer payback period, Project A may still be the preferred project, for example, when the discount rate is 11% (as in Problems 1 and 2). As in problem 5, you should note that the payback period for each project is fixed, but the NPV changes as the discount rate changes. The project with the shorter payback period need not have the higher NPV.

9. NPV = −$3,000 + [$800 × annuity factor(10%, 6 years)]

   $$= -\$3,000 + \$800 \times \left[\frac{1}{0.10} - \frac{1}{0.10 \times (1.10)^6} \right] = \$484.21$$

   At the 10% discount rate, the project is worth pursuing.

   IRR = Discount rate (r) which is the solution to the following equation:

   $$\$800 \times \left[\frac{1}{r} - \frac{1}{r \times (1+r)^6} \right] = \$3,000 \Rightarrow r = IRR = 15.34\%$$

   You can solve for IRR using a financial calculator by entering:
   PV = (−)3000; n = 6; FV = 0; PMT = 800; and then compute i.

   Since the IRR is 15.34%, this is the highest discount rate before project NPV turns negative.

10. Payback period = $2,500/$600 = 4.167 years
This is less than the cutoff, so the firm would accept the project.

$r = 2\% \Rightarrow \text{NPV} = -\$2{,}500 + [\$600 \times \text{annuity factor}(\ 2\%,\ 6\ \text{years})]$

$$= -\$2{,}500 + \$600 \times \left[\frac{1}{0.02} - \frac{1}{0.02 \times (1.02)^6} \right] = \$860.86$$

$r = 12\% \Rightarrow \text{NPV} = -\$2{,}500 + [\$600 \times \text{annuity factor}(12\%,\ 6\ \text{years})]$

$$= -\$2{,}500 + \$600 \times \left[\frac{1}{0.12} - \frac{1}{0.12 \times (1.12)^6} \right] = -\$33.16$$

If $r = 2\%$, the project should be pursued; at $r = 12\%$, it should not be.

11. $\text{NPV} = -\$10{,}000 + \dfrac{\$3{,}000}{1.09} + \dfrac{\$3{,}000}{1.09^2} + \dfrac{\$5{,}000}{1.09^3} + \dfrac{\$5{,}000}{1.09^4} = \$2{,}680.38$

Profitability index = NPV/Investment = 0.2680

12. $\text{NPV} = -\$2.2\ \text{billion} + [\$0.3\ \text{billion} \times \text{annuity factor}(r,\ 15\ \text{years})] - [\$0.9\ \text{billion}/(1 + r)^{15}]$

$$-\$2.2\ \text{billion} + \$0.3\ \text{billion} \times \left[\frac{1}{r} - \frac{1}{r \times (1+r)^{15}} \right] + \frac{\$0.9\ \text{billion}}{(1+r)^{15}}$$

$r = 5\% \Rightarrow \text{NPV} = -\$2.2\ \text{billion} + \$2.681\ \text{billion} = \$0.481\ \text{billion}$

$r = 18\% \Rightarrow \text{NPV} = -\$2.2\ \text{billion} + \$1.452\ \text{billion} = -\$0.748\ \text{billion}$

13. IRR_A = Discount rate (r) which is the solution to the following equation:

$$\$21{,}000 \times \left[\frac{1}{r} - \frac{1}{r \times (1+r)^2} \right] = \$30{,}000 \Rightarrow r = \text{IRR}_A = 25.69\%$$

IRR_B = Discount rate (r) which is the solution to the following equation:

$$\$33{,}000 \times \left[\frac{1}{r} + \frac{1}{r \times (1+r)^2} \right] = \$50{,}000 \Rightarrow r = \text{IRR}_B = 20.69\%$$

The IRR of project A is 25.69%, and that of B is 20.69%. However, project B has the higher NPV and therefore is preferred. The incremental cash flows of B over A are: −$20,000 at time 0; +$12,000 at times 1 and 2. The NPV of the incremental cash flows (discounted at 10%) is $826.45, which is positive and equal to the difference in the respective project NPVs.

14. $NPV = \$5,000 + \dfrac{\$4,000}{1.12} - \dfrac{\$11,000}{(1.12)^2} = -\$197.70$

Because the NPV is negative, you should reject the offer. You should reject the offer despite the fact that the IRR exceeds the discount rate. This is a 'borrowing type' project with positive cash flows followed by negative cash flows. A high IRR in these cases is not attractive: You don't want to borrow at a high interest rate.

15. a. $r = 0\% \Rightarrow NPV = -\$6,750 + \$4,500 + \$18,000 = \$15,750$

$r = 50\% \Rightarrow NPV = -\$6,750 + \dfrac{\$4,500}{1.50} + \dfrac{\$18,000}{1.50^2} = \$4,250$

$r = 100\% \Rightarrow NPV = -\$6,750 + \dfrac{\$4,500}{2.00} + \dfrac{\$18,000}{2.00^2} = \$0$

b. IRR = 100%, the discount rate at which NPV = 0.

16. $NPV = -\$10,000 + \dfrac{\$7,500}{1.12^2} + \dfrac{\$8,500}{1.12^3} = \$2,029.09$

Since the NPV is positive, the project should be accepted.

Alternatively, you can compute the IRR by solving for r, using trial-and-error, in the following equation:

$$-\$10,000 + \dfrac{\$7,500}{(1+r)^2} + \dfrac{\$8,500}{(1+r)^3} = 0 \Rightarrow IRR = 20.61\%$$

Since the IRR of the project is greater than the required rate of return of 12%, the project should be accepted.

17. $NPV_{9\%} = -\$20,000 + [\$4,000 \times \text{annuity factor}(9\%, 8 \text{ periods})]$

$$= -\$20,000 + \$4,000 \times \left[\dfrac{1}{0.09} - \dfrac{1}{0.09 \times (1.09)^8} \right] = \$2,139.28$$

$NPV_{14\%} = -\$20,000 + [\$4,000 \times \text{annuity factor}(14\%, 8 \text{ periods})]$

$$= -\$20,000 + \$4,000 \times \left[\dfrac{1}{0.14} - \dfrac{1}{0.14 \times (1.14)^8} \right] = -\$1,444.54$$

IRR = Discount rate (r) which is the solution to the following equation:

$$\$4,000 \times \left[\frac{1}{r} - \frac{1}{r \times (1+r)^8}\right] = \$20,000 \Rightarrow r = IRR = 11.81\%$$

[Using a financial calculatior, enter: PV = (–)20,000; PMT = 4000; FV = 0; n = 8, and compute i.]

The project will be rejected for any discount rate above this rate.

18. a. The present value of the savings is: $1,000/r

   $r = 0.08 \Rightarrow$ PV = \$12,500 and NPV = –\$10,000 + \$12,500 = \$2,500

   $r = 0.10 \Rightarrow$ PV = \$10,000 and NPV = –\$10,000 + \$10,000 = \$0

   b. IRR = 0.10 = 10%

   At this discount rate, NPV = \$0

   c. Payback period = 10 years

19. a. NPV for each of the two projects, at various discount rates, is tabulated below.

   NPV_A = –\$20,000 + [\$8,000 × annuity factor(r%, 3 years)]

   $$= -\$20,000 + \$8,000 \times \left[\frac{1}{r} - \frac{1}{r(1+r)^3}\right]$$

   $$NPV_B = -\$20,000 + \frac{\$25,000}{(1+r)^3}$$

Discount Rate	NPV_A	NPV_B
0%	$4,000	$5,000
2%	3,071	3,558
4%	2,201	2,225
6%	1,384	990
8%	617	–154
10%	–105	–1,217
12%	–785	–2,205
14%	–1,427	–3,126
16%	–2,033	–3,984
18%	–2,606	–4,784
20%	–3,148	–5,532

From the NPV profile, it can be seen that Project A is preferred over Project B if the discount rate is above 4%. At 4% and below, Project B has the higher NPV.

b. IRR$_A$ = Discount rate (r) which is the solution to the following equation:

$$\$8,000 \times \left[\frac{1}{r} - \frac{1}{r \times (1+r)^3} \right] = \$20,000 \Rightarrow r = IRR_A = 9.70\%$$

IRR$_B$ = Discount rate (r) which is the solution to the following equation:

$$-\$20,000 + \frac{\$25,000}{(1+r)^3} = 0 \Rightarrow IRR_B = 7.72\%$$

Using a financial calculator, find IRR$_A$ = 9.70% as follows: enter PV = (–)20; PMT = 8; FV = 0; n = 3; compute i

Find IRR$_B$ = 7.72% as follows: enter PV = (–)20; PMT = 0; FV = 25; n = 3; compute i

20. We know that the *undiscounted* project cash flows sum to the initial investment because payback equals project life. Therefore, the *discounted* cash flows are less than the initial investment, so NPV is negative.

21. $$NPV = \$100 + \frac{-\$60}{1.12} + \frac{-\$60}{(1.12)^2} = -\$1.40$$

IRR$_B$ = Discount rate (r) which is the solution to the following equation:

$$\$100 + \frac{-\$60}{(1+r)} + \frac{-\$60}{(1+r)^2} = 0 \Rightarrow IRR = 13.07\%$$

Because NPV is negative, you should reject the project. This is so despite the fact that the IRR exceeds the discount rate. This is a 'borrowing type' project with a positive cash flow followed by negative cash flows. A high IRR in these cases is not attractive: You don't want to borrow at a high interest rate.

22. a.

Project	Payback
A	3 years
B	2 years
C	3 years

b. Only Project B satisfies the 2-year payback criterion.

c. All three projects satisfy a 3-year payback criterion.

d. $NPV_A = -\$5,000 + \dfrac{\$1,000}{1.10} + \dfrac{\$1,000}{(1.10)^2} + \dfrac{\$3,000}{(1.10)^3} = -\$1,010.52$

$NPV_B = -\$1,000 + \dfrac{\$1,000}{(1.10)^2} + \dfrac{\$2,000}{(1.10)^3} + \dfrac{\$3,000}{(1.10)^4} = \$3,378.12$

$NPV_C = -\$5,000 + \dfrac{\$1,000}{1.10} + \dfrac{\$1,000}{(1.10)^2} + \dfrac{\$3,000}{(1.10)^3} + \dfrac{\$5,000}{(1.10)^4} = \$2,405.55$

e. False. Payback gives *no* weight to cash flows after the cutoff date.

23. a. The net present values of the project cash flows are:

$$NPV_A = -\$2,100 + \dfrac{\$2,000}{1.22} + \dfrac{\$1,200}{(1.22)^2} = \$345.58$$

$$NPV_B = -\$2,100 + \dfrac{\$1,440}{1.22} + \dfrac{\$1,728}{(1.22)^2} = \$241.31$$

The initial investment for each project is $2,100.

Profitability index (A) = $345.58/$2,100 = 0.1646

Profitability index (B) = $241.31/$2,100 = 0.1149

b. (i)   If you could undertake both projects, you should: Both have a positive profitability index.
   (ii) If you could undertake only one project, choose A for its higher profitability index.

24. a. The less–risky projects should have lower discount rates.

b. First, find the profitability index of each project.

Project	PV of Cash flow	Investment	NPV	Profitability Index
A	$3.79	$3	$0.79	0.26
B	$4.97	$4	$0.97	0.24
C	$6.62	$5	$1.62	0.32
D	$3.87	$3	$0.87	0.29
E	$4.11	$3	$1.11	0.37

Then, select projects with the highest profitability index until the $8 million budget is exhausted. Therefore, choose Projects E and C.

c. All the projects have positive NPV so that all will be chosen if there is no capital rationing.

25. a. $NPV_A = -\$36 + [\$20 \times$ annuity factor(10%, 3 periods)]

$$= -\$36 + \$20 \times \left[\frac{1}{0.10} - \frac{1}{0.10 \times (1.10)^3} \right] = \$13.74$$

$NPV_B = -\$50 + [\$25 \times$ annuity factor(10%, 3 periods)]

$$= -\$50 + \$25 \times \left[\frac{1}{0.10} - \frac{1}{0.10 \times (1.10)^3} \right] = \$12.17$$

Thus Project A has the higher NPV if the discount rate is 10%.

b. Project A has the higher profitability index, as shown in the table below:

Project	PV of Cash flow	Investment	NPV	Profitability Index
A	$49.74	$36	$13.74	0.38
B	$62.17	$50	$12.17	0.24

c. A firm with a *limited* amount of funds available should choose Project A since it has a higher profitability index of 0.38, i.e., a higher 'bang for the buck.' Note that A also has a higher NPV as well.

For a firm with unlimited funds, the possibilities are:

i. If the projects are independent projects, then the firm should choose both projects.
ii. However, if the projects are mutually exclusive, then Project B should be selected. It has the higher NPV.

26. a. $NPV_A = -\$100 + \dfrac{\$30}{1.02} + \dfrac{\$50}{(1.02)^2} + \dfrac{\$70}{(1.02)^3} = \$43.43$

$NPV_B = -\$100 + [\$49 \times$ annuity factor(2%, 3 periods)]

$$= -\$100 + \$49 \times \left[\frac{1}{0.02} - \frac{1}{0.02 \times (1.02)^3} \right] = \$41.31$$

If r = 2%, choose A

b. $NPV_A = -\$100 + \dfrac{\$30}{1.12} + \dfrac{\$50}{(1.12)^2} + \dfrac{\$70}{(1.12)^3} = \$16.47$

$NPV_B = -\$100 + [\$49 \times$ annuity factor(12%, 3 periods)]

$$= -\$100 + \$49 \times \left[\frac{1}{0.12} - \frac{1}{0.12 \times (1.12)^3} \right] = \$17.69$$

If r = 12%, choose B

c. The larger cash flows of project A tend to come later, so the present value of these cash flows is more sensitive to increases in the discount rate.

27. PV of Costs = $10,000 + [$20,000 × annuity factor(10%, 5 years)]

$$= \$10,000 + \$20,000 \times \left[\frac{1}{0.10} - \frac{1}{0.10 \times (1.10)^5} \right] = \$85,815.74$$

The equivalent annual cost is the payment with the same present value. Solve the following equation for C:

$$C \times \left[\frac{1}{0.10} - \frac{1}{0.10 \times (1.10)^5} \right] = \$85,815.74 \Rightarrow C = EAC = \$22,637.98$$

Using a financial calculator, enter: n = 5, i = 10, FV = 0; PV = (–)85,815.74; compute PMT

28. Buy: PV of Costs

$$= \$80,000 + [\$10,000 \times \text{annuity factor}(10\%, 4 \text{ years})] - [\$20,000/(1.10)^4]$$

$$= \$80,000 + \$10,000 \times \left[\frac{1}{0.10} - \frac{1}{0.10 \times (1.10)^4} \right] - \frac{\$20,000}{(1.10)^4}$$

$$= \$80,000 + \$31,698.65 - \$13,660.27 = \$98,038.38$$

The equivalent annual cost is the payment with the same present value. Solve the following equation for C:

$$C \times \left[\frac{1}{0.10} - \frac{1}{0.10 \times (1.10)^4} \right] = \$98,038.38 \Rightarrow C = EAC = \$30,928.25$$

Using a financial calculator, enter: n = 4, i = 10, FV = 0; PV = (–)98,038.38; compute PMT

If you can lease instead for $30,000, then this is the less costly option.

You can also compare the PV of the lease costs to the total PV of buying:

$30,000 × annuity factor(10%, 4 years)

$$= \$30,000 \times \left[\frac{1}{0.10} - \frac{1}{0.10 \times (1.10)^4} \right] = \$95,095.96$$

The PV of the lease costs is less than the PV of the costs when buying the truck.

29. a. The following table shows the NPV profile of the project. NPV is zero at an interest rate between 7% and 8%, and is also equal to zero at an interest rate between 33% and 34%. These are the two IRRs of the project. You can use your calculator to confirm that the two IRRs are, more precisely: 7.16% and 33.67% (as shown below the table).

Discount rate	NPV	Discount rate	NPV
0.00	−2.00	0.21	0.82
0.01	−1.62	0.22	0.79
0.02	−1.28	0.23	0.75
0.03	−0.97	0.24	0.71
0.04	−0.69	0.25	0.66
0.05	−0.44	0.26	0.60
0.06	−0.22	0.27	0.54
0.07	−0.03	0.28	0.47
0.08	0.14	0.29	0.39
0.09	0.29	0.30	0.32
0.10	0.42	0.31	0.24
0.11	0.53	0.32	0.15
0.12	0.62	0.33	0.06
0.13	0.69	0.34	−0.03
0.14	0.75	0.35	−0.13
0.15	0.79	0.36	−0.22
0.16	0.83	0.37	−0.32
0.17	0.85	0.38	−0.42
0.18	0.85	0.39	−0.53
0.19	0.85	0.40	−0.63
0.20	0.84	0.41	−0.74

$$NPV = -\$22 + \frac{\$20}{1.0716} + \frac{\$20}{(1.0716)^2} + \frac{\$20}{(1.0716)^3} - \frac{\$40}{(1.0716)^4} = \$0.00$$

$$NPV = -\$22 + \frac{\$20}{1.3367} + \frac{\$20}{(1.3367)^2} + \frac{\$20}{(1.3367)^3} - \frac{\$40}{(1.3367)^4} = \$0.00$$

b. At 5% the NPV is:

$$NPV = -\$22 + \frac{\$20}{1.05} + \frac{\$20}{1.05^2} + \frac{\$20}{1.05^3} - \frac{\$40}{1.05^4} = -\$0.443$$

Since the NPV is negative, the project is not attractive.

c. At 20% the NPV is:

$$NPV = -\$22 + \frac{\$20}{1.20} + \frac{\$20}{1.20^2} + \frac{\$20}{1.20^3} - \frac{\$40}{1.20^4} = \$0.840$$

Since the NPV is positive, the project is attractive.

At 40% the NPV is:

$$NPV = -\$22 + \frac{\$20}{1.40} + \frac{\$20}{1.40^2} + \frac{\$20}{1.40^3} - \frac{\$40}{1.40^4} = -\$0.634$$

Since the NPV is negative, the project is not attractive.

d. At a low discount rate, the positive cash flows ($20 for 3 years) are not discounted very much. However, the final cash flow of negative $40 does not get discounted very heavily either. The net effect is a negative NPV.

At very high rates, the positive cash flows are discounted very heavily, resulting in a negative NPV. For moderate discount rates, the positive cash flows that occur in the middle of the project dominate and project NPV is positive.

30. a. Econo-cool costs $300 and lasts for 5 years. The annual rental fee with the same PV is $102.53. We solve as follows:

$$C \times \left[\frac{1}{0.21} - \frac{1}{0.21 \times (1.21)^5} \right] = \$300$$

C × annuity factor(21%,5 years) = $300

C × 2.92598 = $300 ⇒ C = EAC = $102.53

The equivalent annual cost of owning *and running* Econo-cool is:

$102.53 + $150 = $252.53

Luxury Air costs $500, and lasts for 8 years. Its equivalent annual rental fee is found as follows:

$$C \times \left[\frac{1}{0.21} - \frac{1}{0.21 \times (1.21)^8} \right] = \$500$$

C × annuity factor(21%,8 years) = $500

C × 3.72558 = $500 ⇒ C = EAC = $134.21

The equivalent annual cost of owning and operating Luxury Air is:

$134.21 + $100 = $234.21

b. Luxury Air is more cost effective. It has the lower equivalent annual cost.

c. The real interest rate is now: (1.21/1.10) – 1 = 0.10 = 10%

Redo (a) and (b) using a 10% discount rate. (Note: Because energy costs would normally be expected to inflate along with all other costs, we should assume that the *real* cost of electric bills is either $100 or $150, depending on the model.)

Equivalent annual real cost to own Econo-cool =	$ 79.14
plus $150 (real operating cost) =	150.00
	$229.14
Equivalent annual real cost to own Luxury Air =	$ 93.72
plus $100 (real operating cost) =	100.00
	$193.72

Luxury Air is still more cost effective.

31.

Time until purchase	Cost	NPV at purchase date[a]	NPV today[b]
0	$400.00	−$31.33	−$31.33
1	320.00	48.67	44.25
2	256.00	112.67	93.12
3	204.80	163.87	123.12
4	163.84	204.83	139.90
5	131.07	237.60	147.53
6	104.86	263.81	148.91
7	83.89	284.78	146.14

Notes:

    a. $-\text{Cost} + [60 \times \text{annuity factor}(10\%, 10 \text{ years})]$

    b. $(\text{NPV at purchase date})/(1.10)^n$

NPV is maximized when you wait six years to purchase the scanner.

32. The equivalent annual cost of the new machine is the 4-year annuity with present value equal to $20,000:

$$C \times \left[\frac{1}{0.15} - \frac{1}{0.15 \times (1.15)^4} \right] = \$20,000$$

$C \times$ annuity factor(15%, 4 years) = $20,000

$C \times 2.85498 = \$20,000 \Rightarrow C = \text{EAC} = \$7,005.30$

This can be interpreted as the extra yearly charge that should be attributed to the purchase of the new machine spread over its life. It does not yet pay to replace the equipment since the incremental cash flow provided by the new machine is:

    $10,000 − $5,000 = $5,000

This is less than the equivalent annual cost of the new machine.

33. a. The equivalent annual cost (EAC) of the *new* machine over its 10-year life is found by solving as follows:

$$C \times \left[\frac{1}{0.04} - \frac{1}{0.04 \times (1.04)^{10}} \right] = \$20,000$$

$C \times$ annuity factor(4%, 10 years) = $20,000

$C \times 8.11090 = \$20,000 \Rightarrow C = \text{EAC} = \$2,465.82$

Together with maintenance costs of $2,000 per year, the equivalent cost of owning *and* operating is: $4,465.82

The old machine costs $5,000 per year to operate, and is already paid for.
(We assume it has no scrap value and therefore no opportunity cost.) The new machine is less costly. You should replace.

b. If r = 12%, then the equivalent annual cost (EAC) is computed as follows:

$$C \times \left[\frac{1}{0.12} - \frac{1}{0.12 \times (1.12)^{10}} \right] = \$20,000$$

$C \times$ annuity factor(12%, 10 years) = \$20,000

$C \times 5.65022 = \$20,000 \Rightarrow C = EAC = \$3,539.68$

The equivalent cost of owning and operating the new machine is now: \$5,539.68
This is higher than that of the old machine. Do not replace.

Your answer changes because the higher discount rate implies that the opportunity
cost of the money tied up in the forklift also is higher.

34. a. Present Value $= \dfrac{\text{Cash flow at end of year}}{\text{Discount rate } - \text{ growth rate}} = \dfrac{\$5,000}{0.10 - 0.05} = \$100,000$

NPV = –\$80,000 + \$100,000 = \$20,000

b. Recall that the IRR is the discount rate that makes NPV equal to zero:

(– Investment) + (PV of cash flows discounted at IRR) = 0

$$-\$80,000 + \frac{\$5,000}{IRR - 0.05} = 0$$

Solving, we find that:

IRR = (\$5,000/\$80,000) + 0.05 = 0.1125 = 11.25%

35. For harvesting lumber, the NPV-maximizing rule is to cut the tree when its growth rate
equals the discount rate. When the tree is young and the growth rate exceeds the discount
rate, it pays to wait: the value of the tree is increasing at a rate that exceeds the discount
rate. When the tree is older and the growth rate is less than r, cutting immediately is better,
since the revenue from the tree can be invested to earn the rate r, which is greater than the
growth rate the tree is providing.

36. a.

Time	Cash flow
0	–\$5 million
1	30 million
2	–28 million

The graph below shows a plot of NPV as a function of the discount rate. NPV = 0
when r equals (approximately) either 15.61% or 384.39%. These are the two IRRs.

b.

Discount rate	NPV	Develop?
10%	−$0.868 million	No
20%	0.556	Yes
350%	0.284	Yes
400%	−0.120	No

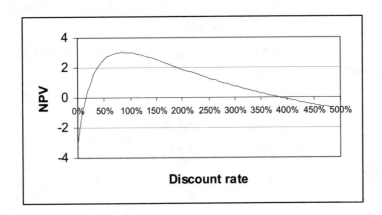

37. a. $NPV = -\$27,000 + \dfrac{(-1500 + (2400 \times \$3.50)}{1.08} + \dfrac{(-1500 + (2400 \times \$4.00)}{1.08^2}$

$+ \dfrac{(-1500 + (2400 \times \$4.50)}{1.08^3} + \dfrac{(-1500 + (2400 \times \$4.50)}{1.08^4} + ...$

$+ \dfrac{(-1500 + (2400 \times \$4.50)}{1.08^{20}} = \$61,058$

b. Using Excel, IRR = 31.37%

c. Cumulative Cash Flows are positive after year 4.

Year	CF	CUM CF
0	−27000	−27000
1	6900	−20100
2	8100	−12000
3	9300	−2700
4	9300	6600

d. The equivalent annual cost of the new machine is the 20-year annuity with present value equal to $27,000:

$$C \times \left[\dfrac{1}{0.08} - \dfrac{1}{0.08 \times (1.08)^{20}} \right] = \$27,000$$

C × annuity factor(8%, 20 years) = $270,000

C × 9.8181 = $27,000 ⇒ C = EAC = $2,750.02

e. The present value of the annual savings is given by the following equation:

$$PV = \frac{(-1500+(2400\times\$3.50))}{1.08} + \frac{(-1500+(2400\times\$4.00))}{1.08^2}$$
$$+\frac{(-1500+(2400\times\$4.50))}{1.08^3} + ... + \frac{(-1500+(2400\times\$4.50))}{1.08^{20}} = \$88,058$$

The equivalent annual annuity for this present value at 8% for 20 years is $8,968.92.

EAA = Present Value of Annual Savings / annuity factor(8%, 20 years)
    = $88,058/9.8181 = $8,968.92

The difference between equivalent annual savings and costs is $6,219 ($8,969 – $2,750). This value is equivalent to an annual annuity with a present value of $61,058, the net present value from part a.

$6,219 × annuity factor(8%, 20 years) = $6,219 × 9.8181 = $61,058.

None of the measures in the summary tables is appropriate for the analysis of this case, although the NPV calculations can be used as the starting point for an appropriate analysis.

The payback period is not appropriate for the same reasons that it is always inappropriate for analysis of a capital budgeting problem: cash flows after the payback period are ignored; cash flows before the payback period are all assigned equal weight, regardless of timing; the cutoff period is arbitrary.

The internal rate of return criterion can result in incorrect rankings among mutually exclusive investment projects when there are differences in the size of the projects under consideration and/or when there are differences in the timing of the cash flows. In choosing between the two different stamping machines, both of these differences exist.

The net present value calculations indicate that the Skilboro machines have a greater NPV ($2.56 million) than do the Munster machines ($2.40 million). However, since the Munster machines also have a shorter life, it is not clear whether the difference in NPV is simply a matter of longevity. In order to adjust for this difference, we can compute the equivalent annual annuity for each:

Munster machines:

$$C \times \left[\frac{1}{0.15} - \frac{1}{0.15 \times (1.15)^7} \right] = \$2.40 \text{ million}$$

$C \times$ annuity factor(15%, 7 years) = $2.40 million

$C \times 4.16042 = \$2.40 \text{ million} \Rightarrow C = EAC = \$0.57686 \text{ million}$

Skilboro machines:

$$C \times \left[\frac{1}{0.15} - \frac{1}{0.15 \times (1.15)^{10}} \right] = \$2.56 \text{ million}$$

$C \times$ annuity factor(15%, 10 years) = $2.56 million

$C \times 5.01877 = \$2.56 \text{ million} \Rightarrow C = EAC = \$0.51009 \text{ million}$

Therefore, the Munster machines are preferred.

Another approach to making this comparison is to compute the equivalent annual annuity based on the cost of the two machines. The cost of the Munster machine is $8 million, so that the equivalent annual annuity is computed as follows:

Munster machines:

$$C \times \left[\frac{1}{0.15} - \frac{1}{0.15 \times (1.15)^7} \right] = \$8 \text{ million}$$

$C \times$ annuity factor(15%, 7 years) = \$8 million

$C \times 4.16042 = \$8$ million $\Rightarrow C = EAC = \$1.92288$ million

For the Skilboro machine, we can treat the reduction in operator and material cost as a reduction in the present value of the cost of the machine:

$$PV = \$500,000 \times \left[\frac{1}{0.15} - \frac{1}{0.15 \times (1.15)^{10}} \right] = \$2.50938 \text{ million}$$

$12.5 million – $2.50938 million = $9.99062 million

$$C \times \left[\frac{1}{0.15} - \frac{1}{0.15 \times (1.15)^{10}} \right] = \$9.99062 \text{ million}$$

$C \times$ annuity factor(15%, 10 years) = \$9.99062 million

$C \times 5.01877 = \$9.99062$ million $\Rightarrow C = EAC = \$1.99065$ million

Here, the equivalent annual cost is less for the Munster machines.

Note that the differences in the equivalent annual annuities for the two methods are equal. (Differences are due to rounding.)

Solutions to Chapter 9

Using Discounted Cash-Flow Analysis to Make Investment Decisions

1. Net income = ($74 − $42 − $10) − [0.35 × ($74 − $42 − $10)] = $22 − $7.7 = $14.3 million

    - revenues − cash expenses − taxes paid = $74 − $42 − $7.7 = $24.3 million

    - after-tax profit + depreciation = $14.3 + $10 = $24.3 million

    - (revenues − cash expenses) × (1 − tax rate) + (depreciation × tax rate)
      = ($32 × 0.65) + ($10 × 0.35) = $24.3 million

2. a. ΔNWC = ΔAccounts Receivable + ΔInventory − ΔAccounts Payable

        = −$1,000 + $500 − $2,000 = −$2,500

    b. Cash flow = $36,000 − $24,000 + $2,500 = $14,500

3. Net income = ($7 − $4 − $1) − [0.35 × ($7 − $4 − $1)] = $2 − $0.7 = $1.3 million

    - revenues − cash expenses − taxes paid = $3 − $0.7 = $2.3 million

    - after-tax profit + depreciation = $1.3 + $1.0 = $2.3 million

    - (revenues − cash expenses) × (1 − tax rate) + (depreciation × tax rate)
      = ($3 × 0.65) + ($1 × 0.35) = $2.3 million

4. While depreciation is a non-cash expense, it has an impact on net cash flow because of its impact on taxes. Every dollar of depreciation expense reduces taxable income by one dollar, and thus reduces taxes owed by $1 times the firm's marginal tax rate. Accelerated depreciation moves the tax benefits forward in time, and thus increases the present value of the tax shield, thereby increasing the value of the project.

5. Gross revenues from new chip = 12 million × $25 = $300 million

    Cost of new chip = 12 million × $8 = $96 million

    Lost sales of old chip = 7 million × $20 = $140 million

    Saved costs of old chip = 7 million × $6 = $42 million

    Increase in cash flow = ($300 − $96) − ($140 − $42) = $106 million

6. | | |
    | --- | ---: |
    | Revenue | $160,000 |
    | Rental costs | 30,000 |
    | Variable costs | 50,000 |
    | Depreciation | 10,000 |
    | Pretax profit | 70,000 |
    | Taxes (35%) | 24,500 |
    | Net income | $ 45,500 |

7. a. net income + depreciation = $45,500 + $10,000 = $55,500

    b. revenue – rental costs – variable costs – taxes

    = $160,000 – $30,000 – $50,000 – $24,500 = $55,500

    c. [(revenue – rental costs – variable costs) × (1–0.35)] + (depreciation × 0.35)

    = [($160,000 – $30,000 – $50,000) × 0.65] + ($10,000 × 0.35)

    = $52,000 + $3,500 = $55,500

8. Change in working capital = ΔAccounts receivable – ΔAccounts payable

    = ($4500 – $1200) – ($300 – $700) = $3,700

    Cash flow = $16,000 – $9,000 – $3,700 = $3,300

9. Incremental cash flows are:

    b. The current market value of the painting (i.e., the cash that *could* have been realized by selling the art).
    d. The reduction in taxes due to its declared tax deduction.

10. | | |
    | --- | ---: |
    | Revenue | $120,000 |
    | Variable costs | 40,000 |
    | Fixed costs | 15,000 |
    | Depreciation | 40,000 |
    | Pretax profit | 25,000 |
    | Taxes (35%) | 8,750 |
    | Net income | 16,250 |
    | Depreciation | 40,000 |
    | Operating cash flow | $ 56,250 |

11. a.

Year	MACRS(%)	Depreciation	Book value (end of year)
1	20.00	$ 8,000	$32,000
2	32.00	12,800	19,200
3	19.20	7,680	11,520
4	11.52	4,608	6,912
5	11.52	4,608	2,304
6	5.76	2,304	0

b. If the machine is sold for $22,000 after 3 years, sales price exceeds book value by:

$$\$22,000 - \$11,520 = \$10,480$$

After-tax proceeds are: $\$22,000 - (0.35 \times \$10,480) = \$18,332$

12. a. If the office space would have remained unused in the absence of the proposed project, then the incremental cash outflow from allocating the space to the project is effectively zero. The incremental cost of the space used should be based on the cash flow given up by allocating the space to this project rather than some other use.

b. One reasonable approach would be to assess a cost to the space equal to the rental income that the firm could earn if it allowed another firm to use the space. This is the opportunity cost of the space.

13. Cash flow = net income + depreciation – increase in NWC

$$1.2 = 1.2 + 0.4 - \Delta NWC \Rightarrow \Delta NWC = \$0.4 \text{ million}$$

14. Cash flow = profit – increase in inventory = $10,000 – $1,000 = $9,000

15. $NWC_{2008} = \$32 + \$25 - \$12 = \$45$ million

$NWC_{2009} = \$36 + \$30 - \$26 = \$40$ million

Net working capital has decreased by $5 million.

16. Depreciation expense per year = $40/5 = $8 million

Book value of old equipment = $40 – (3 × $8) = $16 million

After-tax cash flow = $18 – [0.35 × ($18 – $16)] = $17.3 million

17. Using the seven-year ACRS depreciation schedule, after five years the machinery will be written down to 22.30% of its original value: $0.2230 \times \$10$ million $= \$2.230$ million

If the machinery is sold for $4.5 million, the sale generates a taxable gain of: $2.270 million

This increases the firm's tax bill by: $0.35 \times \$2.270 = \$0.7945$ million

Thus: total cash flow $= \$4.5 - \$0.7945 = \$3.7055$ million

18. a. All values should be interpreted as *incremental* results from making the purchase.

Earnings before depreciation	$1,500
Depreciation	1,000
Taxable income	500
Taxes	200
Net income	300
+ Depreciation	1,000
Operating CF	$1,300 in years 1–6

Net cash flow at time 0 is: $-\$6,000 + [\$2,000 \times (1 - 0.40)] = -\$4,800$

b. NPV $= -\$4,800 + [\$1,300 \times$ annuity factor(16%, 6 years)]

$$= -\$4,800 + \$1,300 \times \left[\frac{1}{0.16} - \frac{1}{0.16 \times (1.16)^6} \right] = -\$9.84$$

c. Incremental CF in each year (using depreciation tax shield approach) is:

$$[\$1,500 \times (1 - 0.40)] + (\text{depreciation} \times 0.40)$$

Year	Depreciation	CF
0	n/a	-$4,800.00
1	$1,200.00	1,380.00
2	1,920.00	1,668.00
3	1,152.00	1,360.80
4	691.20	1,176.48
5	691.20	1,176.48
6	345.60	1,038.24

$$NPV = -\$4,800 + \frac{\$1,380}{1.16} + \frac{\$1,668}{1.16^2} + \frac{\$1,360.80}{1.16^3} + \frac{\$1,176.48}{1.16^4} + \frac{\$1,176.48}{1.16^5} + \frac{\$1,038.24}{1.16^6}$$

$$= \$137.09$$

19. If the firm uses straight-line depreciation, the present value of the cost of buying, net of the annual depreciation tax shield (which equals $1,000 \times 0.40 = \$400$), is:

$6,000 - [\$400 \times$ annuity factor(16%, 6 years)] =

$$\$6,000 - \$400 \times \left[\frac{1}{0.16} - \frac{1}{0.16 \times (1.16)^6} \right] = \$4,526.11$$

The equivalent annual cost (EAC) is therefore determined by:

$C \times$ annuity factor(16%, 6 years) = $4,526.11

$$C \times \left[\frac{1}{0.16} - \frac{1}{0.16 \times (1.16)^6} \right] = \$4,526.11$$

$$C \times 3.68474 = \$4,526.11 \Rightarrow C = EAC = \$1,228.34$$

Note: this is the equivalent annual *cost* of the new washer, and does not include any of the washer's benefits.

20. a. In the following table, we compute the impact on operating cash flows by summing the value of the depreciation tax shield (depreciation $\times$ tax rate) plus the net-of-tax improvement in operating income [$20,000 \times (1 - \text{tax rate})$]. Although the MACRS depreciation schedule extends out to 4 years, the project will be terminated when the machine is sold after 3 years, so we need to examine cash flows for only 3 years.

MACRS	Depreciation	Depreciation $\times$ 0.035	ΔOperating income $\times (1 - 0.35)$	Contribution to operating cash flow
0.3333	$13,332	$4,666.20	$13,000	$17,666.20
0.4445	17,780	6,223.00	13,000	19,223.00
0.1481	5,942	2,073.40	13,000	15,073.40
0.0741				

   b. Total cash flow = Operating cash flow + cash flow associated with investments

   At time 0, the cash flow from the investment is: $-\$40,000$

   When the grill is sold at the end of year 3, its book value will be $2,964, so the sale price, net of tax, will be: $10,000 - [0.35 \times (\$10,000 - \$2,964)] = \$7,537.40$

   Therefore, total cash flows are:

Time	Cash Flow
0	$-\$40,000.00$
1	17,666.20
2	19,223.00
3	22,610.80 [= 15,073.40 + 7,537.40]

   c. The net present value of this cash flow stream, at a discount rate of 12 percent, is $7,191.77, which is positive. So the grill should be purchased.

21. a. Working capital = 20% × $40,000 = $8,000

Initial investment = $45,000 + $8,000 = $53,000

b. <u>All figures in thousands of dollars</u>

Year	Revenues	Expenses	Working Capital	Depreciation	Cash Flow*
1	40	16	6	11.25	20.9
2	30	12	4	11.25	17.3
3	20	8	2	11.25	13.7
4	10	4	0	11.25	10.1

*Cash flow = [(revenues − expenses) × (1 − 0.40)] + (depreciation × 0.40)

+ $2,000 (decrease in working capital from previous year)

c. $NPV = -\$53,000 + \dfrac{\$20,900}{1.12} + \dfrac{\$17,300}{1.12^2} + \dfrac{\$13,700}{1.12^3} + \dfrac{\$10,100}{1.12^4} = -\$4,377.71$

d. To compute IRR, use trial-and-error or a financial calculator to solve for r in the following equation:

$$\dfrac{\$20,900}{1+r} + \dfrac{\$17,300}{(1+r)^2} + \dfrac{\$13,700}{(1+r)^3} + \dfrac{\$10,100}{(1+r)^4} = \$53,000 \Rightarrow IRR = 7.50\%$$

22. a, b, and c. The NPV would be lower by $237, due to higher working capital requirements in each year. (See spreadsheet solution below).

A. Inputs

		Spreadsheet Name
Initial Investment	10,000	Investment
Salvage value	2,000	Salvage
Initial revenue	15,000	Initial_rev
Initial expenses	10,000	Intial_exp
Inflation rate	0.05	Inflation
Discount rate	0.12	Disc_rate
Acct receiv. as % of sales	1/6	A_R
Inven. as % of expenses	0.2	Inv_pct
Tax rate	0.35	Tax_rate

Year:	0	1	2	3	4	5	6
B. Fixed assets							
Investments in fixed assets	10,000						
Sales of fixed assets							1,300
CF, invest. in fixed assets	−10,000	0	0	0	0	0	1,300
C. Operating Cash Flow							
Revenues		15,000	15,750	16,538	17,364	18,233	
Expenses		10,000	10,500	11,025	11,576	12,155	
Depreciation		2,000	2,000	2,000	2,000	2,000	
Pretax profit		3,000	3,250	3,513	3,788	4,078	
Tax		1,050	1,138	1,229	1,326	1,427	
Profit after tax		1,950	2,113	2,283	2,462	2,650	
Cash flow from operations		3,950	4,113	4,283	4,462	4,650	
D. Working capital							
Working capital	2,000	4,600	4,830	5,072	5,325	3,039	0
Change in working capital	2,000	2,600	230	242	254	−2,286	−3,039
CF, invest. in wk capital	−2,000	−2,600	−230	−242	−254	2,286	3,039
E. Project valuation							
Total project cash flow	−12,000	1,350	3,883	4,042	4,209	6,937	4,339
Discount factor	1.0	0.8929	0.7972	0.7118	0.6355	0.5674	0.5066
PV of cash flow	−12,000	1,205	3,095	2,877	2,675	3,936	2,198
Net present value	3,986						

23. The initial investment is $100,000 for the copier plus $10,000 in working capital, for a total outlay of $110,000.

   Depreciation expense = ($100,000 − $20,000)/5 = $16,000 per year

The project saves $20,000 in annual labor costs, so the net operating cash flow (including the depreciation tax shield) is:

   $20,000 × (1 − 0.35) + ($16,000 × 0.35) = $18,600

In year 5, the copier is sold for $30,000, which generates net-of-tax proceeds of:

   $30,000 − (0.35 × $10,000) = $26,500

In addition, the working capital associated with the project is freed up, which releases another $10,000 in cash. So, non-operating cash flow in year 5 totals $36,500.

The NPV is thus:

$$NPV = -\$110{,}000 + [\$18{,}600 \times \text{annuity factor}(8\%, 5 \text{ years})] + [\$36{,}500/(1.08)^5]$$

$$= -\$110{,}000 + \$18{,}600 \times \left[\frac{1}{0.08} - \frac{1}{0.08 \times (1.08)^5}\right] + \frac{\$36{,}500}{(1.08)^5}$$

$$= -\$110{,}000 + \$99{,}105.69 = -\$10{,}894.31$$

Because NPV is negative, Kinky's should not buy the new copier.

24. Find the equivalent annual cost of each alternative:

	Quick and Dirty	Do-It-Right
Operating costs	$ 1 million	$ 1 million
Investment	$10 million	$12 million
Project life	5 years	8 years
Annual depreciation	$ 2 million	$ 1.5 million
Depreciation tax shield	$ 0.700 million	$ 0.525 million
PV(Depreciation tax shield) *	$ 2.523 million	$ 2.608 million
Net capital cost **	$ 7.477 million	$ 9.392 million
EAC of net capital cost *	$ 2.074 million	$ 1.891 million

* annuity discounted at 12%; number of years = project life
** Investment – PV(Depreciation tax shield)

The present value of the depreciation tax shield for each alternative is computed as follows:

$$PV = \$0.700 \text{ million} \times \left[\frac{1}{0.12} - \frac{1}{0.12 \times (1.12)^5}\right] = \$2.523 \text{ million}$$

$$PV = \$0.525 \text{ million} \times \left[\frac{1}{0.12} - \frac{1}{0.12 \times (1.12)^8}\right] = \$2.608 \text{ million}$$

The equivalent annual cost (EAC) for each alternative is computed as follows:

$$C \times \left[\frac{1}{0.12} - \frac{1}{0.12 \times (1.12)^5}\right] = \$7.477 \text{ million} \Rightarrow C = EAC = \$2.074 \text{ million}$$

$$C \times \left[\frac{1}{0.12} - \frac{1}{0.12 \times (1.12)^8}\right] = \$9.392 \text{ million} \Rightarrow C = EAC = \$1.891 \text{ million}$$

Since the operating costs are the same, then Do-It-Right is preferred because it has the lower EAC.

25.   All figures in thousands

	0	1	2	3	4
Net working capital	$176	$240	$112	$40	$ 0
Investment in NWC	176	64	−128	−72	−40
Investment in plant & equipment	200	0	0	0	0
Cash flow from investment activity	−$376	−$ 64	+$128	+$72	+$40

All figures in thousands

	0	1	2	3	4
Revenue		$880.00	$1200.00	$560.00	$200.00
Cost		550.00	750.00	350.00	125.00
Depreciation		66.66	88.90	29.62	14.82
Pretax profit		263.34	361.10	180.38	60.18
Taxes		92.17	126.39	63.13	21.06
Net income		171.17	234.71	117.25	39.12
Depreciation		66.66	88.90	29.62	14.82
Operating cash flow		$237.83	$ 323.61	$146.87	$ 53.94
Total cash flow	−$376.00	$173.83	$ 451.61	$218.87	$ 93.94

$$\text{NPV} = -\$376 + \frac{\$173.83}{1.20} + \frac{\$451.61}{1.20^2} + \frac{\$218.87}{1.20^3} + \frac{\$93.94}{1.20^4} = \$254.440 \text{ or } \$254,440$$

26.   All figures are on an incremental basis:

Labor savings	$125,000
− Operating Cost	35,000
− Depreciation	90,000
EBIT	0
− Taxes	0
Net income	0
+ Depreciation	90,000
Operating cash flow	$ 90,000

$$\text{NPV} = -\$1,000,000 + [\$90,000 \times \text{annuity factor}(8\%, 10 \text{ years})] + [\$100,000/(1.08)^{10}]$$

$$= -\$1,000,000 + \$90,000 \times \left[\frac{1}{0.08} - \frac{1}{0.08 \times (1.08)^{10}}\right] + \frac{\$100,000}{(1.08)^{10}} = -\$349,773.33$$

27.   If the savings are permanent, then the inventory system is worth $250,000 to the firm. The firm can take $250,000 out of the project now without ever having to replace it. So the most the firm should be willing to pay is $250,000.

28. All cash flows are in millions of dollars. Sales price of machinery in year 6 is shown on an after-tax basis as a positive cash flow on the capital investment line.

a.

Year	0	1	2	3	4	5	6
Sales (Traps)		0.5	0.6	1	1	0.6	0.2
Revenue	0	2	2.4	4	4	2.4	0.8
Working capital	0.2	0.24	0.4	0.4	0.24	0.08	0
Change in Working Capital	−0.2	0.04	0.16	0	−0.16	−0.16	−0.08
Revenues		2	2.4	4	4	2.4	0.8
Expense		0.75	0.9	1.5	1.5	0.9	0.3
Depreciation		1	1	1	1	1	1
Pretax profit		0.25	0.5	1.5	1.5	0.5	−0.5
Tax		0.0875	0.175	0.525	0.525	0.175	−0.175
After-tax profit		0.1625	0.325	0.975	0.975	0.325	−0.325
Cash Flow from operations		1.1625	1.325	1.975	1.975	1.325	0.675
Cash Flow: capital invest.	−6						0.325
Cash Flow from WC	−0.2	−0.04	−0.16	0	0.16	0.16	0.08
Cash Flow from operations	0	1.1625	1.325	1.975	1.975	1.325	0.675
Total Cash Flow	−6.2	1.1225	1.165	1.975	2.135	1.485	1.08
PV of Cash Flow at 12%	−6.2	1.002	0.929	1.406	1.357	0.843	0.547
Net present value	−0.11665						

b.

Year	0	1	2	3	4	5	6
Sales (Traps)		0.5	0.6	1	1	0.6	0.2
Revenue	0	2	2.4	4	4	2.4	0.8
Working capital	0.2	0.24	0.4	0.4	0.24	0.08	0
Change in Working Capital	−0.2	0.04	0.16	0	−0.16	−0.16	−0.08
Revenues		2	2.4	4	4	2.4	0.8
Expense		0.75	0.9	1.5	1.5	0.9	0.3
Depreciation		1.2	1.92	1.152	0.6912	0.6912	0.3456
Pretax profit		0.05	−0.42	1.348	1.8088	0.8088	0.1544
Tax		0.0175	−0.147	0.4718	0.63308	0.28308	0.05404
After-tax profit		0.0325	−0.273	0.8762	1.17572	0.52572	0.10036
Cash Flow from operations		1.2325	1.647	2.0282	1.86692	1.21692	0.44596
Cash Flow: capital invest.	−6						0.325
Cash Flow from WC	−0.2	−0.04	−0.16	0	0.16	0.16	0.08
Cash Flow from operations	0	1.2325	1.647	2.0282	1.86692	1.21692	0.44596
Total	−6.2	1.1925	1.487	2.0282	2.02692	1.37692	0.85096
Net present value	−0.00564						

Using the 5-year MACRS schedule the net present value increases by $111,010 (−116,650 − 5,640).

29. If working capital requirements were only one-half of those in the previous problem, then the working capital cash flow forecasts would change as follows:

Year:	0	1	2	3	4	5
Original forecast	−0.20	−0.04	−0.16	0.0	+0.16	+0.24
Revised forecast	−0.10	−0.02	−0.08	0.0	+0.08	+0.12
Change in cash flow	+0.10	+0.02	+0.08	0.0	−0.08	−0.12

The PV of the change in the cash flow stream (at a discount rate of 12%) is: $0.0627 million

30. a. Annual depreciation is: ($115 − $15)/5 = $20 million

   Book value at the time of sale is: $115 − (2 × $20) = $75 million

   Sales price = $80 million, so net-of-tax proceeds from the sale are:

   $80 − (0.35 × $5) = $78.25 million

   Therefore, the net cash outlay at time 0 is: $150 − $78.25 = $71.75 million

   b. The project saves $10 million in operating costs, and increases sales by $25 million. Depreciation expense for the new machine would be $50 million per year. Therefore, including the depreciation tax shield, operating cash flow increases by:

   ($25 + $10) × (1 − 0.35) + ($50 × 0.35) = $40.25 million per year

   c. NPV = −$71.75 + [$40.25 × annuity factor(10%, 3 years)]

   $$= -\$71.75 + \$40.25 \times \left[\frac{1}{0.10} - \frac{1}{0.10 \times (1.10)^3} \right] = \$28.35 \text{ or } \$28.35 \text{ million}$$

   To find the internal rate of return, set the PV of the annuity to $71.75 and solve for the discount rate (r):

   $$\$40.25 \times \left[\frac{1}{r} - \frac{1}{r \times (1+r)^3} \right] = \$71.75 \Rightarrow r = \text{IRR} = 31.33\%$$

31. At the optimistic production level the NPV of the power plant is $453 million:

Year	Revenue	Fuel Costs	Labor & Other	Depreciation	Oper. Prof.	Tax	Cash Flow	Present Value
0							−386	−386
1	398.64	229.52	45.00	14.48	109.65	38.38	85.74	76.56
2	410.60	236.41	46.35	27.87	99.97	34.99	92.85	74.02
3	422.92	243.50	47.74	25.78	105.89	37.06	94.62	67.35
4	435.60	250.80	49.17	23.85	111.77	39.12	96.51	61.33
5	448.67	258.33	50.65	22.04	117.66	41.18	98.52	55.90
6	462.13	266.08	52.17	20.38	123.51	43.23	100.66	51.00
7	476.00	274.06	53.73	18.88	129.33	45.27	102.94	46.56
8	490.28	282.28	55.34	17.45	135.20	47.32	105.33	42.54
9	504.99	290.75	57.00	17.22	140.02	49.01	108.23	39.03
10	520.13	299.47	58.71	17.22	144.73	50.66	111.29	35.83
11	535.74	308.46	60.48	17.22	149.59	52.36	114.45	32.90
12	551.81	317.71	62.29	17.22	154.60	54.11	117.70	30.21
13	568.37	327.24	64.16	17.22	159.75	55.91	121.05	27.74
14	585.42	337.06	66.08	17.22	165.06	57.77	124.50	25.48
15	602.98	347.17	68.07	17.22	170.53	59.68	128.06	23.40
16	621.07	357.58	70.11	17.22	176.16	61.66	131.72	21.49
17	639.70	368.31	72.21	17.22	181.96	63.69	135.49	19.73
18	658.89	379.36	74.38	17.22	187.94	65.78	139.37	18.12
19	678.66	390.74	76.61	17.22	194.09	67.93	143.37	16.65
20	699.02	402.46	78.91	17.22	200.43	70.15	147.49	15.29
21	719.99	414.54	81.28	8.61	215.57	75.45	148.73	13.77
22	741.59	426.97	83.71	0.00	230.90	80.81	150.08	12.40
23	763.84	439.78	86.22	0.00	237.83	83.24	154.59	11.41
24	786.75	452.98	88.81	0.00	244.96	85.74	159.23	10.49
25	810.35	466.57	91.48	0.00	252.31	88.31	164.00	9.65
						NPV:		452.84

The company should go ahead with the project since the NPV is still positive ($24.45 million) at the more realistic production level of 3.624 (6.04 × 0.060) million megawatt hours.

Year	Revenue	Fuel Costs	Labor & Other	Depreciation	Oper. Prof.	Tax	Cash Flow	Present Value
0							−386	−386
1	239.18	137.71	45.00	14.48	42.00	14.70	41.77	37.30
2	246.36	141.84	46.35	27.87	30.30	10.60	47.56	37.92
3	253.75	146.10	47.74	25.78	34.13	11.94	47.97	34.14
4	261.36	150.48	49.17	23.85	37.85	13.25	48.46	30.80
5	269.20	155.00	50.65	22.04	41.52	14.53	49.03	27.82
6	277.28	159.65	52.17	20.38	45.09	15.78	49.69	25.17
7	285.60	164.44	53.73	18.88	48.56	16.99	50.44	22.81
8	294.17	169.37	55.34	17.45	52.01	18.20	51.25	20.70
9	302.99	174.45	57.00	17.22	54.32	19.01	52.52	18.94
10	312.08	179.68	58.71	17.22	56.47	19.76	53.92	17.36
11	321.44	185.07	60.48	17.22	58.68	20.54	55.36	15.91
12	331.09	190.63	62.29	17.22	60.95	21.33	56.84	14.59
13	341.02	196.34	64.16	17.22	63.30	22.15	58.36	13.37
14	351.25	202.23	66.08	17.22	65.72	23.00	59.93	12.26
15	361.79	208.30	68.07	17.22	68.20	23.87	61.55	11.24
16	372.64	214.55	70.11	17.22	70.77	24.77	63.21	10.31
17	383.82	220.99	72.21	17.22	73.41	25.69	64.93	9.46
18	395.33	227.62	74.38	17.22	76.12	26.64	66.70	8.67
19	407.19	234.45	76.61	17.22	78.92	27.62	68.52	7.96
20	419.41	241.48	78.91	17.22	81.81	28.63	70.39	7.30
21	431.99	248.72	81.28	8.61	93.39	32.69	69.31	6.42
22	444.95	256.18	83.71	0.00	105.05	36.77	68.29	5.64
23	458.30	263.87	86.22	0.00	108.21	37.87	70.33	5.19
24	472.05	271.79	88.81	0.00	111.45	39.01	72.44	4.77
25	486.21	279.94	91.48	0.00	114.80	40.18	74.62	4.39

| | | | | | | | NPV: | 24.45 |

Solution to Minicase for Chapter 9

The spreadsheet on the next page shows the cash flows associated with the project.
Rows 1 – 10 replicate the data in Table 9-4, with the exception of the substitution of MACRS depreciation for straight-line depreciation.

Row 12 (capital investment) shows the initial investment of $1.5 million in refurbishing the plant and buying the new machinery.

When the project is shut down after five years, the machinery and plant will be worthless.
But they will not be fully depreciated. The tax loss on each will equal the book value since the market price of each asset is zero. Therefore, tax savings in year 5 (rows 14 and 15) equals:

$0.35 \times$ book value (i.e., original investment minus accumulated depreciation)

The investment in working capital (row 13) is initially equal to $300,000, but in year 5, when the project is shut down, the investment in working capital is recouped.

If the project goes ahead, the land cannot be sold until the end of year 5. If the land is sold for $600,000 (as Mr. Tar assumes it can be), the taxable gain on the sale is $590,000, since the land is carried on the books at $10,000. Therefore, the cash flow from the sale of the land, net of tax at 35%, is $393,500.

The total cash flow from the project is given in row 17. The present value of the cash flows, at a 12% discount rate, is $716,400.

If the land can be sold for $1.5 million immediately, the after-tax proceeds will be:

$1,500,000 - [0.35 \times ($1,500,000 - $10,000)] = $978,500$

So it appears that immediate sale is the better option.

However, Mr. Tar may want to reconsider the estimate of the selling price of the land five years from now. If the land can be sold today for $1,500,000 and the inflation rate is 4%, then perhaps it makes more sense to assume it can be sold in 5 years for:

$1,500,000 \times 1.04^5 = $1,825,000$

In that case, the forecasted after-tax proceeds of the sale of the land in five years increases to $1,190,000, which is $796,500 higher than the original estimate of $393,500; the present value of the proceeds from the sale of the land increases by:

$796,500/1.12^5 = $452,000$

Therefore, under this assumption, the present value of the project increases from the original estimate of $716,400 to a new value of $1,168,400, and in this case the project is more valuable than the proceeds from selling the land immediately.

Year	0	1	2	3	4	5
1. Yards sold		100.00	100.00	100.00	100.00	100.00
2. Price per yard		30.00	30.00	30.00	30.00	30.00
3. Revenue		3,000.00	3,000.00	3,000.00	3,000.00	3,000.00
4. Cost of goods sold		2,100.00	2,184.00	2,271.36	2,362.21	2,456.70
5. Operating cash flow		900.00	816.00	728.64	637.79	543.30
6. Depreciation on machine*		200.00	320.00	192.00	115.20	115.20
7. Depreciation on Plant**		50.00	90.00	72.00	57.60	46.10
8. Income (5 – 6 – 7)		650.00	406.00	464.64	464.99	382.00
9. Tax at 35%		227.50	142.10	162.62	162.75	133.70
10. Net Income		422.50	263.90	302.02	302.24	248.30
11. Cash flow from operations		672.50	673.90	566.02	475.04	409.60
12. Capital investment	−1,500.00					
13. Investment in wk cap	−300.00					300.00
14. Tax savings on machine						20.16
15. Tax savings on plant						64.51
16. Sale of land (after tax)						393.50
17. TOTAL CASH FLOW	−1,800.00	672.50	673.90	566.02	475.04	1,187.77
*5-yr MACRS depreciation		0.2000	0.3200	0.1920	0.1152	0.1152
**10-yr MACRS depreciation		0.1000	0.1800	0.1440	0.1152	0.0922

We compare the NPV of the project to the value of an immediate sale of the land. This treats the problem as two competing mutually exclusive investments: sell the land now versus pursue the project. The investment with higher NPV is selected. Alternatively, we could treat the after-tax cash flow that can be realized from the sale of the land as an opportunity cost at year 0 if the project is pursued. In that case, the NPV of the project would be reduced by the initial cash flow given up by not selling the land. Under this approach, the decision rule is to pursue the project if the NPV is positive, accounting for that opportunity cost. This approach would result in the same decision as the one we have presented.

Solutions to Chapter 10

Project Analysis

1. a. The capital budget mitigates the problem of over-optimism by project sponsors by awarding lower-level managers on the basis of net present value and contribution to value.

    b. The capital budget mitigates the problem of inconsistent forecasts of macroeconomic variables by establishing forecasts of economic indicators, both macro-level and business-specific, that are used in all project analyses.

    c. The capital budget mitigates the problem of a bottom-up process by reflecting both capital budgeting and strategic planning. Senior managers sometimes impose capital rationing, forcing subunits to choose among projects, or by asking lower-levels questions that identify the competitive advantage in each positive-NPV project.

2. The extra 2 million burgers increase total costs by $1.0 million.

    Therefore: variable cost = $0.50 per burger

    Fixed costs must then be $2.5 million, since the first 2 million burgers result in total cost of $3.5 million.

3. a. For production of 1 million burgers, fixed costs are $2.5 million.

    Variable costs = $0.50 × 1,000,000 = $0.5 million

    Average cost = $3.00 million/1 million = $3.00/burger

    b. Average cost = $3.50 million/2 million = $1.75/burger

    c. The fixed costs are spread across more burgers — thus the average cost falls.

4. a. (Revenue – expenses) changes by: $1 million – $0.5 million = $0.5 million

    After-tax profits increase by: $0.5 million × (1 – 0.35) = $0.325 million

    Because depreciation is unaffected, cash flow changes by the same amount.

    b. Expenses increase from $5 million to $6.5 million.

    After-tax income and cash flow decrease by:

    $1.5 million × (1 – 0.35) = $0.975 million

5. The 12%, 10-year annuity factor is: $\left[\dfrac{1}{0.12} - \dfrac{1}{0.12 \times (1.12)^{10}}\right] = 5.65022$

The effect on NPV equals the change in CF $\times$ 5.65022

a. $0.325 million $\times$ 5.65022 = $1.836 million
$0.975 million $\times$ 5.65022 = $5.509 million

b. Fixed costs can increase up to the point at which the higher costs (after taxes) reduce NPV by $2 million:

Increase in fixed costs $\times$ (1 – T) $\times$ annuity factor(12%, 10 years) = $2 million

Increase in fixed costs $\times$ (1 – 0.35) $\times$ 5.65022 = $2 million

Increase in fixed costs = $544,567

c. Accounting profits are currently: $(10 – 5 – 2) million $\times$ (1 – 0.35) = $1.95 million

Fixed costs can increase by this amount before pretax profits are reduced to zero.

6. Revenue = Price $\times$ quantity = $2 $\times$ 6 million = $12 million
Expense = Variable cost + fixed cost = ($1 $\times$ 6 million) + $2 million = $8 million
Depreciation expense = $5 million/5 years = $1 million per year
Cash flow = (1 – T) $\times$ (Revenue – expenses) + (T $\times$ depreciation)
$\qquad$ = [0.60 $\times$ ($12 million – $8 million)] + (0.4 $\times$ $1 million) = $2.8 million

a. NPV = –$5 million + [$2.8 million $\times$ annuity factor(10%, 5 years)]

$\qquad$ = –$5 million + $2.8 million$\times\left[\dfrac{1}{0.10} - \dfrac{1}{0.10\times(1.10)^5}\right] = 5.61 million

b. If variable cost = $1.20, then expenses increase to:

($1.20 $\times$ 6 million) + $2 million = $9.2 million

CF = [0.60 $\times$ ($12 million – $9.2 million)] + (0.4 $\times$ $1 million) = $2.08 million

NPV = –$5 million + [$2.08 million $\times$ annuity factor(10%, 5 years)]

$\qquad$ = –$5 million + $2.08 million$\times\left[\dfrac{1}{0.10} - \dfrac{1}{0.10\times(1.10)^5}\right] = 2.88 million

c. If fixed costs = $1.5 million, expenses fall to:

($1 × 6 million) + $1.5 million = $7.5 million

Cash flow = [0.60 × ($12 million – $7.5 million)] + (0.4 × $1 million) = $3.1 million

NPV = –$5 million + [$3.1 million × annuity factor(10%, 5 years)]

$$= -\$5 \text{ million} + \$3.1 \text{ million} \times \left[\frac{1}{0.10} - \frac{1}{0.10 \times (1.10)^5} \right] = \$6.75 \text{ million}$$

d. Call P the price per jar. Then:

Revenue = P × 6 million

Expense = ($1 × 6 million) + $2 million = $8 million

Cash flow = [(1 – 0.40) × (6P – 8)] + (0.40 × 1) = 3.6P – 4.4

NPV = –5 + [(3.6P – 4.4) × annuity factor(10%, 5 years)]

$$= -5 + \left[(3.6P - 4.4) \times \left[\frac{1}{0.10} - \frac{1}{0.10 \times (1.10)^5} \right] \right]$$

$$= -5 + [(3.6P - 4.4) \times 3.7908] = -21.6795 + 13.6469P = 0 \Rightarrow P = \$1.59 \text{ per jar}$$

7.

	Base Case	Best Case	Worst Case
Price	$ 50	$ 55	$ 45
Variable cost	$ 30	$ 27	$ 33
Fixed cost	$300,000	$270,000	$330,000
Sales	30,000 units	33,000 units	27,000 units

Cash flow = [(1 – T) × (Revenue – Cash Expenses)] + (T × Depreciation)

Depreciation expense = $1 million/10 years = $100,000 per year

Best-case CF = 0.65 × [33,000 × ($55 – $27) – $270,000] + (0.35 × $100,000) = $460,100

Worst-case CF = 0.65 × [27,000 × ($45 – $33) – $330,000] + (0.35 × $100,000) = $31,100

$$12\%, \text{ 10-Year Annuity factor} = \left[\frac{1}{0.12} - \frac{1}{0.12 \times (1.12)^{10}} \right] = 5.65022$$

Best-case NPV = (5.65022 × $460,100) – $1,000,000 = $1,599,666

Worst-case NPV = (5.65022 × $ 31,100) – $1,000,000 = –$824,278

8. If price is higher, for example because of inflation, variable costs may also higher. Similarly, if price is high because of strong demand for the product, then sales may be higher. It doesn't make sense to formulate a scenario analysis in which uncertainty in each variable is treated independently of all other variables.

9. At the break-even level of sales (60,000 units) profit would be zero:

    Profit = [60,000 × (2 – variable cost per unit)] – 20,000 – 10,000 = 0

    Solve to find that variable cost per unit = $1.50

10. a. Each dollar of sales generates $0.60 of pretax profit. Depreciation expense is $100,000 per year and fixed costs are $200,000. Therefore:

    Accounting break-even revenue = ($200,000 + $100,000)/0.60 = $500,000
    The firm must sell 5,000 diamonds annually.

    b. Let Q = the number of diamonds sold

    Cash flow equals = [(1 – 0.35) × (Revenue – expenses)] + (0.35 × depreciation)

    $$= [0.65 \times (100Q - 40Q - 200,000) + (0.35 \times 100,000)$$

    $$= 39Q - 95,000$$

    $$12\%, \text{10-Year Annuity factor} = \left[\frac{1}{0.12} - \frac{1}{0.12 \times (1.12)^{10}} \right] = 5.65022$$

    Therefore, for NPV to equal zero:

    $(39Q - 95,000) \times 5.65022 = \$1,000,000 \Rightarrow Q = 6,974$ diamonds per year

11. a. The accounting break-even point would increase because the depreciation charge will be higher, thereby reducing net profit.

    b. The break-even point would decrease because the present value of the depreciation tax shield will be higher when all depreciation charges can be taken in the first five years.

12. The accounting break-even point would be unaffected since taxes paid are zero when pretax profit is zero, regardless of the tax rate.

    The break-even point would increase since the after-tax cash flow corresponding to any level of sales falls when the tax rate increases.

13. Cash flow = Net income + depreciation

If depreciation is positive, then cash flow will be positive even when net income = 0. Therefore the level of sales necessary for cash flow break-even is less than the level of sales necessary for zero-profit break-even.

14. If cash flow = 0 for the entire life of the project, then the present value of cash flows = 0, and project NPV will be negative in the amount of the required investment.

15. a. Variable cost = 75% of sales revenue

Therefore, additional profit per $1 of additional sales = $0.25

Depreciation expense = $3,000/5 = $600 per year

Break-even level of sales =

$$\frac{\text{Fixed costs including depreciation}}{\text{Additional profit from each additional dollar of sales}} = \frac{\$1,000 + \$600}{0.25} = \$6,400 \text{ per year}$$

This sales level corresponds to a production level of: $6,400/$80 per unit = 80 units

To find the economic break-even level of sales, first calculate cash flow.

With no taxes: Cash flow = $(0.25 \times \text{Sales}) - 1,000$

The 10%, 5-year annuity factor is: $\left[\dfrac{1}{0.10} - \dfrac{1}{0.10 \times (1.10)^5} \right] = 3.79079$

Therefore, if project NPV equals zero:

PV(cash flows) – Investment = 0

$[3.79079 \times ((0.25 \times \text{Sales}) - 1000)] - 3000 = 0$

$(0.94770 \times \text{Sales}) - 3790.79 - 3000 = 0 \Rightarrow \text{Sales} = \$7,166$

This sales level corresponds to a production level of: $7,166/$80 = almost 90 units

b. Now taxes are 35% of profits. Accounting break-even is unchanged since taxes are zero when profits = 0.

To find NPV break-even, recalculate cash flow:

Cash flow = $[(1 - T) \times (\text{Revenue} - \text{Cash Expenses})] + (T \times \text{Depreciation})$

$= 0.65 \times [(0.25 \times \text{Sales}) - 1000] + (0.35 \times 600) = (0.1625 \times \text{Sales}) - 440$

The annuity factor is 3.79079, so we find NPV as follows:

$3.79079 \times [(0.1625 \times \text{Sales}) - 440] - 3000 = 0 \Rightarrow \text{Sales} = \$7,578$

This corresponds to production of: $7,578/$80 = almost 95 units

16. a. Accounting break-even level of sales increases: MACRS results in higher depreciation charges in the early years of the project, requiring a higher sales level for the firm to break even in terms of accounting profits.

   b. NPV break-even level of sales decreases. The accelerated depreciation increases the present value of the tax shield, and thus reduces the level of sales necessary to achieve zero NPV.

   c. MACRS makes the project more attractive. The PV of the tax shield is higher, so the NPV of the project at any given level of sales is higher.

17.

Sales	$16,000,000	
– Variable costs	12,800,000	(80% of sales)
– Fixed costs	2,000,000	
– Depreciation	500,000	(includes depreciation on new checkout equipment)
= Pretax profit	700,000	
– Taxes (at 40%)	280,000	
= Profit after tax	$ 420,000	
+ Depreciation	500,000	
= Cash flow from operations	$ 920,000	

   a. Cash flow increases by $140,000 [from $780,000 (see Table 9-1) to $920,000]. The cost of the investment is $600,000. Therefore:

   $$NPV = -\$600,000 + [\$140,000 \times \text{annuity factor}(8\%, 12 \text{ years})]$$

   $$= -\$600,000 + \$140,000 \times \left[\frac{1}{0.08} - \frac{1}{0.08 \times (1.08)^{12}} \right]$$

   $$= -\$600,000 + \$140,000 \times 7.53608 = \$455,051$$

   b. The equipment reduces variable costs from 81.25% of sales to 80% of sales. Pretax savings are therefore equal to (0.0125 × Sales). On the other hand, annual depreciation expense increases by: $600,000/12 = $50,000. Therefore, accounting profits are unaffected if sales equal: $50,000/0.0125 = $4,000,000

   c. The project reduces variable costs from 81.25% of sales to 80% of sales. Pretax savings are therefore equal to (0.0125 × Sales). Annual depreciation expense increases by $50,000. Therefore, after-tax cash flow increases by:

   $$[(1 - T) \times (\Delta\text{Revenue} - \Delta\text{Expenses})] + (T \times \Delta\text{Depreciation})$$

   $$= [(1 - 0.4) \times (0.0125 \times \text{Sales})] + (0.4 \times 50,000) = (0.0075 \times \text{Sales}) + 20,000$$

For NPV to equal zero, the increment to cash flow times the 12-year annuity factor must equal the initial investment:

$$\Delta \text{cash flow} \times 7.53608 = 600,000 \Rightarrow \Delta \text{cash flow} = \$79,617$$

Therefore: $(0.0075 \times \text{Sales}) + 20,000 = 79,617 \Rightarrow \text{Sales} = \$7,948,933$

NPV break-even is nearly double accounting break-even.

18. NPV will be negative. We've shown in the previous problem that the accounting break-even level of sales is less than the economic break-even level of sales.

19. Percentage change in profits = percentage change in Sales × DOL
   A decline of $0.5 million in sales represents a change of: $0.5/$4 = 12.5 percent
   Profits will decrease by: 8 × 12.5% = 100%, from $1 million to zero.
   Similarly, a sales increase will increase profits to $2 million.

20. $\text{DOL} = 1 + \dfrac{\text{fixed costs (including depreciation)}}{\text{profits}}$

   a. Profit = Revenues − variable costs − fixed costs − depreciation
      = $7,000 − $5,250 − $1,000 − $600 = $150

   $$\text{DOL} = 1 + \frac{\$1,600}{\$150} = 11.67$$

   b. Profit = Revenues − variable costs − fixed costs − depreciation
      = $12,000 − $9,000 − $1,000 − $600 = $1,400

   $$\text{DOL} = 1 + \frac{\$1,600}{\$1,400} = 2.14$$

   c. DOL is higher when profits are lower because a $1 change in sales leads to a greater percentage change in profits.

21. $\text{DOL} = 1 + \dfrac{\text{fixed costs (including depreciation)}}{\text{profits}}$

   If profits are positive, DOL cannot be less than 1.0. At sales = $7,000, profits for Modern Artifacts (if fixed costs and depreciation were zero) would be: $7,000 × 0.25 = $1,750

   At sales of $12,000, profits would be: $12,000 × 0.25 = $3,000

   Profit is one-quarter of sales regardless of the level of sales. If sales increase by 1%, so will profits. Thus DOL = 1.

22.   a.   Pretax profits currently equal:

Revenue − variable costs − fixed costs − depreciation =

$6,000 − $4,000 − $1,000 − $500 = $500

If sales increase by $600, expenses will increase by $400, and pretax profits will increase by $200, an increase of 40%.

b. $$DOL = 1 + \frac{fixed\ costs\ (including\ depreciation)}{profits} = 1 + \frac{\$1,500}{\$500} = 4$$

c.   Percentage change in profits = DOL × percentage change in sales = 4 × 10% = 40%

23.   We compare expected NPV with and without testing. If the field is large, then:

NPV = $8 million − $3 million = $5 million.

If the field is small, then: NPV = $2 million − $3 million = −$1 million

If the test is performed, and the field is found to be small, then the project is abandoned, and NPV = zero (minus the cost of the test, which is $0.1 million).

Therefore, without testing:

NPV = (0.5 × $5 million) + [0.5 × (−$1 million)] = $2 million

With testing, expected NPV is higher:

NPV = −$0.1 million + (0.5 × $5 million) + (0.5 × 0) = $2.4 million

Therefore, it pays to perform the test.

The decision tree is as follows:

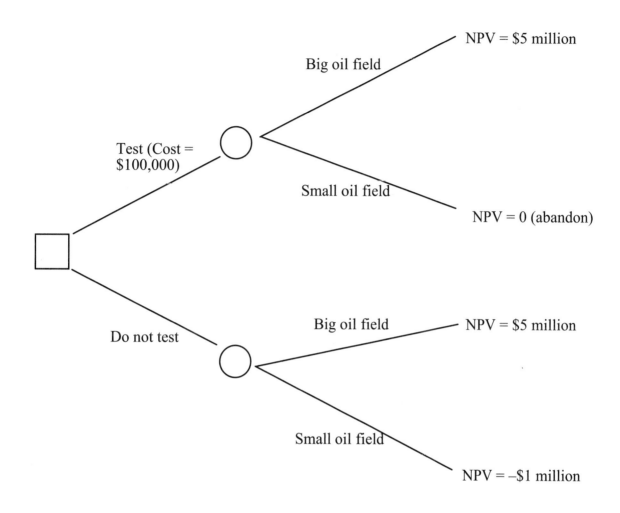

24. a. Expenses = (10,000 × $8) + $10,000 = $90,000
Revenue is either: 10,000 × $12 = $120,000

or: 10,000 × $6 = $60,000

Average cash flow = [0.5 × ($120,000 – $90,000)] + [0.5× ($60,000 – $90,000)] = 0

b. If you can shut down the mine, CF in the low-price years will be zero. In that case:
Average cash flow = [0.5 × ($120,000 – $90,000)] + [0.5 × $0] = $15,000

(We assume fixed costs are incurred only if the mine is operating. The fixed costs do not rise with the amount of silver extracted, but are not incurred unless the mine is in production.)

25. a. Expected NPV = [0.5 × ($140 – $100)] + [0.5 × ($50 – $100)] = –$5 million

Therefore, you should not build the plant.

b. Now the worst-case value of the installed project is $95 million rather than $50 million. Expected NPV increases to a positive value:

[0.5 × ($140 – $100)] + [0.5 × ($95 – $100)] = $17.5 million

Therefore, you should build the plant.

c.

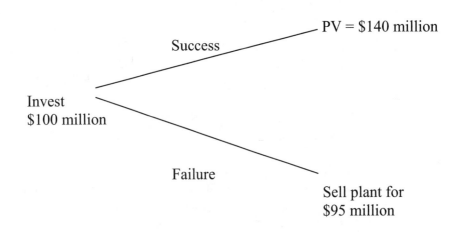

26. Options provide the ability to cut losses or to extend gains. You benefit from good outcomes, but can limit damage from bad outcomes. The ability to *change* your actions (e.g., to abandon or to expand or to change timing) is most important when the ultimate best course of action is most difficult to forecast.

27. a.

	Optimistic	Pessimistic
Price	$ 60	$ 55
Sales	50,000 units	30,000 units
Variable cost	$30	$30

Cash flow = [(1 – T) × (Revenue – Cash expenses)] + [T × Depreciation]

Optimistic CF = 0.65 × [($60 – $30) × 50,000] + [0.35 × $600,000] = $1,185,000

NPV = –$6,000,000 + [$1,185,000 × annuity factor(12%, 10 years)]

$$= -\$6,000,000 + \$1,185,000 \times \left[\frac{1}{0.12} - \frac{1}{0.12 \times (1.12)^{10}} \right] = \$695,514$$

Pessimistic CF = 0.65 [($55 – $30) × 30,000] + [0.35 × $600,000] = $697,500

NPV = –$6,000,000 + [$697,500 × annuity factor(12%, 10 years)]

$$= -\$6,000,000 + \$697,500 \times \left[\frac{1}{0.12} - \frac{1}{0.12 \times (1.12)^{10}} \right] = -\$2,058,969$$

Expected NPV = $(0.5 \times \$695,514) + [0.5 \times (-\$2,058,969)] = -\$681,728$

The firm will reject the project.

b. If the project can be abandoned after one year, then it will be sold for $5.4 million. (There will be no taxes on the sale because this also is the depreciated value of the equipment.)

Cash flow (at t = 1) = Cash flow from project + sales price:

$$\$697,500 + \$5,400,000 = \$6,097,500$$

$$PV = \frac{\$6,097,500}{1.12} = \$5,444,196$$

NPV in the abandonment scenario is:

$$\$5,444,196 - \$6,000,000 = -\$555,804$$

Note that this NPV is not as disastrous as the result in part (a).

Expected NPV is now positive:

$$(0.5 \times \$695,514) + [0.5 \times (-\$555,804)] = \$69,855$$

Because of the abandonment option, the project is now worth pursuing.

28. The additional after-tax cash flow from the expanded sales in the successful outcome for the project is:

$$0.65 \times [25,000 \times (\$60 - \$35)] = \$406,250$$

As in the previous problem, we assume that the firm decides whether to expand production after it learns the first-year sales results. At that point, the project will have a remaining life of nine years. The present value *as of the end of the first year* is thus calculated using the nine-year annuity factor at an interest rate of 12%:

$$12\%, \text{9-Year Annuity factor} = \left[\frac{1}{0.12} - \frac{1}{0.12 \times (1.12)^9}\right] = 5.32825$$

Therefore, in this scenario, the increase in NPV *as of year 1* is:

$$5.32825 \times \$406,250 = \$2,164,601$$

The increase in NPV *as of time 0* is: $\$2,164,601/1.12 = \$1,932,679$

The probability of this outcome is 0.5, so the increase in expected NPV is $966,340.

Oil Price

29. a.

Annual Sales	80	100	120
25	−3369.59	−1156.06	1057.47
30	−3325.32	−669.08	1987.15
35	−3281.05	−182.11	2916.84

The price of oil is the greatest source of uncertainty in the project.

b. Given a $100 per barrel price, the annual level of sales necessary for an NPV break-even is 36.87 million barrels. The value was found using Excel's Goal Seek shown below:

Investment (mil):	4000
Annual Expenses (mil)	100
Input Costs Today	78
Oil Prices Today	100
Output (mil barrels)	36.86976
Inflation:	0
Discount Rate:	0.12
Tax Rate:	0.35

Year	Revenue	Input Costs	Expenses	Depreciation	Oper. Prof.	Tax	Cash Flow	Present Value
0							−4000	−4000
1	3686.98	2875.84	100.00	400.00	311.13	108.90	602.24	537.71
2	3686.98	2875.84	100.00	720.00	−8.87	−3.10	714.24	569.39
3	3686.98	2875.84	100.00	576.00	135.13	47.30	663.84	472.51
4	3686.98	2875.84	100.00	460.80	250.33	87.62	623.52	396.26
5	3686.98	2875.84	100.00	368.80	342.33	119.82	591.32	335.53
6	3686.98	2875.84	100.00	294.80	416.33	145.72	565.42	286.46
7	3686.98	2875.84	100.00	262.00	449.13	157.20	553.94	250.57
8	3686.98	2875.84	100.00	262.00	449.13	157.20	553.94	223.73
9	3686.98	2875.84	100.00	262.40	448.73	157.06	554.08	199.81
10	3686.98	2875.84	100.00	262.00	449.13	157.20	553.94	178.35
11	3686.98	2875.84	100.00	131.20	579.93	202.98	508.16	146.08
12	3686.98	2875.84	100.00	0.00	711.13	248.90	462.24	118.64
13	3686.98	2875.84	100.00	0.00	711.13	248.90	462.24	105.93
14	3686.98	2875.84	100.00	0.00	711.13	248.90	462.24	94.58
15	3686.98	2875.84	100.00	0.00	711.13	248.90	462.24	84.45

c.

Year	Acct. BE	test
0		
1	22.73	
2	37.27	
3	30.73	
4	25.49	
5	21.31	
6	17.95	
7	16.45	
8	16.45	
9	16.47	
10	16.45	
11	10.51	
12	4.55	
13	4.55	
14	4.55	
15	4.55	

The accounting break-even level of sales changes each year with the changes in depreciation expense. Given that depreciation is a non-cash expense, the true break-even level of sales should not vary if prices are unchanged.

d. The expected NPV of –$669.08 million is found as an equally weighted average for all NPV values given in part a.

	Oil Price		
Annual Sales	80	100	120
25	–3369.59	–1156.06	1057.47
30	–3325.32	–669.08	1987.15
35	–3281.05	–182.11	2916.84
Expected NPV		–669.0833	

e. The facility may be worth building if discount rate adequately accounts for the risk of prices being lower than $120 per barrel.

Solution to Minicase for Chapter 10

You will find an Excel spreadsheet solution for this minicase at the Online Learning Center (www.mhhe.com/bmm6e).

The spreadsheet at the Online Learning Center presents the base-case analysis for the mining project. Inflation is assumed to be 3.5%, but most costs increase in line with inflation. Thus, we deal with real quantities in the spreadsheet, and keep all quantities except for depreciation at their constant real values. The real value of the depreciation expense thus falls by 3.5% per year. For example, real depreciation for the expensive design in year t is:

$$\text{real depreciation} = \frac{\$10\,\text{million}/\,7}{(1.035)^t}$$

The real discount rate is: $(1.14/1.035) - 1 = 0.10 = 10\%$

Notice that the cheaper design seems to dominate the more expensive one. Even if the expensive design ends up costing $10 million, which appears to be the best-case outcome, the cheaper design saves $1.7 million up front, which results in higher net present value. If the cost overruns on the expensive design, the advantage of the cheap design will be even more dramatic.

We are told that the two big uncertainties are construction costs and the price of the transcendental zirconium (TZ). The following table does a sensitivity analysis of the impact of these two variables on the NPV of the expensive design. The range of initial costs represents a pessimistic outcome of a 15% overrun (i.e., $1.5 million) combined with environmental regulation costs of an additional $1.5 million. The optimistic outcome, which we arbitrarily take to entail costs of only $8 million, is probably less relevant. It seems from the case description that there is little chance of costs coming in below $10 million.

Variable	Range of input variables			Resultant net present values		
	Pessimistic	Expected	Optimistic	Pessimistic	Expected	Optimistic
Initial cost	$13 m	$10 m	$8 m	−$0.72m	$1.63m	$3.20m
TZ Price	$7,500	$10,000	$14,000	−$1.06m	$1.63m	$5.94m

The following table repeats this analysis for the cheaper design. Here, the uncertainty in initial cost is due solely to the environmental regulations. We are told that this design will not be subject to significant other cost overruns.

Variable	Range of input variables			Resultant net present values		
	Pessimistic	Expected	Optimistic	Pessimistic	Expected	Optimistic
Initial cost	$9.8 m	$8.3 m	NA	$0.68m	$1.63m	NA
TZ Price	$7,500	$10,000	$14,000	−$0.83m	$1.86m	$6.16m

Notice that the NPV of the cheaper design exceeds the NPV of the expensive one by about $0.22 million regardless of the price of TZ.

In this case, there do not seem to be any inherent relationships among the chief uncertainties of this project. The price of TZ is likely to be unaffected by the cost of opening a new mine. Thus, scenario analysis does not add much information beyond that provided by sensitivity analysis.

One can make a case for delaying construction. If the firm waits a year to see how the price of TZ evolves, the firm may avoid the negative NPV that would result from a low price. Whether it is worth waiting depends on the likelihood that the price will fall.

There is less of a case to be made for delaying construction over the uncertainty of cost overruns. It is unlikely that much of the uncertainty regarding initial cost would be resolved by waiting — the firm probably needs to go into production to learn if there will be overruns.

If the firm goes ahead with the cheaper design, it does not seem necessary to wait to see how the environmental regulations turn out. NPV is positive regardless of the outcome for this variable, so it would not affect the decision of whether to go ahead with the project. The option to walk away from the project would be irrelevant, at least with regard to this variable.

Solutions to Chapter 11

Introduction to Risk, Return, and the Opportunity Cost of Capital

1. Rate of return $= \dfrac{\text{capital gain} + \text{dividend}}{\text{initial share price}} = \dfrac{(\$44 - \$40) + \$2}{\$40} = 0.15 = 15.0\%$

   Dividend yield = dividend/initial share price = \$2/\$40 = 0.05 = 5%

   Capital gains yield = capital gain/initial share price = \$4/\$40 = 0.10 = 10%

2. Dividend yield = \$2/\$40 = 0.05 = 5%

   The dividend yield is unaffected; it is based on the initial price, not the final price.

   Capital gain = \$36 – \$40 = –\$4

   Capital gains yield = –\$4/\$40 = –0.10 = –10%

3. a. Rate of return $= \dfrac{\text{capital gain} + \text{dividend}}{\text{initial share price}} = \dfrac{(\$38 - \$40) + \$2}{\$40} = 0\%$

   Real rate of return $= \dfrac{1 + \text{nominal rate of return}}{1 + \text{inflation rate}} - 1 = \dfrac{1 + 0}{1 + 0.04} - 1 = -0.0385 = -3.85\%$

   b. Rate of return $= \dfrac{(\$40 - \$40) + \$2}{\$40} = 0.05 = 5\%$

   Real rate of return $= \dfrac{1 + \text{nominal rate of return}}{1 + \text{inflation rate}} - 1 = \dfrac{1.05}{1.04} - 1 = 0.0096 = 0.96\%$

   c. Rate of return $= \dfrac{(\$42 - \$40) + \$2}{\$40} = 0.10 = 10\%$

   Real rate of return $= \dfrac{1 + \text{nominal rate of return}}{1 + \text{inflation rate}} - 1 = \dfrac{1.10}{1.04} - 1 = 0.0577 = 5.77\%$

4. $$\text{Real rate of return} = \frac{1 + \text{nominal rate of return}}{1 + \text{inflation rate}} - 1$$

Costaguana: $\text{Real return} = \dfrac{1.95}{1.80} - 1 = 0.0833 = 8.33\%$

U.S.: $\text{Real return} = \dfrac{1.12}{1.02} - 1 = 0.0980 = 9.80\%$

The U.S. provides the higher real rate of return despite the lower nominal rate of return.

Notice that the approximate relationship between real and nominal rates of return is valid only for low rates:

real rate of return ≈ nominal rate of return – inflation rate

This approximation incorrectly suggests that the Costaguanan real rate was higher than the U.S. real rate.

5. We use the following relationship:

$$\text{Real rate of return} = \frac{1 + \text{nominal rate of return}}{1 + \text{inflation rate}} - 1$$

Asset class	Nominal rate of return	Inflation rate	Real rate of return
Treasury bills	4.0%	3.0%	0.97%
Treasury bonds	5.3%	3.0%	2.23%
Common stocks	11.6%	3.0%	8.35%

6. The nominal interest rate cannot be negative. If it were, investors would choose to hold cash (which pays a rate of return equal to zero) rather than buy a Treasury bill providing a negative return. On the other hand, the *real* expected rate of return is negative if the inflation rate exceeds the nominal return.

7.

Quarter	Average price of stocks in market	Index (using DJIA method)	Total market value of stocks	Index (using S&P method)
1	875.83	100	663,736	100
2	857.50	97.91	654,456	98.60
3	906.67	103.52	691,336	104.16
4	911.67	104.09	685,256	103.24

8. a. For the period 1900–2007, Average rate of return = 11.6% (See Table 11-1)

    b. For the period 1900–2007, Average risk premium = 7.6% (See Table 11-1)

    c. For the period 1900–2007, Standard deviation of returns = 19.7%. (See Table 11-5)

9. a.

Year	Stock market return	T-bill return	Risk premium	Deviation from mean	Squared deviation
2003	31.64	1.02	30.62	19.146	366.57
2004	12.62	1.2	11.42	−0.054	0.00
2005	6.38	2.98	3.4	−8.074	65.19
2006	15.77	4.8	10.97	−0.504	0.25
2007	5.62	4.66	0.96	−10.514	110.54
	Average		11.474		542.56

    b. The average risk premium was: 11.474%

    c. The variance (the average squared deviation from the mean) was 409.2538 (without correcting for the lost degree of freedom).

    Therefore: standard deviation = $\sqrt{542.56}$ = 23.29%

10. In 2007, the Dow was substantially more than four times its 1990 level. Therefore, in 2007, a 40-point movement was far less significant in percentage terms than it was in 1990. We would expect to see more 40-point days in 2007 even if market risk as measured by percentage returns is no higher than it was in 1990.

11. Investors would not have invested in bonds during the period 1977–1981 if they had expected to earn negative average returns. *Unanticipated* events must have led to these results. For example, inflation and nominal interest rates during this period rose to levels not seen for decades. These increases, which resulted in large capital losses on long-term bonds, were almost certainly unanticipated by investors who bought those bonds in prior years.

The results for this period demonstrate the perils of attempting to measure 'normal' maturity (or risk) premiums from historical data. While experience over long periods may be a reasonable guide to normal premiums, the realized premium over short periods may contain little information about expectations of future premiums.

12. If investors become less willing to bear investment risk, they will require a higher risk premium to compensate them for holding risky assets. Security prices of risky investments will fall until the *expected* rates of return on those securities rise to the now-higher *required* rates of return.

13. Based on the historical risk premium of the S&P 500 (7.6 percent) and the current level of the risk-free rate (about 3.5 percent), one would predict an expected rate of return of 11.1 percent. If the stock has the same systematic risk, it also should provide this expected return. Therefore, the stock price equals the present value of cash flows for a one-year horizon.

$$P_0 = \frac{\$2 + \$50}{1.111} = \$46.80$$

14. Boom: $\dfrac{\$5 + (\$195 - \$80)}{\$80} = 150.00\%$

   Normal: $\dfrac{\$2 + (\$100 - \$80)}{\$80} = 27.50\%$

   Recession: $\dfrac{\$0 + (\$0 - \$80)}{\$80} = -100.00\%$

   $r = \dfrac{150 + 27.50 + (-100)}{3} = 25.83\%$

   Variance $= \dfrac{1}{3} \times (150 - 25.83)^2 + \dfrac{1}{3} \times (27.50 - 25.83)^2 + \dfrac{1}{3} \times (-100 - 25.83)^2 = 10,418.06$

   Standard deviation $= \sqrt{\text{variance}} = 102.07\%$

15. The bankruptcy lawyer does well when the rest of the economy is floundering, but does poorly when the rest of the economy is flourishing and the number of bankruptcies is down. Therefore, the Leaning Tower of Pita is a risk-reducing investment. When the economy does well and the lawyer's bankruptcy business suffers, the stock return is excellent, thereby stabilizing total income.

16. Boom: $\dfrac{\$0+(\$18-\$25)}{\$25}=-28.00\%$

Normal: $\dfrac{\$1+(\$26-\$25)}{\$25}=8.00\%$

Recession: $\dfrac{\$3+(\$34-\$25)}{\$25}=48.00\%$

$r=\dfrac{(-28)+8+48}{3}=9.33\%$

$\text{Variance}=\dfrac{1}{3}\times(-28-9.33)^2+\dfrac{1}{3}\times(8-9.33)^2+\dfrac{1}{3}\times(48-9.33)^2=963.56$

$\text{Standard deviation}=\sqrt{\text{variance}}=31.04\%$

Portfolio Rate of Return
Boom: $(-28+150)/2=61.00\%$

Normal: $(8+27.5)/2=17.75\%$

Recession: $(48-100)/2=-26.0\%$

Expected return $=17.58\%$

Standard deviation $=35.52\%$

17.   a.   Interest rates tend to fall at the outset of a recession and rise during boom periods. Because bond prices move inversely with interest rates, bonds provide higher returns during recessions when interest rates fall.

   b. $r_{stock}=[0.2\times(-5\%)]+(0.6\times15\%)+(0.2\times25\%)=13.0\%$

   $r_{bonds}=(0.2\times14\%)+(0.6\times8\%)+(0.2\times4\%)=8.4\%$

   $\text{Variance(stocks)}=[0.2\times(-5-13)^2]+[0.6\times(15-13)^2]+[0.2\times(25-13)^2]=96$

   $\text{Standard deviation}=\sqrt{96}=9.80\%$

   $\text{Variance(bonds)}=[0.2\times(14-8.4)^2]+[0.6\times(8-8.4)^2]+[0.2\times(4-8.4)^2]=10.24$

   $\text{Standard deviation}=\sqrt{10.24}=3.20\%$

   c.   Stocks have both higher expected return and higher volatility. More risk averse investors will choose bonds, while those who are less risk averse might choose stocks.

18. a. Recession $(-5\% \times 0.6) + (14\% \times 0.4) = 2.6\%$

            Normal economy $(15\% \times 0.6) + (8\% \times 0.4) = 12.2\%$

            Boom $(25\% \times 0.6) + (4\% \times 0.4) = 16.6\%$

    b. Expected return $= (0.2 \times 2.6\%) + (0.6 \times 12.2\%) + (0.2 \times 16.6\%) = 11.16\%$

$$\text{Variance} = [0.2 \times (2.6 - 11.16)^2] + [0.6 \times (12.2 - 11.16)^2]$$
$$+ [0.2 \times (16.6 - 11.16)^2] = 21.22$$

       Standard deviation $= \sqrt{21.22} = 4.61\%$

    c. The investment opportunities have these characteristics:

	Mean Return	Standard Deviation
Stocks	13.00%	9.80%
Bonds	8.40%	3.20%
Portfolio	11.16%	4.61%

The best choice depends on the degree of your aversion to risk. Nevertheless, we suspect most people would choose the portfolio over stocks since the portfolio has almost the same return with much lower volatility. This is the advantage of diversification.

19. If we use historical averages to compute the "normal" risk premium, then our estimate of "normal" returns and "normal" risk premiums will fall when we include a year with a negative market return. This makes sense if we believe that each additional year of data reveals new information about the "normal" behavior of the market portfolio. We should update our beliefs as additional observations about the market become available.

20. Risk reduction is most pronounced when the stock returns vary against each other. When one firm does poorly, the other will tend to do well, thereby stabilizing the return of the overall portfolio.

21. a. General Steel ought to have greater sensitivity to broad market movements. Steel production is more sensitive to changes in the economy than is food consumption.

    b. Club Med sells a luxury good (expensive vacations) while General Cinema sells movies, which are less sensitive to changes in the economy. Club Med will have greater market risk.

22. a. The expected rate of return on the stock is 4 percent. The standard deviation is 24 percent.

    b. Because the stock offers a risk premium of zero (its expected return is the same as the expected return for Treasury bills), it must have no market risk. All the risk must be diversifiable, and therefore of no concern to investors.

23. Sassafras is *not* a risky investment for a diversified investor. Its return is better when the economy enters a recession. Therefore, the company risk offsets the risk of the rest of the portfolio. Sassafras is a portfolio *stabilizer* despite the fact that there is a 90 percent chance of loss.

    Compare Sassafras to purchasing an insurance policy. Most of the time, you lose money on your insurance policy. But the policy pays off big if you suffer losses elsewhere — for example, if your house burns down. For this reason, we view insurance as a risk-reducing hedge, not as speculation. Similarly, Sassafras may be viewed as analogous to an insurance policy on the rest of your portfolio since it tends to yield higher returns when the rest of the economy fares poorly.

    In contrast, the Leaning Tower of Pita has returns that are positively correlated with the rest of the economy. It does best in a boom and goes out of business in a recession. For this reason, Leaning Tower would be a risky investment for a diversified investor since it increases exposure to the macroeconomic or market risk to which the investor is already exposed.

24. a. Using Excel's AVERAGE and STDEV functions gives:

	Wal-Mart	BP	Shell
Average	0.0037	0.01373	0.01524
Standard Deviation	0.0451	0.0571	0.06317

    b. Using Excel's CORREL Function gives:

	Wal-Mart	BP	Shell
Wal-Mart	1		
BP	–0.14232	1	
Shell	–0.19658	0.82379	1

    Not surprisingly, two firms from the same industry, Shell Oil and British Petroleum, have the highest correlation at 0.82.

c. Using Excel, the standard deviation for an equally-weighted portfolio of Wal-Mart and Shell is 0.03502. Using the values from part a, the average standard deviation for the two stocks is $0.05414 = (0.0451 + 0.0632)/2$.

d. Using Excel, the standard deviation for an equally-weighted portfolio of BP and Shell is 0.05744. Using the values from part a, the average standard deviation for the two stocks is $0.06014 = (0.0571 + 0.0632)/2$. Pairing Wal-Mart with Shell provides greater benefits from diversification because the correlation in their returns is most highly negative (–0.19658).

Solutions to Chapter 12

Risk, Return, and Capital Budgeting

1. a. False. Investors require higher expected rates of return on investments with high *market* risk, not high *total* risk. Variability of returns is a measure of total risk.

    b. False. If beta = 0, then the asset's expected return should equal the risk-free rate, not zero.

    c. False. The portfolio is invested one-third in Treasury bills and two-thirds in the market. Its beta will be:

    $$(1/3 \times 0) + (2/3 \times 1.0) = 2/3$$

    d. True.

    e. True.

2. The risks of deaths of individual policyholders are largely independent, and are therefore diversifiable. The insurance company is satisfied to charge a premium that reflects actuarial probabilities of death, without an additional risk premium. In contrast, flood damage is not independent across policyholders. If my coastal home floods in a storm, there is a greater chance that my neighbor's will too. Because flood risk is not diversifiable, the insurance company may not be satisfied to charge a premium that reflects only the expected value of payouts.

3. The actual returns for the Snake Oil fund exhibit considerable variation around the regression line. This indicates that the fund is subject to diversifiable risk: it is not well diversified. The variation in the fund's returns is influenced by more than just market-wide events.

4. Investors would buy shares of firms with high levels of diversifiable risk, and earn high risk premiums. But by holding these shares in diversified portfolios, they would not necessarily bear a high degree of portfolio risk. This would represent a profit opportunity, however. As investors seek these shares, we would expect their prices to rise, and the expected rate of return to investors buying at these higher prices to fall. This process would continue until the reward for bearing diversifiable risk dissipated.

5. a. Required return $= r_f + \beta(r_m - r_f) = 4\% + [0.6 \times (14\% - 4\%)] = 10\%$

    With an IRR of 14%, the project should be accepted.

    b. If beta = 1.6, then required return increases to:

    $$4\% + [1.6 \times (14\% - 4\%)] = 20\%$$

    This is greater than the project IRR. You should now reject the project.

    c. Given its IRR, the project is attractive when its risk and therefore its required return are low. At a higher risk level, the IRR is no longer higher than the expected return on comparable-risk assets available elsewhere in the capital market.

6. a. The expected cash flows from the firm are in the form of a perpetuity. The discount rate is:

    $$r_f + \beta(r_m - r_f) = 4\% + 0.4 \times (11\% - 4\%) = 6.8\%$$

    Therefore, the value of the firm would be:

    $$P_0 = \frac{\text{Cash flow}}{r} = \frac{\$10,000}{0.068} = \$147,058.82$$

    b. If the true beta is actually 0.6, the discount rate should be:

    $$r_f + \beta(r_m - r_f) = 4\% + [0.6 \times (11\% - 4\%)] = 8.2\%$$

    Therefore, the value of the firm is:

    $$P_0 = \frac{\text{Cash flow}}{r} = \frac{\$10,000}{0.082} = \$121,951.22$$

    By underestimating beta, you would overvalue the firm by:
    $$\$147,058.82 - \$121,951.22 = \$25,107.60$$

7. Required return $= r_f + \beta(r_m - r_f) = 6\% + [1.25 \times (13\% - 6\%)] = 14.75\%$

    Expected return = 16%

    The security is underpriced. Its expected return is greater than the required return given its risk.

8. Beta tells us how sensitive the stock return is to changes in market performance. The market return was 4 percent less than your prior expectation (10% versus 14%). Therefore, the stock would be expected to fall short of your original expectation by:

    $$0.8 \times 4\% = 3.2\%$$

    The 'updated' expectation for the stock return is: $12\% - 3.2\% = 8.8\%$

9. a. A diversified investor will find the lowest-beta stock safest. This is Newmong Mining, which has a beta of 0.84.

    b. McDonald's has the lowest total volatility; the standard deviation of its returns is 20.3%.

    c. $\beta = (2.46 + 0.84 + 1.45)/3 = 1.58$

    d. The portfolio will have the same beta as Ford (2.46). The total risk of the portfolio will be (2.46 times the total risk of the market portfolio) because the effect of firm-specific risk will be diversified away. Therefore, the standard deviation of the portfolio is: $2.46 \times 20\% = 49.2\%$

    e. Using the CAPM, we compute the expected rate of return on each stock from the equation: $r = r_f + \beta(r_m - r_f)$

        In this case: $r_f = 4\%$ and $(r_m - r_f) = 8\%$

        Ford: $r = 4\% + (2.46 \times 8\%) = 23.68\%$

        Newmont Mining: $r = 4\% + (0.84 \times 8\%) = 10.72\%$

        Microsoft: $r = 4\% + (1.45 \times 8\%) = 15.60\%$

10. The following table shows the *average* return on Tumblehome for various values of the market return. It is clear from the table that, when the market return increases by 1%, Tumblehome's return increases, on average, by 1.5%. Therefore, $\beta = 1.5$. If you prepare a plot of the return on Tumblehome as a function of the market return, you will find that the slope of the line through the points is 1.5.

Market return(%)	Average return on Tumblehome(%)
−2	−3.0
−1	−1.5
0	0.0
1	1.5
2	3.0

11. a. Beta is the responsiveness of each stock's return to changes in the market return. Then:

$$\beta_A = \frac{\Delta r_A}{\Delta r_m} = \frac{38 - (-10)}{32 - (-8)} = \frac{48}{40} = 1.2$$

$$\beta_D = \frac{\Delta r_D}{\Delta r_m} = \frac{24 - (-6)}{32 - (-8)} = \frac{30}{40} = 0.75$$

Stock D is considered a more defensive stock than Stock A because the return of Stock D is less sensitive to the return of the overall market. In a recession, Stock D will usually outperform both Stock A and the market portfolio.

b. We take an average of returns in each scenario to obtain the expected return:

$r_m = (32\% – 8\%)/2 = 12\%$

$r_A = (38\% – 10\%)/2 = 14\%$

$r_D = (24\% – 6\%)/2 = 9\%$

c. According to the CAPM, the expected returns investors will demand of each stock, given the stock betas and the expected return on the market, are determined as follows:

$r = r_f + \beta(r_m – r_f)$

$r_A = 4\% + [1.2 \times (12\% – 4\%)] = 13.6\%$

$r_D = 4\% + [0.75 \times (12\% – 4\%)] = 10.0\%$

d. The return you *actually* expect for Stock A (14%) is above the fair return (13.6%). The return you expect for Stock D (9%) is below the fair return (10%). Therefore stock A is the better buy.

12. Figure shown below.

Beta	Cost of capital (from CAPM)
0.75	$4\% + (0.75 \times 7\%) = 9.25\%$
1.75	$4\% + (1.75 \times 7\%) = 16.25\%$

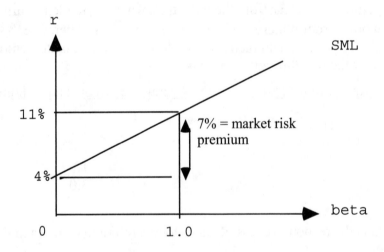

Beta	Cost of capital	IRR	NPV
1.0	11.0%	14%	+
0.0	4.0%	6%	+
2.0	18.0%	18%	0
0.4	6.8%	7%	+
1.6	15.2%	20%	+

13. The appropriate discount rate for the project is:

$$r = r_f + \beta(r_m - r_f) = 4\% + 1.4 \times (12\% - 4\%) = 15.2\%$$

Therefore:

NPV = –$100 + [$15 × annuity factor(15.2%, 10 years)]

$$= -\$100 + \$15 \times \left[\frac{1}{0.152} - \frac{1}{0.152 \times (1.152)^{10}} \right] = -\$25.29$$

You should reject the project.

14. Find the discount rate (r) which:

$15 × annuity factor(r, 10 years) = 100

$$\$15 \times \left[\frac{1}{r} - \frac{1}{r \times (1+r)^{10}} \right] = \$100$$

Solving this equation using trial-and-error or a financial calculator, we find that the project IRR is 8.14%. The IRR is less than the opportunity cost of capital (15.2%). Therefore you should reject the project, just as you found from the NPV rule.

15. From the CAPM, the appropriate discount rate is:

$$r = r_f + \beta(r_m - r_f) = 4\% + (0.75 \times 7\%) = 9.25\%$$

$$r = 0.0925 = \frac{\text{DIV} + \text{capital gain}}{\text{price}} = \frac{2 + (P_1 - 50)}{50} \Rightarrow P_1 = \$52.625$$

16. If investors believe the year-end stock price will be $52, then the expected return on the stock is:

$$\frac{\$2 + (\$52 - \$50)}{\$50} = 0.08 = 8.0\%$$

This is less than the opportunity cost of capital. Alternatively, the 'fair' price of the stock (that is, the present value of the investor's expected cash flows) is:

($2 + $52)/1.0925 = $49.43

This is less than the current price. Investors will want to sell the stock, in the process reducing its price until it reaches $49.43. At that point, the expected return is a 'fair' .25%:

$$\frac{\$2 + (\$52 - \$49.43)}{\$49.43} = 0.0925 = 9.25\%$$

17. a. The expected return of the portfolio is equal to the weighted average of the returns on the S&P 500 and T-bills. Similarly, the beta of the portfolio is equal to the weighted average of the beta of the S&P (which is 1.0) and the beta of T-bills (which is zero):

   (i) $E(r) = (0 \times 13\%) + (1.0 \times 5\%) = 5\%$ $\beta = (0 \times 1) + (1 \times 0) = 0$

   (ii) $E(r) = (0.25 \times 13\%) + (0.75 \times 5\%) = 7\%$ $\beta = (0.25 \times 1) + (0.75 \times 0) = 0.25$

   (iii) $E(r) = (0.50 \times 13\%) + (0.50 \times 5\%) = 9\%$ $\beta = (0.50 \times 1) + (0.50 \times 0) = 0.50$

   (iv) $E(r) = (0.75 \times 13\%) + (0.25 \times 5\%) = 11\%$ $\beta = (0.75 \times 1) + (0.25 \times 0) = 0.75$

   (v) $E(r) = (1.00 \times 13\%) + (0 \times 5\%) = 13\%$ $\beta = (1.0 \times 1) + (0 \times 0) = 1.0$

   b. For every increase of 0.25 in the β of the portfolio, the expected return increases by 2%. The slope of the relationship (additional return per unit of additional risk) is therefore: 2%/0.25 = 8%

   c. The slope of the return per unit of risk relationship is the market risk premium:

   $$r_m - r_f = 13\% - 5\% = 8\%$$

   This is exactly what the SML predicts, i.e., that the risk premium equals beta times the market risk premium.

18. a. Call the weight in the S&P 500 w and the weight in T-bills $(1 - w)$. Then w must satisfy the equation:

   $$w \times 10\% + (1 - w) \times 4\% = 8\% \Rightarrow w = 2/3$$

   Therefore, invest 2/3 in the S&P 500 and 1/3 in T-bills.

   b. To form a portfolio with beta = 0.4, use a weight of 0.40 in the S&P 500 and a weight of 0.60 in T-bills. Then, the portfolio beta is:

   $$\beta = (0.40 \times 1) + (0.60 \times 0) = 0.40$$

   c. Both portfolios have the same ratio of risk premium to beta:

   $$\frac{8\% - 4\%}{\frac{2}{3}} = \frac{6.4\% - 4\%}{0.4} = 6\%$$

   Notice that the ratio of risk premium to risk (i.e., beta) equals the market risk premium (6%) for both stocks.

19. If the systematic risk were comparable to that of the market, the discount rate would be 12.5%. The property would be worth: $50,000/0.125 = $400,000

20. The CAPM states that: $r = r_f + \beta(r_m - r_f)$

If $\beta < 0$ then $r < r_f$

Investors would invest in a security with an expected return below the risk-free rate because of the hedging value such a security provides for the rest of the portfolio. Investors get their 'reward' in terms of risk reduction rather than in the form of high expected return.

21. We can use the CAPM to derive the cost of capital for these firms:

$$r = r_f + \beta(r_m - r_f) = 5\% + (\beta \times 7\%)$$

	Beta	Cost of capital
Cisco	1.54	15.78%
Citigroup	1.21	13.47%
Merck	1.23	13.61%
Walt Disney	.66	9.62%

22. $r = r_f + \beta(r_m - r_f)$

$5 = r_f + 0.5(r_m - r_f)$ (stock A)

$13 = r_f + 1.5(r_m - r_f)$ (stock B)

Solve these simultaneous equations to find that: $r_f = 1\%$ and $r_m = 9\%$

23. $r = r_f + \beta(r_m - r_f)$

$10 = 6 + \beta(13 - 6) \Rightarrow \beta = 4/7 = 0.5714$

24. Cisco should use the beta of Merck (which is 1.23) to find that the required rate of return is 13.61%. The project is a pharmaceutical venture and the beta of Merck reflects the risk of pharmaceutical firms. The beta of Cisco does not reflect that risk.

25. a. False. The stock's risk premium, not its expected rate of return, is twice as high as the risk premium of the market portfolio.

    b. True. The stock's unique risk does not affect its contribution to portfolio risk.

    c. False. A stock plotting below the SML offers too low an expected return relative to the expected return indicated by the CAPM. The stock is *over*priced.

d. True. If the portfolio is diversified to such an extent that it has negligible unique risk, then the only source of volatility is its market exposure. A beta of 2 then implies twice the volatility of the market portfolio.

e. False. An *undiversified* portfolio has *more* than twice the volatility of the market. In addition to the fact that it has double the sensitivity to market risk, it also has volatility due to unique risk.

26. The CAPM implies that the expected rate of return that investors will demand of the portfolio is:

$$r = r_f + \beta(r_m - r_f) = 4\% + 0.8 \times (14\% - 4\%) = 12\%$$

If the portfolio is expected to provide only an 11% rate of return, it's an unattractive investment. The portfolio does not provide an expected return that is sufficiently high relative to its risk.

27. A portfolio that is invested 80% in a stock index mutual fund (with a beta of 1.0) and 20% in a money market mutual fund (with a beta of zero) would have the same beta as this manager's portfolio:

$$\beta = (0.80 \times 1.0) + (0.20 \times 0) = 0.80$$

However, it would provide an expected return of:

$$(0.80 \times 14\%) + (0.20 \times 4\%) = 12\%$$

This is better than the portfolio manager's expected return.

28. The security market line provides a benchmark expected return that an investor can earn by mixing index funds with money market funds. Before an investor places funds with a professional mutual fund manager, the investor must be convinced that the mutual fund can earn an expected return (net of fees) in excess of the expected return available on an equally risky index fund strategy.

29. a. $r = r_f + \beta(r_m - r_f) = 5\% + [(-0.2) \times (15\% - 5\%)] = 3\%$

   b. Portfolio beta = $(0.90 \times \beta_{market}) + (0.10 \times \beta_{law\ firm})$

$$= (0.90 \times 1.0) + [0.10 \times (-.2)] = 0.88$$

30.   Expected income on stock fund: $2 million × 0.12 = $0.24 million
      Interest on borrowed funds: $1 million × 0.04 = $0.04 million
      Net expected earnings: $0.20 million
      Expected rate of return on the $1 million you invest is:

$$\frac{\$0.20\,million}{\$1\,million} = 0.20 = 20.0\%$$

Risk premium = 20% – 4% = 16%

This is double the risk premium of the market index fund.

The risk is also double that of holding ay market index fund. You have $2 million at risk, but the net value of your portfolio is only $1 million. A 1% change in the rate of return on the market index will change your profits by: 0.01 × $2 million = $20,000
But this changes the rate of return on your portfolio by: $20,000/$1,000,000 = 2%
This is double that of the market. So your risk is in fact double that of the market index.

31.   a.   The beta for Consolidated Edison and Dell computer are 0.516 and 1.2051, respectively. See charts below:

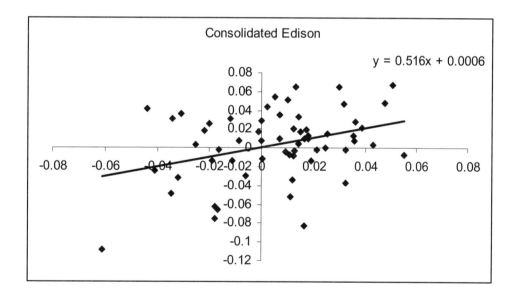

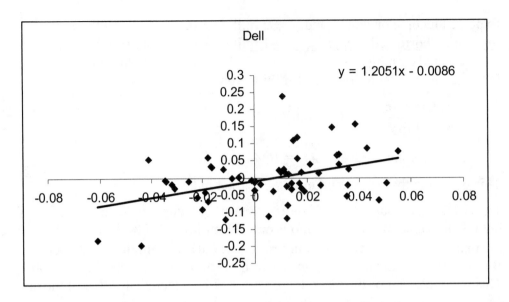

b. The return on Dell's stock is relatively more volatile than that of Consolidated Edison. The resulting higher beta for Dell makes sense as the business risk for this computer company is higher than that of a regulated utility such as Consolidated Edison.

Solutions to Chapter 13

The Weighted Average Cost of Capital and Company Valuation

1. The yield to maturity for the bonds (since maturity is now 19 years) is the interest rate (r) that is the solution to the following equation:

    [$80 × annuity factor(r, 19 years)] + [$1,000/(1 + r)^{19}] = $1,050

    $$\$80 \times \left[\frac{1}{r} - \frac{1}{r \times (1+r)^{19}} \right] + \frac{\$1,000}{(1+r)^{19}} = \$1,050 \Rightarrow r = 7.50\%$$

    Using a financial calculator, enter: n = 19, FV = 1000, PV = (–)1050, PMT = 90, and then compute i = 7.50%
    Therefore, the after-tax cost of debt is: $7.50\% \times (1 - 0.35) = 4.88\%$

2. $r = \dfrac{DIV}{P_0} = \dfrac{\$4}{\$40} = 0.100 = 10.0\%$

3. $\text{WACC} = \left[\dfrac{D}{V} \times r_{debt} \times (1 - T_C) \right] + \left[\dfrac{P}{V} \times r_{preferred} \right] + \left[\dfrac{E}{V} \times r_{equity} \right]$

    $= [0.3 \times 7.50\% \times (1 - 0.35)] + [0.2 \times 10\%] + [0.5 \times 12.0\%] = 9.46\%$

4. $r = \dfrac{DIV_1}{P_0} + g = \dfrac{DIV_0(1+g)}{P_0} + g = \dfrac{\$5 \times 1.05}{\$60} + 0.05 = 0.1375 = 13.75\%$

5. The total value of the firm is $80 million. The weights for each security class are as follows:

    Debt: D/V = 20/80 = 0.250
    Preferred: P/V = 10/80 = 0.125
    Common: E/V = 50/80 = 0.625

    $\text{WACC} = \left[\dfrac{D}{V} \times r_{debt} \times (1 - T_C) \right] + \left[\dfrac{P}{V} \times r_{preferred} \right] + \left[\dfrac{E}{V} \times r_{equity} \right]$

    $= [0.250 \times 6\% \times (1 - 0.35)] + [0.125 \times 8\%] + [0.625 \times 12.0\%] = 9.475\%$

6. Executive Fruit should use the WACC of Geothermal, not its own WACC, when evaluating an investment in geothermal power production. The risk of the project determines the discount rate, and in this case, Geothermal's WACC is more reflective of the risk of the project in question. The proper discount rate, therefore, is not 12.3%. It is more likely to be 11.4%.

7. a. The weighted average cost of capital, with a tax rate of 40%, is:

$$\text{WACC} = \left[\frac{D}{V} \times r_{debt} \times (1 - T_C) \right] + \left[\frac{E}{V} \times r_{equity} \right]$$

$$= [0.30 \times 6\% \times (1 - 0.40)] + [0.70 \times 11\%] = 8.78\%$$

Free cash flow next year is: $68 million – $30 million = $38 million
Since the cash flows are in the form of a growing perpetuity, with a growth rate of 4%, the total value of Icarus is:

$$PV = \frac{\$38 \text{ million}}{r - g} = \frac{\$38 \text{ million}}{0.0878 - 0.04} = \$795 \text{ million}$$

b. Since management will maintain the company's debt at 30% of the present value of the company, the company's equity is:

0.70 × $795 million = $389.55 million

8. The rate on Buildwell's debt is 5 percent. The cost of equity capital is the required rate of return on equity, which can be calculated from the CAPM as follows:

4% + (0.90 × 8%) = 11.2%

The weighted average cost of capital, with a tax rate of 40%, is:

$$\text{WACC} = \left[\frac{D}{V} \times r_{debt} \times (1 - T_C) \right] + \left[\frac{E}{V} \times r_{equity} \right]$$

$$= [0.30 \times 5\% \times (1 - 0.40)] + [0.70 \times 11.2\%] = 8.74\%$$

9. The internal rate of return, which is 12%, exceeds the cost of capital. Therefore, BCCI should accept the project.

The present value of the project cash flows is:

$100,000 × annuity factor(8.74%, 8 years) =

$$\$100,000 \times \left[\frac{1}{0.0874} - \frac{1}{0.0874 \times (1.0874)^8} \right] = \$558,870.94$$

This is the most BCCI should pay for the project.

10. Line numbers in the table below are from the text:

	Year 1	2	3	4
3. EBITDA	80	100	115	120
4. Depreciation	20	30	35	40
5. Profit before tax = 3 – 4	60	70	80	80
6. Tax at 40%	24	28	32	32
7. Profit after tax = 5 – 6	36	42	48	48
8. Operating cash flow = 4 + 7	56	72	83	88
9. Investment	12	15	18	20
10. Free cash flow = 8 – 9	44	57	65	68

Since free cash flow from year 5 onward will remain unchanged at year-4 levels, the horizon value at year 4 is:

$$\frac{\$68\text{ million}}{r} = \frac{\$68\text{ million}}{0.0874} = \$778 \text{ million}$$

The company's total value is:

$$PV = \frac{\$44}{1.0874} + \frac{\$57}{(1.0874)^2} + \frac{\$65}{(1.0874)^3} + \frac{\$68}{(1.0874)^4} + \frac{\$778}{(1.0874)^4} = \$744.3 \text{ million}$$

Since the capital structure is 30% debt, the value of the firm's debt is:

$$0.30 \times \$744.3 \text{ million} = \$223.3 \text{ million}$$

The value of the equity is:

$$0.70 \times \$744.3 \text{ million} = \$521.0 \text{ million}$$

11.

Security	Market Value	Explanation
Debt	$ 5.5 million	1.10 × par value of $5 million
Equity	$15.0 million	$30 per share × 500,000 shares *
Total	$20.5 million	

$$*\text{Number of shares} = \frac{\$10\text{ million book value}}{\$20\text{ book value per share}} = 500{,}000$$

$$\text{WACC} = \left[\frac{D}{V} \times r_{debt} \times (1 - T_C)\right] + \left[\frac{E}{V} \times r_{equity}\right]$$

$$= \left[\frac{5.5}{20.5} \times 9\% \times (1 - 0.40)\right] + \left[\frac{15}{20.5} \times 15\%\right] = 12.42\%$$

12. Since the firm is all-equity financed: asset beta = equity beta = 0.8
The WACC is the same as the cost of equity, which can be calculated using the CAPM:

$$r_{equity} = r_f + \beta(r_m - r_f) = 4\% + (0.80 \times 10\%) = 12\%$$

13. The 12.5% value calculated by the analyst is the current yield of the firm's outstanding debt: interest payments/bond value. This calculation ignores the fact that bonds selling at discounts from, or premiums over, par value provide expected returns determined in part by expected price appreciation or depreciation. The analyst should be using yield to maturity instead of current yield to calculate cost of debt. [This answer assumes the value of the debt provided is the market value. If it is the book value, then 12.5% would be the average coupon rate of outstanding debt, which would also be a poor estimate of the required rate of return on the firm's debt.]

14. a. Using the recent growth rate of 30% and the dividend yield of 2%, one estimate would be:

$$DIV_1/P_0 + g = 0.02 + 0.30 = 0.32 = 32\%$$

Another estimate, based on the CAPM, would be:

$$r = r_f + \beta(r_m - r_f) = 4\% + (1.2 \times 8\%) = 13.6\%$$

b. The estimate of 32% seems far less reasonable. It is based on an historic growth rate that is impossible to sustain. The $[DIV_1/P_0 + g]$ rule requires that the growth rate of dividends per share must be viewed as highly stable over the foreseeable future. In other words, it requires the use of the sustainable growth rate.

15. a. The 9% coupon bond has a yield to maturity of 10% and sells for 93.86% of face value, as shown below:

$$PV = \$90 \times \left[\frac{1}{0.10} - \frac{1}{0.10(1.10)^{10}} \right] + \frac{\$1,000}{1.10^{10}} = \$938.55$$

Using a financial calculator, enter: n = 10, i = 10%, PMT = 90, FV = 1000, compute PV = $938.55

Therefore, the market value of the issue is:

0.9386 × $20 million = $18.77 million

The 10% coupon bond sells for 94% of par value, and has a yield to maturity of 10.83%, as shown below:

$$\$940 = \$100 \times \left[\frac{1}{r} - \frac{1}{r \times (1+r)^{15}} \right] + \frac{\$1,000}{(1+r)^{15}} \Rightarrow r = 10.83\%$$

Using a financial calculator, enter: n = 15, PV = (–)940, PMT = 100, FV = 1000, compute i = 10.83%

The market value of the issue is: 0.94 × $25 million = $23.50 million

Therefore, the weighted-average before-tax cost of debt is:

$$\left[\frac{18.77}{18.77 + 23.50} \times 10\%\right] + \left[\frac{23.50}{18.77 + 23.50} \times 10.83\%\right] = 10.46\%$$

b. The after-tax cost of debt is: (1 – 0.35) × 10.46% = 6.80%

16. The bonds are selling below par value because the yield to maturity is greater than the coupon rate.

The price per $1,000 par value is:

$$PV = [\$80 \times \text{annuity factor}(9\%, 10 \text{ years})] + (\$1,000/1.09^{10})$$

$$= \$80 \times \left[\frac{1}{0.09} - \frac{1}{0.09(1.09)^{10}}\right] + \frac{\$1,000}{1.09^{10}} = \$935.82$$

The total market value of the bonds is:

$$\$10 \text{ million par value} \times \frac{\$935.82 \text{ market value}}{\$1,000 \text{ par value}} = \$9.36 \text{ million}$$

There are: $2 million/$20 = 100,000 shares of preferred stock.

The market price of the preferred stock is $15 per share, so that the total market value of the preferred stock is $1.5 million.

There are: $0.1 million/$0.10 = 1 million shares of common stock.

The market price of the common stock is $20 per share, so that the total market value of the common stock is $20 million.

Therefore, the capital structure is:

Security	Market Value	Percent
Bonds	$ 9.36 million	30.3%
Preferred Stock	$ 1.50 million	4.9%
Common Stock	$20.00 million	64.8%
Total	$30.86 million	100.0%

17. The yield to maturity for the firm's debt is: $r_{debt} = 9\%$

The rate for the preferred stock is: $r_{preferred} = \$2/\$15 = 0.1333 = 13.33\%$

The rate for the common stock is:

$r_{equity} = r_f + \beta(r_m - r_f) = 6\% + (0.8 \times 10\%) = 14\%$

Using the capital structure derived in the previous problem, we can calculate WACC as:

$$WACC = \left[\frac{D}{V} \times r_{debt} \times (1 - T_C)\right] + \left[\frac{P}{V} \times r_{preferred}\right] + \left[\frac{E}{V} \times r_{equity}\right]$$

$$= [0.303 \times 9\% \times (1 - 0.40)] + [0.049 \times 13.33\%] + [0.648 \times 14\%] = 11.36\%$$

18. The IRR on the computer project is less than the WACC of firms in the computer industry. Therefore, the project should be rejected. However, the WACC of the firm (based on its existing mix of projects) is only 11.36%. If the firm uses this figure as the hurdle rate, it will incorrectly go ahead with the venture in home computers.

19. a. $r = r_f + \beta(r_m - r_f)$ $r = 4\% + (1.2 \times 10\%) = 16\%$

   b. Weighted average beta $= (0.4 \times 0) + (0.6 \times 1.2) = 0.72$

   c. $$WACC = \left[\frac{D}{V} \times r_{debt} \times (1 - T_C)\right] + \left[\frac{E}{V} \times r_{equity}\right]$$

   $$= [0.4 \times 4\% \times (1 - 0.4)] + [0.6 \times 16\%] = 10.56\%$$

   d. If the company plans to expand its present business, then the WACC is a reasonable estimate of the discount rate since the risk of the proposed project is similar to the risk of the existing projects. Use a discount rate of 10.56%.

   e. The WACC of optical projects should be based on the risk of those projects. Using a beta of 1.4, the discount rate for the new venture is:

   $r = 4\% + 1.4 \times 10\% = 18\%$

20. If Big Oil does not pay taxes, then the after-tax and before-tax costs of debt are identical. WACC would then become:

$$WACC = \left[\frac{D}{V} \times r_{debt} \times (1 - T_C)\right] + \left[\frac{E}{V} \times r_{equity}\right]$$

$$= [0.243 \times 9\% \times (1 - 0)] + [0.757 \times 12.0\%] = 11.27\%$$

If Big Oil issues new equity and uses the proceeds to pay off all of its debt, the cost of equity will decrease. There is no longer any leverage, so the equity becomes safer and therefore commands a lower risk premium. In fact, with all-equity financing, the cost of equity would be the same as the firm's WACC, which is 11.27%. This is less than the previous value of 12.0%. (We use the WACC derived in the absence of interest tax shields since, for the all-equity firm, there is no interest tax shield.)

21. The net effect of Big Oil's transaction is to leave the firm with $200 million more debt (because of the borrowing) and $200 million less equity (because of the dividend payout). Total assets and business risk are unaffected. The WACC will remain unchanged because business risk is unchanged. However, the cost of equity will increase. With the now higher leverage, the business risk is spread over a smaller equity base, so each share is now riskier.

The new financing mix for the firm is: E = $1,000 and D = $585.7
Therefore:

$$\frac{D}{V} = \frac{\$585.7}{\$1,585.7} = 0.369 \text{ and } \frac{E}{V} = \frac{\$1,000}{\$1,585.7} = 0.631$$

If the cost of debt is still 9%, then we solve for the new cost of equity as follows. Use the fact that, even at the new financing mix, WACC must still be 11.27%.

$$WACC = \left[\frac{D}{V} \times r_{debt} \times (1 - T_C) \right] + \left[\frac{E}{V} \times r_{equity} \right]$$

$$= [0.369 \times 9\% \times (1 - 0)] + [0.631 \times r_{equity}] = 11.27\%$$

We solve to find that: r_{equity} = 12.60%

22. Even if the WACC were lower when the firm's tax rate is higher, this does not imply that the firm would be worth more. The after-tax cash flows the firm would generate for its owners would also be lower. This would reduce the value of the firm even if the cash flows were discounted at a lower rate. If the tax authority is collecting more income from the firm, the value of the firm will fall.

23. This reasoning is faulty in that it implicitly treats the discount rate for the project as the cost of debt if the project is debt financed, and as the cost of equity if the project is equity financed. In fact, if the project poses risk comparable to the risk of the firm's other projects, the proper discount rate is the firm's cost of capital, which is a weighted average of the costs of both debt and equity.

Bernice needs to explain to her boss, Mr. Brinestone, that appropriate rates of return for cost of capital calculations are the rates of return that investors can earn on comparable risk investments in the capital market. Mr. Brinestone's estimate of the cost of equity is his target value for the book return on equity; it is not the expected rate of return that investors demand on shares of stock with the same risk as Sea Shore Salt.

Bernice's CAPM calculation indicates that the correct value for the equity rate is 10.5%. This value is broadly consistent with the rate one would infer from the constant growth dividend discount model (which seems appropriate for a mature firm like this one with stable growth prospects). The dividend discount model implies a cost of equity of a bit more than 11 percent:

$$r_{equity} = \frac{DIV_1}{P_0} + g = \frac{\$2}{\$40} + 0.067 = 0.117 = 11.7\%$$

Thus, it appears that Bernice's calculation is correct.

Similarly, Mr. Brinestone's returns for other securities should be modified to reflect the expected returns these securities currently offer to investors. The bank loan and bond issue offer pre-tax rates of 8% and 7.75%, respectively, as in Mr. Brinestone's memo. The preferred stock, however, is not selling at par, so Mr. Brinestone's assertion that the rate of return on preferred is 6% is incorrect. In fact, with the preferred selling at $70 per share, the rate of return is:

$$r_{preferred} = \frac{DIV}{P_0} = \frac{\$6}{\$70} = 0.086 = 8.6\%$$

This makes sense: the pre-tax return on preferred should exceed that on the firm's debt.

Finally, the weights used to calculate the WACC should reflect market, not book, values. These are the prices that investors would pay to acquire the securities. The market value weights are computed as follows:

	Comment	Amount (millions)	Percent of total	Rate of return (%)
Bank loan	valued at face amount	$120	17.91	8.00
Bond issue	valued at par	80	11.94	7.75
Preferred stock	$70 × 1 million shares	70	10.45	8.60
Common stock	$40 × 10 million shares	400	59.70	10.50
		$670	100.00	

Therefore, the WACC, which serves as the corporate hurdle rate, should be 8.70%:

$$WACC = [0.1791 \times 8\% \times (1 - 0.35)] + [0.1194 \times 7.75\% \times (1 - 0.35)]$$

$$+ (0.1045 \times 8.6\%) + (0.5970 \times 10.5\%) = 8.70\%$$

Solutions to Chapter 14

Introduction to Corporate Financing

1. a. Number of Shares = Par value of issued stock/par value per share
    = $60,000/$1.00 = 60,000 shares

    b. Outstanding shares = Issued shares – Treasury stock
    = 60,000 – 2,000 = 58,000 shares

    c. The firm can issue up to a total of 100,000 shares. Because 60,000 shares have been issued, another 40,000 shares can be issued without approval from share holders.

2. a. The issue of 10,000 shares would increase the par value of common stock by:
    10,000 shares × $1.00 = $10,000

    Additional paid-in capital increases by:

    10,000 shares × $3.00 per share = $30,000

    The new accounts would be as follows:

Common stock	$70,000
Additional paid-in capital	40,000
Retained earnings	30,000
Common equity	140,000
Treasury stock	5,000
Net common equity	$135,000

    b. If the company bought back 1,000 shares, Treasury stock would increase by the amount spent on the stock: $4,000. The accounts would be:

Common stock	$60,000
Additional paid-in capital	10,000
Retained earnings	30,000
Common equity	100,000
Treasury stock	9,000
Net common equity	$91,000

3. a. funded

    b. eurobond

    c. subordinated

    d. sinking fund

    e. call

f. prime rate

g. floating rate

h. private placement, public issue

i. lease

j. convertible

k. warrant

4. a. True

   b. True

   c. True

5. Preferred stock is like long-term debt in that it commits the firm to paying the security holder a fixed sum -- either a specified interest payment in the case of bonds or a specified dividend in the case of preferred stock. Like equity and unlike debt, however, failure to pay the dividend on preferred stock does not set off bankruptcy.

6. a. Under majority voting, the shareholder can cast a maximum of 100 votes for a favorite candidate.

   b. Under cumulative voting with 10 candidates, the maximum number of votes a shareholder can cast for a favorite candidate is: $10 \times 100 = 1,000$

7. a. If the company has majority voting, each candidate is voted on in a separate election. To ensure that your candidate is elected, you need to own at least half the shares, or 200,000 shares (or 200,001 shares, in order to ensure a strict majority of the votes).

   b. If the company has cumulative voting, all candidates are voted on at once, and the number of votes cast is: $5 \times 400,000 = 2,000,000$ votes

   If your candidate receives one-fifth of the votes, that candidate will place at least fifth in the balloting and will be elected to the board. Therefore, you need to cast 400,000 votes for your candidate, which requires that you own 80,000 shares.

8. a. Par value of common shares will increase by:

    10 million shares × $0.25 par value per share = $2.5 million

    Additional paid-in capital will increase by:

    ($40.00 – $0.25) × 10 million = $397.5 million

    Table 14-2 becomes:

Common shares ($0.25 par value per share)	$ 110.5
Additional paid-in capital	978.5
Retained earnings	5,779.0
Treasury shares at cost	(4,406.0)
Other	(219.0)
Net common equity	$2,243.0

    b. Treasury shares will increase by: 500,000 × $50 = $25 million

Common shares ($0.25 par value per share)	$ 110.5
Additional paid-in capital	978.5
Retained earnings	5,779.0
Treasury shares at cost	(4,381.0)
Other	(219.0)
Net common equity	$2,268.0

9. Common shares (par value) = 200,000 × $2.00 = $400,000

    Additional paid in capital = funds raised – par value = $2,000,000 – $400,000 = $1,600,000

    Because net common equity of the firm is $2,500,000 and the book value of outstanding stock is $2,000,000, then retained earnings equals $500,000.

10. Lease obligations are like debt in that both legally obligate the firm to make a series of specified payments. Bondholders would like the firm to limit its lease obligations for the same reason that bondholders desire limits on debt: to keep the firm's financial burden at manageable levels and to make the already existing debt safer.

11. a. A call provision gives the firm a valuable option. The call provision will require the firm to compensate the investor by promising a higher yield to maturity.

    b. A restriction on further borrowing protects bondholders. Bondholders will therefore require a lower yield to maturity.

    c. Collateral protects the bondholder and results in a lower yield to maturity.

    d. The option to convert gives bondholders a valuable option. They will therefore be satisfied with a lower promised yield to maturity.

12. Income bonds are like preferred stock in that the firm promises to make specified payments to the security holder. If the firm cannot make those payments, however, the firm is not forced into bankruptcy. For the firm, the advantage of income bonds over preferred stock is that the bond interest payments are tax-deductible expenses.

13. In general, the fact that preferred stock has lower priority in the event of bankruptcy reduces the price of the preferred stock and increases its yield compared to bonds. On the other hand, the fact that 70 percent of the preferred stock dividend payments are free of taxes to corporate holders increases the price and reduces the yield of the preferred stock. For strong firms, the default premium is small and the tax effect dominates, so that the preferred stock has a lower yield than the bonds. For weaker firms, the default premium dominates.

Solutions to Chapter 15

Venture Capital, IPOs, and Seasoned Offerings

1. a. A rights issue can be used for subsequent issues of stock. A rights issue requires that there are already existing shareholders.

   b. Seasoned offerings are security issues by firms that are already publicly traded. Publicly traded firms usually find it advantageous to sell new shares in a public offering because the public offering is less costly than a private placement. In contrast, even publicly traded firms may find it advantageous to use a private placement of bonds. Such bonds can be issued with unusual terms and can allow the firm to negotiate directly with the bondholders should the firm later wish to make changes in the terms of the debt. Therefore, it is more likely that the private placement is used for the bond issue.

   c. Shelf registration is more likely to be used for bonds issued by a large industrial company.

2. a. C

   b. A

   c. B

3. a. A large issue involves proportionately lower costs due to economies of scale. See Figure 15-1.

   b. A bond issue is less expensive.

   c. Private placements are less expensive for small amounts.

4. Issue costs for debt are less than for equity for several reasons. Underwriting spreads are lower because there is less risk to the underwriters concerning the price at which the debt can be placed. Debt is more standard than equity, so it can be evaluated by, and marketed to, the public more easily. Underpricing is much less of a concern because debt issues are far less likely to signal management assessments of the value of the firm relative to the market price.

5. Advancing money in stages rather than fully funding a project all at once serves at least two goals. First, it keeps the entrepreneur on a 'short leash.' There will not be any excess funds available to squander on luxuries. Moreover, the firm will have to show good evidence of progress and likely success in order to proceed successfully to the next stage of financing. Second, staged financing limits the amount of money initially put at risk by the venture capitalist. New money will not be committed until evidence of the likely success of the firm is forthcoming.

6. You should be suspicious. If the issue were underpriced, preferred customers would be likely to snap up the offering. If the underwriters have to aggressively market the issue to the general public, it could be a sign that more knowledgeable investors are staying away because they view the issue as overpriced.

7. a. Average underpricing can be estimated as the average initial return on the sample of IPOs:

$$(7\% + 12\% - 2\% + 23\%)/4 = 10\%$$

   b. The average initial return, weighted by the amount invested in each issue, is calculated as follows:

	Investment (Shares × price)	Initial Return	Profit (% return × investment)
A	$5,000	7%	$350
B	4,000	12%	480
C	8,000	−2%	−160
D	0	23%	0
Total	$17,000		$670

   Average return = $670/$17,000 = 0.0394 = 3.94%

   Alternatively, you can calculate average return as:

$$\left(\frac{5,000}{17,000} \times 7\%\right) + \left(\frac{4,000}{17,000} \times 12\%\right) + \left(\frac{8,000}{17,000} \times (-2\%)\right) = 3.94\%$$

   c. The average return is far below the average initial return for the sample of IPOs. This is because I have received smaller allocations of the best performing IPOs and larger allocations of the poorly performing IPOs. I have suffered the winner's curse: On average, I have been awarded larger allocations of the IPOs that other players in the market knew to stay away from, and my average performance has suffered as a result.

8. Underwriting costs for Moonscape:

   Underwriting spread: $0.50 × 3 million = $1.5 million

   Underpricing: $4.00 × 3 million = $12.0 million

   Other direct costs = $0.1 million

   Total = $13.6 million

   Funds raised = $8 × 3 million = $24 million

$$\frac{\text{Flotation costs}}{\text{Funds raised}} = \frac{13.6}{24} = 0.567 = 56.7\%$$

From Figure 15-1, average direct costs for IPOs in the range of $20 to $40 million have been only 10%. Moonscape's direct costs are:

$$\frac{1.5 + 0.1}{24} = 0.0667 = 6.67\%$$

Direct costs are below average, but the underpricing is very large, as indicated by the first-day return: $4/\$8 = 50\%$

9. a. The offering is both a primary and a secondary offering. The firm is selling 500,000 shares (primary) and the existing shareholders are selling 300,000 shares (secondary).

    b. Direct costs are as follows:

    Underwriting spread: $1.30 × 800,000 = $1.04 million
    Other direct costs = $0.40 million
                    Total = $1.44 million

    Funds raised = $12 × 800,000 = $9.6 million

    $$\frac{\text{Direct costs}}{\text{Funds raised}} = \frac{1.44}{9.60} = 0.15 = 15.0\%$$

    From Figure 15-1, direct costs for IPOs in the range of $2 to $10 million have been approximately 17%. Direct costs for IPOs in the range of $10 to $20 million have been approximately 12%. The direct costs of this $9.6 million IPO, at 15%, seem about in line with the size of the issue.

    c. If the stock price increases from $12 to $15 per share, we infer underpricing of $3 per share. Direct costs per share are: $1.44 million/800,000 = $1.80
    Therefore, total costs are: $3.00 + $1.80 = $4.80 per share
    This is equal to: $4.80/\$15 = 0.32 = 32\%$ of the market price

    d. Emma Lucullus will sell 25,000 shares and retain 375,000 shares. She will receive $12 for each of her shares, less $1.80 per share direct costs:
    ($12 − $1.80) × 25,000 = $255,000

    Her remaining shares, selling at $15 each, will be worth: $15 × 375,000 = $5,625,000

10. Unlike interest payments, which are made annually, the issue cost is a one-time cost. Rather than adjust the cost of capital, the issue costs should be deducted from the project's NPV. Remember that the cost of capital is the required rate of return to investors in a project with a given level of risk. While flotation costs reduce the NPV of a project because an extra cash outflow is required, flotation costs do not affect the rate of return commensurate with the project's risk.

11. a. The price of each share, net of the underwriting spread, was: $21 – $1.31 = $19.69

   Therefore, by selling new stock in the primary issue, the company received:

   2 million × $19.69 = $39.38 million

   b. The existing shareholders sold their 800,000 shares to the underwriters for total proceeds of: 800,000 × $19.69 = $15.752 million

   c. If the underwriters had paid $30 per share, the number of new shares the company would have needed to sell is: $39.38 million/$30 = 1.313 million

   d. If the existing shareholders had sold their 800,000 shares to the underwriters for $30 per share, rather than $19.69, the increase in their proceeds would have been:

   800,000 × ($30.00 –$19.69) = $8.248 million

12. The lost value to the original shareholders is: 0.02 × $600 million = $12 million
    This is 12 percent of the value of the funds raised.

13. a. The firm will receive: $30 × (1 – 0.06) = $28.20 per share

    The firm will need to issue: $3,000,000/$28.20 = 106,383 shares

    The gross proceeds from the issue will be: 106,383 × $30 = $3,191,490

    The firm will be left with $3,000,000 (which it uses in part to pay the other direct costs of the issue).

    b. The underwriting spread costs the firm $191,490. Therefore, total direct costs are:
    $191,490 + $60,000 = $251,490

    c. The total market value of the stock is $30 million. If the share price falls by 3% on the announcement of the offering, the existing shareholders suffer a loss in value of: 0.03 × $30 million = $0.9 million = $900,000

    This loss is more than three times the direct costs of the offering.

14. a. Net proceeds of public issue = $10,000,000 – $150,000 – $80,000 = $9,770,000
    Net proceeds of private placement = $9,970,000

    b. The extra interest paid on the private placement is:

    0.005 × $10 million = $50,000 per year

The present value is:

$$\$50,000 \times \text{annuity factor}(8.5\%, 10 \text{ years}) =$$

$$\$50,000 \times \left[\frac{1}{0.085} - \frac{1}{0.085 \times (1.085)^{10}} \right] = \$328,067$$

This exceeds the savings in direct issue costs ($200,000) so the public issue appears to be the better deal.

(Note that we use a discount rate of 8.5%, rather than 9%, because 8.5% is the yield to maturity at which public investors are willing to invest in the bond when the company pays the cost of the issue directly to the underwriters. In the private placement, part of the 9% coupon rate should be considered compensation for issuance costs that are not charged for explicitly.)

    c.   The private placement is more expensive, but it has the advantages that the terms of the debt can be custom-tailored and the terms can be more easily renegotiated.

15.   a.   The number of new shares is: $10 million/$4 = 2.5 million
            Each share is sold for $5, so new money raised is $12.5 million.

    b.   After the issue, there are 12.5 million shares. The total value of the firm is:

          $60 million (the original value of the firm) plus $12.5 million

       The new share price is: $72.5 million/12.5 million shares = $5.80 per share

16.   If the new stock were issued at $4 a share, the company would have needed to issue:

          $12.5 million/$4 per share = 3.125 million shares

The stock would then sell for: $72.5/13.125 = $5.5238 per share

(The firm will need to issue 3.125 million rights, meaning that one new share can be purchased for every 3.2 shares currently held.)

Despite the lower stock price, the shareholders are just as well off. In the original plan, an investor who owns 1,000 shares would have the right to buy 250 additional shares for $5 per share. The total value of the position would be:

          $(1,000 \times \$5.80) + [250 \times (\$5.80 - \$5.00)] = \$6,000$

In the modified plan the investor will be able to buy:

          1,000/3.2 = 312.5 shares for $4 each

Total value is the same:

          $(1,000 \times \$5.5238) + [312.5 \times (\$5.5238 - \$4.00)] = \$6,000$

17. a. $2 million/200,000 = $10 per share

   b. The total value of the firm currently is $20 million, and there are 1 million shares outstanding. When the rights are exercised, the firm will raise $2 million, and total value will increase to $22 million. Shares outstanding will increase to 1.2 million. Price per share will be: $22 million/1.2 million = $18.3333

   c. The value of each right is the difference between the value of each share after exercise ($18.3333) and the $10 subscription price (the price the right holder pays for each share). Therefore, each right is worth: $8.3333

   d. An investor who holds 1,000 shares would receive 200 rights. (The firm distributes 200,000 rights among its 1 million shares, or 1 right per 5 shares.)

   e. Before the announcement of the rights offering, the 1,000 shares were worth $20,000. After the announcement, the stock price falls and the shares fall in value to $18,333. However, the rights are worth: $200 \times \$8.3333 = \$1,667$

   The value of the rights plus the value of the shares is $20,000. Wealth is unchanged.

18. a. Number of new shares = 50,000 since one new share will be issued for every two of the outstanding 100,000 shares.

   b. New investment = 50,000 shares × $10 per share = $500,000

   c. Value of company = $4,000,000 original value
                       + 500,000 new investment
                       $4,500,000 total value of company after issue

   d. Total number of shares = 100,000 original shares
                             + 50,000 new shares
                             150,000 total shares

   e. Share price after issue = $4.5 million/150,000 = $30

19. The payoffs in year 5 to George Pickwick and First Cookham Venture Partners (FC) are as follows:

a. *FC buys 2 million shares at $1*

   This gives FC two-thirds of Pickwick Electronics. Thus the possible payoffs at the end of five years are determined by splitting up the company value in proportions of 1/3 and 2/3:

	Company value in 5 years after stage-2 financing	
	$ 2 million	$12 million
Payoff to:		
G. Pickwick (1 million shares)	$0.67 million	$ 4 million
FC (2 million shares)	$1.33 million	$ 8 million

b. *FC buys 1 million shares now and invests an additional $1 million in shares in year 5*

	Company value in 5 years after stage-2 financing	
	$ 2 million	$12 million
Company value in 5 years *before* issue of $1 million in stage-2 financing	$1 million	$11 million
Price per share (Price = value/2 million shares)	$0.50	$5.50
No. of new shares issued to FC	$1m/$0.50 = 2 million	$1m/$5.50 = 0.182 million
Total shares outstanding	4 million	2.182 million
Total shares owned by FC	3 million	1.182 million
% of shares owned by Pickwick	25%	45.83%
% of all shares owned by FC	75%	54.17%
Payoff* to:		
G. Pickwick (1 million shares)	$0.5 million	$5.5 million
FC	$1.5 million	$6.5 million

*Payoff equals percentage ownership times total value of firm after issue of stage 2 financing.

Note that, by putting up only part of the money now, FC takes on less risk. If the company does not do well (future value = $2 million), then FC can buy a large number of shares for the $1 million of stage-2 financing. If the firm does well, FC receives fewer shares. Staged financing gives George Pickwick more risk and makes it more important for him to make a success of stage 1.

Solution to Minicase for Chapter 15

Underwriting costs for Mutt.com (including costs to the existing shareholders) are:

Underwriting spread: $1.25 × 1.25 million shares = $ 1.56 million

Other direct expenses: = $ 1.30 million

Underpricing*: $6 × 1.25 million shares   = $ 7.50 million

      TOTAL $10.36 million

*Underpricing based on the assumption that the shares could be sold for $24 rather than $18.

Funds raised = $18 × 1.25 million shares = $22.5 million

Value of shares issued = $24 × 1.25 million shares = $30 million

$$\frac{\text{Direct costs}}{\text{Funds raised}} = \frac{2.86}{22.5} = 0.127 = 12.7\%$$

$$\frac{\text{Underpricing costs}}{\text{Funds raised}} = \frac{7.5}{22.5} = 0.333 = 33.3\%$$

$$\frac{\text{Total flotation costs}}{\text{Value of shares issued}} = \frac{10.36}{30} = 0.345 = 34.5\%$$

Notice that we follow convention by reporting the direct costs as a percentage of the issue price ($18), but total costs as a percentage of the market value of the shares ($24).

Figure 15-1 shows that the average direct costs for IPOs in the range of $40 to $60 million have been about 10%, less than the direct costs for Mutt.com. Moreover, Mutt.com's underpricing is higher than the average 23% underpricing for IPOs reported in the text.

The underwriter's comments miss the point. Of course managers and shareholders prefer a high price to a low price. For any *given* price at which the shares are issued, they still prefer the stock price to rise. However, a very high initial-day return (i.e., evidence of considerable underpricing) indicates that the shares could have been issued at a higher price - in other words, that the company "left some money on the table." To the extent that the shares are issued at a lower-than-necessary price, the firm gives up some value to the new shareholders. This is correctly considered a cost of the issue.

Moreover, this is a cost to existing shareholders whether or not they plan to sell their shares. Underpricing means the firm must sell more new shares to raise the same amount of cash. Consequently, the existing shareholders end up owning a smaller fraction of the firm than they would if the shares were issued at a higher price. Their wealth is lower.

Solutions to Chapter 16

Debt Policy

1. a. True.

    b. False. As financial leverage increases, the expected rate of return on equity rises by just enough to compensate for its higher risk. The value of the firm and stockholders' wealth are unaffected.

    c. False. The sensitivity of equity returns to business risk, and therefore the cost of equity, increases with leverage even without a change in the risk of financial distress.

    d. True.

2. While the cost of debt and the cost of equity both increase, the weight applied to debt in the cost of capital formula also increases. Applying a higher weight to the lower-cost source of capital offsets the increase in the cost of debt and the cost of equity.

3. The interest tax shield is the reduction in corporate income taxes due to the fact that interest is treated as an expense that reduces taxable income. To the extent that the government collects less tax, there is a bigger pie of after-tax income available to the debt and equity holders.

    Example: Assume operating income is $100,000, the interest rate on debt is 10%, and the tax rate is 35%. Compare income for an unlevered firm versus a firm that borrows $400,000:

	Zero-debt firm	$400,000 of debt
Operating income	$100,000	$100,000
Interest on debt	0	40,000
Before-tax income	100,000	60,000
Tax at 35%	35,000	21,000
After-tax income	65,000	39,000
Sum of debt interest plus after-tax income	$ 65,000	$ 79,000

    The combined debt interest plus equity income is higher for the levered firm. The difference equals $14,000, which is also the difference in taxes paid by the two firms.

4. $$\text{PV(Tax shield)} = \frac{0.35 \times (0.076 \times \$800)}{0.076} = 0.35 \times \$800 = \$280 \text{ million}$$

5. a. False. In liquidation, equityholders generally receive nothing. Therefore, they have nothing to lose in a reorganization, which allows equityholders (and junior creditors) to "play for time," hoping for a reversal of fortunes. If the firm is ultimately liquidated, equityholders may still receive nothing, but they have not lost anything either.

    b. True.

    c. False. Claims for payment of expenses incurred after the bankruptcy filing receive first priority, followed by employee claims for wages and benefits. IRS claims (along with some claims for debts owed to government agencies) are next in line.

    d. True.

    e. False. If the firm is liquidated, tax-loss carry-forwards disappear. In a reorganization, the new entity is entitled to any tax-loss carry-forwards of the old firm.

6. The tradeoff theory of capital structure holds that the optimal debt ratio is determined by striking a balance between the advantages and disadvantages of debt financing. The advantage of debt financing is the interest tax shield. The disadvantages are the various costs of financial distress. As leverage increases, the marginal tax shield from each dollar of additional borrowing falls. This is a consequence of the increasing probability that, with higher interest expense, the firm will not have positive taxable income and therefore will not pay taxes. At the same time, the expected costs of financial distress increase with leverage. As leverage increases, the marginal cost of financial distress eventually outweighs the interest tax shield. At the optimal debt ratio, the increase in the present value of tax savings from additional borrowing is exactly offset by increases in the present value of the costs of financial distress.

7. • Direct costs of bankruptcy such as legal or administrative costs.

    • Indirect costs due to the problems encountered when managing a firm in bankruptcy proceedings (e.g., interference by creditors or difficulties buying supplies on credit).

    • Poor investment decisions resulting from conflicts of interest between creditors and stockholders.

8. The pecking order theory states that firms prefer to raise funds through internal finance, and if external finance is required, that they prefer debt to equity issues. This preference – or pecking – order results from the fact that investors may interpret security issues – equity issues in particular – as a signal that managers think the firm is currently overvalued by the market; therefore, investors will reduce their valuation of the firm in response to news of a stock issue.

    If the pecking order theory is correct, we would expect firms with the highest debt ratios to be those with low profits, because internal finance is less available to these firms.

9. Financial slack refers to a firm's access to cash, marketable securities, bank financing, or debt financing. Financial slack is valuable because it means financing will be quickly available to take advantage of positive-NPV investment opportunities.

    Too much financial slack can be detrimental if it allows managers to take it easy, to empire build, or to use excess cash on their own perquisites.

10. Number of shares = 75,000
    Price per share = $10
    Market value of shares = $750,000
    Market value of debt = $250,000

	State of the Economy		
	Slump	Normal	Boom
Operating income	$75,000	$125,000	$175,000
Interest	$25,000	$ 25,000	$ 25,000
Equity earnings	$50,000	$100,000	$150,000
Earnings per share	$ 0.667	$ 1.333	$ 2.000
Return on shares	6.67%	13.33%	20.00%

11. The investor can sell one-fourth of her holdings in the firm, and then invest the proceeds in debt. Suppose she has $10,000 currently invested in the firm. She could sell $2,500 worth of shares, using the proceeds to buy bonds yielding 10%. The return on her portfolio in any economic scenario is:

	State of the Economy		
	Slump	Normal	Boom
Return on Shares	6.67%	13.33%	20.00%
Return on Debt	10.00%	10.00%	10.00%
Portfolio Return*	7.50%	12.50%	17.50%

*Portfolio Return = (0.25 × return on debt) + (0.75 × return on shares)

The portfolio return is precisely the same as it was when the $10,000 was invested in the unlevered firm.

12. Share price = $10

    With no leverage, there are 100,000 shares outstanding:

    $$\text{Expected earnings per share} = \frac{\$125,000}{100,000} = \$1.25$$

    P/E = $10/$1.25 = 8

With leverage, there are 75,000 shares outstanding:

$$\text{Expected earnings per share} = \frac{\$100,000}{75,000} = \$1.333$$

P/E = $10/$1.333 = 7.5

P/E decreases because the equity is now riskier. Although earnings per share are expected to rise from $1.25 to $1.333, the value of each share of equity is no higher. The increase in risk offsets the increase in expected earnings.

13. After-tax income for all-equity firm:

	State of the Economy		
	Slump	Normal	Boom
Operating income	$75,000	$125,000	$175,000
Tax at 35%	$26,250	$ 43,750	$ 61,250
After-tax income	$48,750	$ 81,250	$113,750

After-tax income assuming $250,000 of debt financing:

	State of the Economy		
	Slump	Normal	Boom
Operating income	$75,000	$125,000	$175,000
Debt interest at 10%	25,000	25,000	25,000
Before-tax income	50,000	100,000	150,000
Tax at 35%	17,500	35,000	52,500
After-tax income	32,500	65,000	97,500
Combined debt & equity income (debt interest + after-tax income)	57,500	90,000	122,500
After-tax income (all-equity case)	$48,750	$ 81,250	$113,750
Difference in income	$ 8,750	$ 8,750	$ 8,750

In all states of the economy, the difference in total income to all security holders is $8,750. This is exactly equal to the tax shield from debt:

$$T_c \times \text{Interest expense} = 0.35 \times \$25,000 = \$8,750$$

14. Expected return on assets is:

$$r_{assets} = (0.08 \times 30/100) + (0.16 \times 70/100) = 0.136 = 13.6\%$$

The new return on equity is:

$$r_{equity} = r_{assets} + [D/E \times (r_{assets} - r_{debt})]$$

$$= 0.136 + [20/80 \times (0.136 - 0.08)] = 0.15 = 15\%$$

15. a. Market value of firm is: $100 \times 10,000 = \$1,000,000$

    With the low-debt plan, equity falls by $200,000, so:

    $$D/E = \$200,000/\$800,000 = 0.25$$

    8,000 shares remain outstanding.

    With the high-debt plan, equity falls by $400,000, so:

    $$D/E = \$400,000/\$600,000 = 0.67$$

    6,000 shares remain outstanding.

    b. <u>Low-debt plan</u>

EBIT	$ 90,000	$130,000
Interest	20,000	20,000
Equity Earnings	70,000	110,000
EPS [Earnings/8,000]	$ 8.75	$ 13.75

    Expected EPS = ($8.75 + $13.75)/2 = $11.25

    <u>High-debt plan</u>

EBIT	$ 90,000	$130,000
Interest	40,000	40,000
Equity Earnings	50,000	90,000
EPS [Earnings/6000]	$ 8.33	$ 15.00

    Expected EPS = ($8.33 + $15)/2 = $11.67

    Although the high-debt plan results in higher expected EPS, it is not necessarily preferable because it also entails greater risk. The higher risk shows up in the fact that EPS for the high-debt plan is lower than EPS for the low-debt plan when EBIT is low, but EPS for the high-debt plan is higher when EBIT is higher.

    c.

	Low-debt plan	High-debt plan
EBIT	$100,000	$100,000
Interest	20,000	40,000
Equity Earnings	80,000	60,000
EPS	$ 10.00	$ 10.00

    EPS is the same for both plans because EBIT is 10% of assets which is equal to the rate the firm pays on its debt. When $r_{assets} = r_{debt}$, EPS is unaffected by leverage.

16. Currently, with no outstanding debt: $\beta_{equity} = 1.0$

    Therefore: $\beta_{assets} = 1.0$

    Also: $r_{equity} = 10\% \Rightarrow r_{assets} = 10\%$

    Finally: $r_{debt} = 5\%$

The firm plans to refinance, resulting in a debt-to-equity ratio of 1.0, and debt-to-value ratio: debt/(debt + equity) = 0.5

a. $(\beta_{equity} \times 0.5) + (\beta_{debt} \times 0.5) = \beta_{assets} = 1$

$(\beta_{equity} \times 0.5) + 0 = 1 \Rightarrow \beta_{equity} = 1/0.5 = 2.0$

b. $r_{equity} = r_{assets} = 10\%$

risk premium $= r_{equity} - r_{debt} = 10\% - 5\% = 5\%$

(Note that the debt is risk-free.)

c. $r_{equity} = r_{assets} + [D/E \times (r_{assets} - r_{debt})] = 10\% + [1 \times (10\% - 5\%)] = 15\%$

risk premium $= r_{equity} - r_{debt} = 15\% - 5\% = 10\%$

d. 5%

e. $r_{assets} = (0.5 \times r_{equity}) + (0.5 \times r_{debt}) = (0.5 \times 15\%) + (0.5 \times 5\%) = 10\%$

This is unchanged.

f. Suppose total equity before the refinancing was $1,000. Then expected earnings were 10% of $1000, or $100. After the refinancing, there will be $500 of debt and $500 of equity, so interest expense will be $25. Therefore, earnings fall from $100 to $75, but the number of shares is now only half as large. Therefore, EPS increases by 50%:

$$\frac{\text{EPS after}}{\text{EPS before}} = \frac{75/(\text{Original shares}/2)}{100/\text{Original shares}} = 1.5$$

g. The stock price is unchanged, but earnings per share have increased by a factor of 1.5. Therefore, the P/E ratio must decrease by a factor of 1.5, from 10 to:

$10/1.5 = 6.67$

So, while expected earnings per share increase, the earnings multiple decreases, and the stock price is unchanged.

17. $r_{assets} = (0.8 \times 12\%) + (0.2 \times 6\%) = 10.8\%$

After the refinancing, the package of debt and equity must still provide an expected return of 10.8% so that:

$10.8\% = (0.6 \times r_{equity}) + (0.4 \times 6\%) \Rightarrow r_{equity} = (10.8\% - 2.4\%)/0.6 = 14\%$

18. This is not a valid objection. MM's Proposition II explicitly allows for the rates of return on both debt and equity to increase as the proportion of debt in the capital structure increases. The rate on debt increases because the debtholders take on more of the risk of the firm; the rate on the common stock increases because of increasing financial leverage.

19. a. Under Proposition I, the cost of capital of the firm (r_{assets}) is not affected by the choice of capital structure. The reason the stated argument *seems* to be true is that it does not account for the changing *proportions* of the firm financed by debt and equity. As the debt-equity ratio increases, it is true that both the costs of equity and debt increase; but a larger portion of the firm is financed by debt. The overall effect is to leave the firm's cost of capital unchanged.

b. Moderate borrowing does not significantly affect the probability of financial distress, but it does increase the variability (and also the market risk) borne by stockholders. *This* additional risk must be offset by a higher expected rate of return to stockholders.

c. If the opportunity were the firm's *only* asset, this would be a good deal. Stockholders would put up no money and would therefore have nothing to lose. The trouble is, rational lenders will not advance 100 percent of the asset's value for an 8 percent promised return unless other assets are put up as collateral.

Sometimes firms find it convenient to borrow all the cash required for certain investments. But these investments don't support all of the additional debt; the lenders are protected by the firm's other assets too. In any case, if firm value is independent of leverage, then any asset's contribution to firm value must be independent of how it is financed. Note also that the statement ignores the effect on the stockholders of an increase in financial leverage.

d. This is not an important reason for conservative debt levels. So long as MM's proposition holds, the company's overall cost of capital is unchanged despite increasing interest rates paid as the firm borrows more. (However, the increasing interest rates may signal an increasing probability of financial distress — and that can be important.)

20. The ratio of debt to firm value is: $\dfrac{D}{D+E} = \dfrac{1}{1+2} = \dfrac{1}{3}$

$$r_{assets} = (1/3 \times 6\%) + (2/3 \times 12\%) = 10\%$$

If the firm reduces its debt-equity ratio to 1/3, then:

$$r_{equity} = r_{assets} + [D/E \times (r_{assets} - r_{debt})] = 10\% + \left[\frac{1}{3} \times (10\% - 6\%)\right] = 11.33\%$$

21 Although both debt and equity are riskier, and therefore command higher expected rates of return, the fraction of the firm financed by lower-cost debt is now higher. So the weighted average of the debt and equity rates can in fact remain unchanged. The higher expected returns for each source of financing are offset by the re-weighting towards debt, which has a lower expected return than equity.

22. Pepsi's interest expense is given in Table 3-2 as \$152 million. Its annual interest tax shield is: $0.35 \times \$152 = \$53.2$ million

If the company plans to maintain its current debt level indefinitely, then we can find the present value of the stream of tax savings using the no-growth valuation model. (See Chapter 6.) The discount rate for the tax shield is 8%. Therefore, the present value of the perpetuity of tax savings is:

$$PV = \frac{\text{Interest tax shield}}{r} = \frac{\$58.45 \text{ million}}{0.08} = \$730.625 \text{ million}$$

23. a. $\text{WACC} = \left[\frac{8}{27} \times 7\% \times (1 - 0.35) \right] + \left[\frac{19}{27} \times 14\% \right] = 11.20\%$

    b. If the firm has no debt, the market value of the firm would decrease by the present value of the tax shield: $0.35 \times \$800 = \$280$

    The value of the firm would be \$2,420. The long-term assets of the firm (which previously included the present value of the tax shield) will also decrease by \$280. The new market value balance sheet is therefore as follows:

Net working capital	\$ 550	Debt	\$ 0
Long-term assets	1,870	Equity	2,420
Value of firm	\$2,420	Total	\$2,420

24. a. PV tax shield $= 0.35 \times \text{Debt} = 0.35 \times \$40 = \$14$

    b. $\text{WACC} = \left[\frac{40}{160} \times 8\% \times (1 - 0.35) \right] + \left[\frac{120}{160} \times 15\% \right] = 12.55\%$

    c. Annual tax shield $= 0.35 \times \text{Interest expense} = 0.35 \times (0.08 \times \$40) = \$1.12$

    PV tax shield $= \$1.12 \times \text{annuity factor}(8\%, 5 \text{ years})$

    $$= \$1.12 \times \left[\frac{1}{0.08} - \frac{1}{0.08 \times (1.08)^5} \right] = \$4.47$$

    The total value of the firm falls by: $\$14 - \$4.47 = \$9.53$

    The total value of the firm $= \$160.00 - \$9.53 = \$150.47$

25. Firms operating close to bankruptcy face two general types of problems. First, other firms they do business with will try to protect themselves, in the process, impeding the firm's business. For example, suppliers will not extend credit to the firm. Banks and other lenders will be less willing to lend money even if the firm has identified attractive investment opportunities.

In addition, as the firm nears bankruptcy, its *own* incentives to invest become distorted. The firm may inappropriately favor high-risk investments, reasoning that the creditors bear a large portion of the risk. Or the firm may be less willing to raise new equity to finance a project, reasoning that if the firm subsequently goes under, the debtholders will capture all or part of the new funds raised.

26. Equity can sometimes have a positive value even when companies petition for bankruptcy because there is generally some chance for the company to recover from the financial distress that led to the bankruptcy petition. If the firm does recover to the point of being able to pay off its debts and emerge from bankruptcy, then the equity will have increased value.

27. a. If SOS runs into financial difficulties, the additional funds contributed by the equityholders to finance the new project will end up being available to pay the debtholders. To the extent that the financing for the new project increases the value of debt, it represents a transfer of wealth from stockholders to bondholders.

    b. If the new project is sufficiently risky, it may increase the expected payoff to equity holders. To see this, imagine the following extreme case:

    The face value of SOS's debt is $100 and the market value of its assets is $90. The assets are risk free and therefore SOS is certain to default and the equity currently is valueless. But suppose the stockholders use $10 of the firm's cash to invest in a very risky new project. The project will pay off $100 with probability 0.09 and $0 with probability 0.91. (Notice that the expected payoff from the project is $9, which is less than its cost so that project NPV is negative.) If the project is successful, the value of the assets of the firm will be $190, and the equity holders will have a claim worth $90. Therefore, if they pursue the project, their expected payoff is: $0.09 \times \$90 = \$8.10$

    The project is a long shot, but it is obviously preferable to the equityholders' current position in which they are guaranteed to receive nothing.

28. Financial distress can lead to distorted investment incentives. For example, a firm in distress might be tempted to engage in a highly risky negative-NPV venture, reasoning that the bondholders bear the risk if things go poorly but the equity-holders keep the upside if things go well. (This is called "bet the bank's money" in the text.) Or, a firm on the brink of insolvency might be unwilling to engage in a positive-NPV venture if it requires additional capital, reasoning that even if the project goes well, the firm's creditors will capture much of the returns. (This is called "don't bet your own money" in the text.) These conflicts of interest lead to costs of financial distress since the potential for poor decisions (which reduce firm value) is reflected in the stock price that investors see as reasonable for the firm.

29. The computer software company would experience higher costs of financial distress if its business became shaky. Its assets – largely the skills of its trained employees – are intangible. In contrast, the shipping company could sell off some of its assets if demand for its product was slack. In the event of financial distress, the shipping company would find a market in which it could sell off its assets. This is not true of the software company.

30. a. $V = \dfrac{\text{EBIT} \times (1 - T_c)}{r} = \dfrac{\$25{,}000 \times (1 - 0.35)}{0.10} = \$162{,}500$

    b. The value of the firm increases by the present value of the interest tax shield:

$$0.35 \times \$50{,}000 = \$17{,}500$$

    c. The expected cost of bankruptcy is: $0.30 \times \$200{,}000 = \$60{,}000$

The present value of this cost is: $\$60{,}000/(1.10)^3 = \$45{,}079$

Since this is greater than the present value of the potential tax shield, the firm should not issue the debt.

31. Alpha Corp is more profitable and is therefore able to rely to a greater extent on internal finance (retained earnings) as a source of capital. It will therefore have less dependence on debt, and the lower debt ratio.

32. Sealed Air started with considerable financial slack. Unlike most firms, it was a net lender. The value of such slack is that it could enable the firm to take advantage of any investment opportunities that might arise without the need to raise funds in the securities market. However, top management realized that there could be too much slack, so that managers had become complacent about seeking to enhance efficiency. The dramatic change in capital structure put the firm under great pressure to enhance efficiency, and employees responded to the new pressure. The success of the restructuring says that, even in a pecking order world, there may be a tradeoff between the advantages of slack and the incentive effects of debt. We would not recommend that all firms restructure as Sealed Air did. This restructuring made sense because the firm had an unusual amount of slack to start with, and top management felt that it had an unusual amount of room for improvement in employees' sense of urgency toward instituting productive change.

33. a. Stockholders gain and bondholders lose. Bond value decreases because the value of assets securing the bond has decreased.

    b. If we assume the cash is left in Treasury bills, then bondholders gain. The bondholders are sure to receive $26 plus interest. This is greater than the $25 market value of the debt. Stockholders lose; in fact stock value falls to zero, because there is now no chance that firm value can increase above the $50 face value of the debt.

    c. The bondholders lose and the stockholders gain. The firm adds assets worth $10 and debt worth $10. This increases the debt ratio, leaving the old bondholders more exposed. The old bondholders' loss is the stockholders' gain.

    d. The original stockholders lose and bondholders gain. There are now more assets backing the bondholders' claim. Since the bonds are worth more, the market value of all outstanding stock must have increased by less than the additional investment in the firm. This implies a loss to stockholders. However, because the *new* stockholders will invest only if they receive stock with value at least equal to their investment, the loss must be borne by the old shareholders.

34. a. Masulis's results are consistent with the view that debt is always preferable because of its tax advantage, but are *not* consistent with the trade-off theory, which holds that management strikes a balance between the tax advantage of debt and the costs of possible financial distress. In the trade-off theory, exchange offers would be undertaken to move the firm's debt level toward the optimum. That ought to be good news, if anything, regardless of whether leverage is increased or decreased.

    b. The results are consistent with the evidence on the announcement effects of security issues and repurchases. You can view a debt-for-equity exchange as equivalent to two separate transactions: (i) issue debt (no news) and (ii) repurchase stock (good news).

35. Suppose the firm has assets in place that can generate cash flows with present value of $100 million, but the market believes the assets are actually worth $110 million. If there are 1 million shares outstanding, the shares will sell for $110. The managers (but not the shareholders) know that the stock price will fall to $100 when the market reassesses the value of the firm's project. But if the firm issues new shares while the stock is overpriced, this can benefit the current shareholders.

    Suppose the firm sells an additional 100,000 shares at $110 and invests the proceeds in a zero-NPV project. The new project is thus worth exactly:

    $110 \times 100,000$ shares $= \$11$ million

    Now look at the market value balance sheet of the firm *after* the market reassesses the value of the firm (therefore using the true value of the original assets) and assuming there is no debt outstanding:

Assets		Liabilities & Shareholders' equity	
Original assets	$100 million		
New assets	$ 11 million	Shareholders' equity	$111 million

    There are now 1.1 million shares outstanding, so the price per share is:

    $111 million/1.1 million $= \$100.91$

    The original shareholders now have a claim worth:

    1 million $\times \$100.91 = \$100.91$ million

    The new shareholders have a claim worth: $100,000 \times \$100.91 = \$10.09$ million

    Thus, the total gain to the original shareholders is $0.91 million (the true value of the firm was originally $100 million, but the value of their shares is now $100.91 million), while the new shareholders lose $0.91 million (they paid $11 million for shares worth only $10.09 million). This transfer of wealth occurs because the new shareholders invested when the shares were overpriced.

36. Because debtholders share in the success of the firm only to a minimal extent (i.e., to the extent that bankruptcy risk falls), an issue of debt is not usually taken as a signal that a firm's management has concluded that the market is overvaluing the firm. Thus debt issues are not signals of the firm's future success and they therefore do not induce investors to reassess the value of the firm.

37. Suppose the firm's tax bracket is 35% while shareholders' tax bracket is 27%. The firm has EBIT per share of $5. Compare two situations, one in which the interest on the firm's borrowing is $1 per share, the other in which the investor has borrowed and pays an amount of interest equal to $1 per share.

In the case that the firm has not borrowed, but the investor has, the investor's total after-tax income (on a per share basis) is computed as follows:

EBIT	$5.00
Taxes	1.75
Net income earned per share	3.25
Less interest per share paid by investor (after tax)	0.73 [= $1 × (1 − 0.27)]
Net income earned per share	$2.52

Now consider the case that the firm has borrowed and pays interest of $1 per share, but the investor has not borrowed:

EBIT	$5.00
Interest paid	1.00
Taxable income	4.00
Taxes	1.40
Net income earned per share	$2.60

Total after-tax income going to the investor is $0.08 per share higher when the firm, rather than the investor, borrows. This is because the difference in the tax rate is 8% (i.e., 35% − 27%). The difference in the tax payments going to the government is $0.08 per dollar of interest paid. When individuals are in a lower tax bracket than the firm is, there is an advantage to switching borrowing from the individual to the firm.

38. If there is a tax advantage to firm borrowing, there must be a symmetric disadvantage to firm *lending*. If the firm lends, it pays taxes on its interest income. If its tax bracket is higher than the personal bracket of the shareholder, then lending increases the total tax burden. If the shareholders were to lend instead, the tax rate on the interest income would be less than the 35% tax rate paid by the firm on the interest income.

39. a. In the absence of taxes, WACC and r_{debt} do not change. The r_{equity} increases with increased leverage,

Debt-Equity Ratio	D/(D+E)	r_{equity}	WACC	r_{debt}
0	0.000	0.125	0.125	0.100
0.1	0.091	0.128	0.125	0.100
0.2	0.167	0.130	0.125	0.100
0.3	0.231	0.133	0.125	0.100
0.4	0.286	0.135	0.125	0.100
0.5	0.333	0.138	0.125	0.100
0.6	0.375	0.140	0.125	0.100
0.7	0.412	0.143	0.125	0.100
0.8	0.444	0.145	0.125	0.100
0.9	0.474	0.148	0.125	0.100
1	0.500	0.150	0.125	0.100
1.1	0.524	0.153	0.125	0.100
1.2	0.545	0.155	0.125	0.100
1.3	0.565	0.158	0.125	0.100
1.4	0.583	0.160	0.125	0.100
1.5	0.600	0.163	0.125	0.100
1.6	0.615	0.165	0.125	0.100
1.7	0.630	0.168	0.125	0.100
1.8	0.643	0.170	0.125	0.100
1.9	0.655	0.173	0.125	0.100
2	0.667	0.175	0.125	0.100
2.1	0.677	0.178	0.125	0.100
2.2	0.688	0.180	0.125	0.100
2.3	0.697	0.183	0.125	0.100
2.4	0.706	0.185	0.125	0.100
2.5	0.714	0.188	0.125	0.100

b. When the corporate tax rate is 35% the WACC cost declines with increases in leverage. The optimal capital structure seems to be 100% debt financing.

Debt-Equity Ratio	D/(D+E)	r_{equity}	WACC	r_{debt}
0	0.000	0.125	0.125	0.100
0.1	0.091	0.128	0.122	0.100
0.2	0.167	0.130	0.119	0.100
0.3	0.231	0.133	0.117	0.100
0.4	0.286	0.135	0.115	0.100
0.5	0.333	0.138	0.113	0.100
0.6	0.375	0.140	0.112	0.100
0.7	0.412	0.143	0.111	0.100
0.8	0.444	0.145	0.109	0.100
0.9	0.474	0.148	0.108	0.100
1	0.500	0.150	0.108	0.100
1.1	0.524	0.153	0.107	0.100
1.2	0.545	0.155	0.106	0.100
1.3	0.565	0.158	0.105	0.100
1.4	0.583	0.160	0.105	0.100
1.5	0.600	0.163	0.104	0.100
1.6	0.615	0.165	0.103	0.100
1.7	0.630	0.168	0.103	0.100
1.8	0.643	0.170	0.103	0.100
1.9	0.655	0.173	0.102	0.100
2	0.667	0.175	0.102	0.100
2.1	0.677	0.178	0.101	0.100
2.2	0.688	0.180	0.101	0.100
2.3	0.697	0.183	0.101	0.100
2.4	0.706	0.185	0.100	0.100
2.5	0.714	0.188	0.100	0.100

c. What is not considered in the optimal capital structure seemingly implied by part c is the increased risk associated with higher debt levels - r_{debt} will increase with the debt-equity ratio.

Solution to Minicase for Chapter 16

First we confirm some of the numbers cited in the case:

Market value of bonds:

$$PV = \$10 \times \left[\frac{1}{0.05} - \frac{1}{0.05(1.05)^{20}} \right] + \frac{\$100}{1.05^{20}} = \$162 \text{ million}$$

[Using a financial calculator, enter: n = 20; PMT = 10; FV = 100; i = 5%, compute PV = 162]

Value of shares = $10 × 10 million = $100 million

Long-term debt ratio = 162/(100 + 162) = 0.62

With additional borrowing of $15 million, the long-term debt ratio will increase to:

177/(100 + 177) = 0.64

Solution

At a debt ratio of 62%, a firm in an industry with volatile profits probably should not issue much more debt. (The 45% debt ratio cited by the chief executive is based on book values of debt and equity.) A $15 million increase in debt would increase the debt ratio to 64%.

Johnson's arguments are based on the pecking order theory of capital structure. He is right that investors may interpret an issue of stock as a signal that management views shares as currently overpriced. If the stock price declines at the announcement of the equity offer, equity would indeed be a very expensive source of financing.

Explaining the reasons for the equity offer to investors will go only so far. Actions speak louder than words; a concrete signal of management's confidence in the firm would be more helpful. Thus, Johnson's suggestion of a dividend increase makes sense. If management commits to the higher dividend level, it must anticipate that the firm will generate enough cash flow to pay the dividend. Otherwise, the firm will have to make repeated costly trips to the capital market to raise the additional cash necessary to pay the dividends. Thus, an increase in dividends would corroborate management's stated belief that the firm is doing well, and should serve to mitigate investors' fears that an equity issue is a bad signal.

LA's chief executive raises several false concerns about the equity issue. The fact that the stock price is down relative to recent levels does not make equity a more expensive source of financing. Equity is more expensive only if management has reasons to believe (reasons not also known to public investors) that the stock price has fallen *too much* and will soon recover.

Similarly, the dividend yield on the stock does not indicate whether equity is an expensive source of financing. The dividend yield does not indicate anything about the expected total rate of return investors expect on the equity. That rate of return includes capital gains, and is not affected by how the return is divided between capital gains and dividends.

Moreover, according to the Modigliani-Miller propositions, even if equity has a higher expected rate of return than debt, it is not a more expensive source of financing. Debt has an implicit cost that LA's chief executive does not recognize: the issue of more debt makes both the existing debt and the existing equity riskier. So the observation that the yield to maturity on the firm's bonds is only 5% is irrelevant to the issue of whether equity or debt is the better financing alternative.

Nor is the chief executive's concern about the book value of the equity warranted. This value has nothing to do with the value of the firm as an ongoing business. As long as the stock is fairly priced, the firm will be issuing equity at fair terms. Changes in the book value per share of equity — the chief executive's concern about dilution — have no effect on the share price or stockholders' wealth.

To calculate the required rate of return on the new planes, we use the weighted average cost of capital. Market values of financing sources are as follows:

Debt: $50 million bank loan + $162 million bonds = $212 million

Equity: Value of shares = 10×10 million = $100 million

Therefore, debt (including short-term debt) comprises: 212/312 = 67.9% of total financing

Equity is 32.1% of total financing.

The expected return on debt is 5% and the expected return on equity is (using data from the notes to the financial statements):

$$r_f + \beta(r_m - r_f) = 4\% + 1.25 \times 8\% = 14\%$$

Therefore:

$$WACC = [0.679 \times 5\% \times (1 - 0.35)] + (0.321 \times 14\%) = 6.70\%$$

A slightly more sophisticated approach to calculating WACC would recognize that when calculating the company's capital structure, the company's $20 million cash holdings should be netted out against the bank loan. In that case, net debt equals: $212 – 20 = $192 million Therefore, debt (including short-term debt) comprises:

192/(192 + 100) = 65.8% of total financing

Equity is 34.2% of total financing.

Therefore:

$$WACC = [0.658 \times 5\% \times (1 - 0.35)] + [0.342 \times 14\%] = 6.93\%$$

Solutions for Chapter 17

Payout Policy

1. a. May 7:   Declaration date
        June 6:   Last with-dividend date
        June 7:   Ex-dividend date
        June 11:   Record date
        July 2:   Payment date

    b. The stock price will fall on the ex-dividend date, June 7. The price falls on this day because, as the stock goes ex-dividend, the shareholders are no longer entitled to receive the dividend.

    c. The annual dividend is: $\$0.075 \times 4 = \$0.30$

        The dividend yield is: $\$0.30/\$27 = 0.0111 = 1.11\%$

    d. The percentage payout rate was: $\$0.30/\$1.90 = 0.1579 = 15.79\%$

    e. A 10 percent stock dividend is equivalent to a 1.10 for 1 stock split. The number of shares outstanding increases by 10%, while the firm's assets are unchanged. The stock dividend therefore will reduce the stock price to: $\$27/1.10 = \$24.55$

2. a. The stock price will fall to: $\$80 \times 4/5 = \$64$

    b. The stock price will fall by a factor of 1.25 to: $\$80/1.25 = \$64$

    c. A share repurchase will have no effect on price per share.

3. a. True.

    b. False. Investors realize the special dividends probably won't be repeated.

    c. True. The effective rate can be less than the stated rate because the realization of gains can be deferred, which reduces the present value of the tax obligation.

    d. False. Firms have long-run target payout ratios. The payout may vary from year to year.

    e. True.

    f. False. The repurchase program announcement may signal managers have no good use for the funds.

4. Your dividend income will increase from $1,500 to $3,000. If you view the dividend as excessive, you can invest the extra $1,500 in the firm. When the stock goes ex-dividend, the share price will fall by $1.50 instead of $.75, but you will increase the number of shares you hold, and thereby offset the impact of the higher payout policy.

5. Mr. Donoso should cut this year's dividend as forecasted earnings are expected to decline such the dividend payout is greater than target. Given a target payout ratio of 50% and earnings are expected to remain at the current level of $5.00 per share, the firm should increase dividends from $2.20 to $2.50 ($5.00 × 0.50). However, if future earnings are forecasted at only $4.00 per share, the dividend should be cut to $2.00. If expected earnings are $3.00 per share, dividends should again be cut to ($3.00 × 0.50 = $1.50). If earnings are expected to average $7.00 per share, dividends should be gradually increased to $3.50.

6. Dividend increases are typically good news for investors as they signal manager's confidence in the future cash flow from operations of the firm. A dividend cut conveys a lack of confidence on the part of managers and is therefore typically bad news for investors.

7. If dividends are taxes more heavily than capital gains the firms should not pay generous cash dividends.

8. The manager cannot be correct. If all shareholders have the right to buy additional shares at the deep discount, then none of them individually can benefit. As the additional shares are sold at below-market prices, the share price will gradually fall, precisely offsetting the value of the discount. This is analogous to the firm issuing rights to existing shareholders to buy additional shares at a discount. The value of the right is offset by the fall in the share price. The firm cannot create value by selling discounted shares.

   One benefit of the program that the manager does not mention is that, if the DRIP elicits a significant cash inflow, then the firm may not need to issue equity in the future, thereby saving the costs of a future equity issue.

9. a. P = $1,000,000/20,000 = $50

   b. The price tomorrow will be $0.50 per share lower, or $49.50.

10. a. After the repurchase, the market value of equity falls to $990,000, and the number of shares outstanding falls by: $10,000/$50 = 200 shares
    There are 19,800 shares outstanding, so price per share is: $990,000/19,800 = $50

Price per share is unchanged. An investor who starts with 100 shares and sells one share to the company ends up with $4,950 in stock and $50 in cash, for a total of $5,000.

b. If the firm pays a dividend, the investor would have 100 shares worth $49.50 each and $50 cash, for a total of $5,000. This is identical to the investor's position after the stock repurchase.

11. A one percent stock dividend has no cash implications. The total market value of equity remains $1,000,000, and shares outstanding increase to: $20,000 \times 1.01 = 20,200$

Price per share falls to: $1,000,000/20,200 = 49.50

The investor will end up with 101 shares worth: $101 \times $49.50 = $5,000$

The value of the position is the same as under the cash dividend or repurchase, but the allocation between shares and cash differs.

12. Compare a $10 dividend to a share repurchase. After the first $10 cash dividend is paid (at the end of the year), the shareholders can look forward to a perpetuity of further $10 dividends. The share price in one year (just after the firm goes ex-dividend) will be $100, and the investors will have just received a $10 cash dividend.

If instead the firm does a share repurchase in year 1 (just before the stock would have gone ex-dividend), the share price will be $110 (representing the value of a perpetuity due, with the first payment to be received immediately). For $10 million, the firm could repurchase 90,909 shares. After the repurchase, the total value of outstanding shares will be $100 million, exactly the same as if the firm had paid out the $10 million in a cash dividend. With only 909,091 shares now outstanding, each share will sell for:

$100 million/909,091 shares = 110

Thus, instead of receiving a $10 dividend, shareholders see the value of each share increase by $10. In the absence of taxes, shareholders are indifferent between the two outcomes.

13. The announcement of an increase in Growler Corporation's regular dividend would have the greatest impact on stock price. Dividend increases are typically good news for investors as they signal manager's confidence in the future cash flow from operations of the firm. A share repurchase will have no effect on price per share and investors realize that these programs and special dividends probably won't be repeated.

14. a. $1,000 \times 1.25 = 1,250$ shares

Price per share will fall to: $100/1.25 = 80

Initial value of equity is: $1,000 \times $100 = $100,000$

The value of the equity position remains at: $1,250 \times $80 = $100,000$

b. A 5-for-4 split will have precisely the same effect on price per share, shares held, and the value of your equity position as the 25% stock dividend. In both cases, the number of shares held increases by 25%.

15. If Arborio Farms paid cash dividends at 1/3 of earnings each the dividend per share would vary significantly over the next six years.

	2008	2009	2010	2011	2012	2013	2014
Earnings	$3.60	$3.30	$3.60	$4.00	$4.68	$4.00	$4.05
Target Payout	0.33333	0.33333	0.33333	0.33333	0.33333	0.33333	0.33333
Dividend	$1.20	$1.10	$1.20	$1.33	$1.56	$1.33	$1.35

The average earnings over the next six years are $3.94 per share suggesting a cash dividend of $1.31. However, earnings are forecasted to decline next year. Arborio maintain the current dividend next year and gradually increase its dividend to $1.31 per share.

16. a. After the dividend is paid, total market value of the firm will be $90,000, representing $45 per share. In addition, the investor will receive $5 per share. So the value of the share today is $50.

b. If the dividend is taxed at 30 percent, then the investor will receive an after-tax cash flow of: $5 \times (1 - 0.30) = 3.50

The price today will be: $45 + $3.50 = 48.50

This is less than the value in part (a) by the amount of taxes investors pay on the dividend.

17. a. The repurchase will have no tax implications. Because the repurchase does not create a tax obligation for the shareholders, the value of the firm today is the value of the firm's assets ($100,000) divided by 2,000 shares, or $50 per share. The firm will repurchase 200 shares for $10,000. After the repurchase, the stock will sell at a price of: $90,000/1800 = $50 per share

The price is the same as before the repurchase.

b. An investor who owns 200 shares and sells 20 shares to the firm will receive: $20 \times $50 = $1,000$ in cash

This investor will be left with 180 shares worth $9,000, so the total value of the investor's position is $10,000. In the absence of taxes, this is precisely the cash and share value that would result if the firm paid a $5 per share cash dividend. If the firm had paid the dividend, the investor would have received a cash payment of: $200 \times $5 = $1,000$

Each of the 200 shares would be worth $45, as we found in Problem 14.a.

c. We compute the value of the shares once the firm announces its intention to repurchase shares or to pay a dividend.

If the firm repurchases shares, then today's share price is $50, and the value of the firm is: $50 \times 2000 = \$100,000$

If instead the firm pays a dividend, then the with-dividend stock price is $48.50 (see Problem 14.b) so the value of the firm is only $97,000. This is $3,000 less than the value that would result if the firm repurchased shares. The $3,000 difference represents the taxes on the $10,000 in dividends ($5 \times 2000$ shares).

18. a. $\text{Price} = \text{PV(after-tax dividend plus final share price)} = \dfrac{[\$2 \times (1 - 0.30)] + \$20}{1.10} = \$19.45$

b. $\text{Before tax rate of return} = \dfrac{\text{Dividend} + \text{Capital gain}}{\text{Price}}$

$= \dfrac{\$2 + (\$20 - \$19.45)}{\$19.45} = 0.1311 = 13.11\%$

c. $\text{Price} = \text{PV(after-tax dividend plus final share price)} = \dfrac{[\$3 \times (1 - 0.30)] + \$20}{1.10} = \$20.09$

d. $\text{Before-tax rate of return} = \dfrac{\text{Dividend} + \text{Capital gain}}{\text{Price}}$

$= \dfrac{\$3 + (\$20 - \$20.09)}{\$20.09} = 0.1448 = 14.48\%$

The before-tax return is higher because the larger dividend creates a greater tax burden. The before-tax return must increase in order to provide the same after-tax return of 10%.

19. a. The pension fund pays no taxes. The corporation pays taxes equal to 35 percent of capital gains income and: $35\% \times (1 - 0.70) = 10.5\%$ of dividend income.
The individual pays 15% taxes on dividends and 10% taxes on capital gains.
Therefore, the after-tax rate of return for each investor equals:

$$\dfrac{\text{dividend} \times (1 - \text{dividend tax}) + \text{capital gains} \times (1 - \text{capital gains rate})}{\text{price}}$$

We can use this formula to construct the following table of after-tax returns:

Stock	Investor		
	Pension	Corporation	Individual
A	10.00%	6.500%	9.00%
B	10.00%	7.725%	8.75%
C	10.00%	8.950%	8.50%

b. The after-tax proceeds equal: [dividend $\times (1 - 0.5)$] + [capital gain $\times (1 - 0.2)$]

If these proceeds are to provide an 8% after-tax return, then:

$$0.08 \times P_0 = (\text{dividend} \times 0.5) + (\text{capital gain} \times 0.8)$$

$$P_0 = \frac{(\text{dividend} \times 0.5) + (\text{capital gain} \times 0.8)}{0.08}$$

Using this formula for each stock, we find:

Stock A: $P_0 = \dfrac{(\$0 \times 0.5) + (\$10 \times 0.8)}{0.08} = \$100$

Stock B: $P_0 = \dfrac{(\$5 \times 0.5) + (\$5 \times 0.8)}{0.08} = \$81.25$

Stock C: $P_0 = \dfrac{(\$10 \times 0.5) + (\$0 \times 0.8)}{0.08} = \$62.50$

Notice that a larger proportion of before-tax returns paid in the form of dividends results in a lower stock price.

20. The increase in stock prices reflects the positive information contained in the dividend increase. The stock price increase can be interpreted as a reflection of a new assessment of the firm's prospects, not as a reflection of investors' preferences for high dividend payout ratios.

21. a. The risk in the firm is determined by the variability in cash flows, not payout policy. Managers can stabilize dividends and cannot control stock prices so dividends are stable and capital gains less predictable. However, the risks of the firm are unchanged by its payout policy. As long as investment policy and borrowing are held constant, a firm's overall cash flows are the same regardless of payouts as dividends or repurchases.

b. The causation in this statement is reversed - safer companies pay more generous dividends because their forecasted cash flows are more predictable. Again, the risks of the firm are unchanged by its payout policy. A firm cannot change the outcomes of its investment policy by changing its payout policy.

22. Prowler should reduce its equity through share a special dividend or share repurchase. First, as a capital gain, the tax effect to shareholders is lower. Capital gains have a tax advantage for investors as the investor pays no tax until he or she actually sells shares. The longer he or she waits before the sale, the lower the present value of the tax. Second, since there is no change to operations or investment policy of the firm there is no expected change in cash flow. Without an expected increase in cash flow management has no incentive to increase the regular dividend.

23. a. If the firm pays a dividend, the stock price will fall to $19 per share. If the firm repurchases stock, the market value of equity will fall to $19,000 and the number of shares will fall by: $1,000/$20 = 50 shares

The stock price will remain at: $19,000/950 = $20 per share

b. If the firm pays a dividend, earnings per share will be: $2,000/1,000 = $2

If the firm repurchases stock, then: EPS = $2,000/950 = $2.105

c. If the dividend is paid, the price-earnings ratio will be: $19/$2 = 9.50
    If the stock is repurchased, the price-earnings ratio will be: $20/$2.105 = 9.50

The price-earnings ratio is the same whether the dividend is paid or the stock is repurchased.

d. We have just shown that dividends per se do not have an effect on the price-earnings ratio. The stock sells at the same P/E multiple regardless of whether the firm pays a dividend or repurchases shares.

The most likely reason that firms with high dividend payout ratios have high price-earnings ratios is that both ratios are computed using current earnings rather than trend or long-run earnings. If earnings are temporarily low, the ratio of price to *current* earnings will be temporarily high. The ratio of dividends to current earnings will also be temporarily high because firms set dividend levels based on long-run earnings prospects. Therefore, we observe a correlation between P/E ratios and payout ratios.

Another reason firms with high dividend payout ratios sell at higher price-earnings multiples is that these firms tend to be in more mature industries with lower risk. If investors thus demand a lower risk premium, they will value the stock at a higher multiple of current dividends and earnings.

24. a. If the entire return on the shares is in the form of dividends the investor earns 8.5% after-tax each year (10% × (1 – 15%)) regardless of the holding period.

b. If all of the pre-tax return of 10% is in the form of capital gains, the annualized after-tax return is dependent on the holding period.

c. Capital gains may be preferred to dividends even when the tax rates are equal because taxes on gains can be deferred. As shown in the table below, after-tax returns rise with longer holding periods as the gain, and corresponding tax, is deferred.

Period	Total Return	Annualized Return %	Annualized After-Tax Return %
1	110.00	10.00%	8.50%
5	161.05	12.21%	10.38%
10	259.37	15.94%	13.55%
20	672.75	28.64%	24.34%

Solution to Minicase for Chapter 17

You will find an Excel spreadsheet solution for this minicase at the Online Learning Center (http://www.mhhe.com/bmm6e).

The statement of cash flows indicates that, in spite of substantial capital expenditures in 2008 ($2.063 billion), Penn Schumann's cash balance increased by $1.510 billion in 2008. This increase in cash led to substantial increases in liquidity ratios and decreases in leverage, as shown in the Excel spreadsheet. Dividend payout fell from 42% of net income in 2007 to 35% in 2008 despite a $328 million increase in dividends. If the entire $1.510 billion increase in cash had been instead paid out as dividends, then liquidity would still have increased and leverage would still have decreased (as shown in the spreadsheet), although the changes would of course have been less substantial. The dividend payout ratio would have increased to over 66%.

Ms. Rodriquez is probably correct when she states: "I don't think we should commit to paying out high dividends, but perhaps we could use some of our cash to repurchase stock." A payout ratio of 66.5% is likely too high to be maintained in the future, but a share repurchase might send a positive signal to the markets without creating the expectation of continued high dividend payout. Should other opportunities arise in the future (i.e., a drug for treatment of liver diseases or an acquisition in the biotech field), Penn Schumann would have the option to retain a larger portion of income without reducing the payout ratio. In addition, since debt ratios would improve even with a share repurchase (as shown in the spreadsheet), Penn Schumann may also have additional borrowing capacity to finance such ventures. A payout in the form of a share repurchase would also serve to alleviate the impression that "we fritter away cash on easy living."

Solutions to Chapter 18

Long-Term Financial Planning

1. a. False. Financial planning is a process of deciding which risks to take.

    b. False. Financial planning is concerned with possible surprises as well as the most likely outcomes.

    c. True. Financial planning considers both the financing and investment decisions. This is one (but not the only) reason that financial planning is necessary.

    d. False. A typical horizon for long-term planning is five years.

    e. True. Investments are usually aggregated by category.

    f. True. Perfect accuracy is unlikely to be obtainable, but the firm needs to produce the most accurate possible consistent forecasts.

    g. False. Excessive detail distracts attention from the crucial decisions.

2. Some of the dangers and disadvantages of using a financial model are:

    •   Most models are accounting-based and do not recognize firm value maximization as the objective of the firm.

    •   Often the relationships among variables specified by the model are somewhat arbitrary, and the decisions they imply are not considered explicitly once the model has been constructed. For example, firms have considerably more flexibility in their decisions than would be reflected in a percentage of sales model.

    •   Models are expensive to build and maintain.

    •   Models are often so complicated that it is difficult to use them or to make changes to them efficiently.

3. The ability to meet or exceed the targets embodied in a financial plan is obviously a reassuring indicator of management talent and motivation. Moreover, the financial plan focuses attention on the specific targets that top management deems most important. There are, however, several dangers.

    •   Financial plans are usually accounting-based, and thus are subject to the biases inherent in book profitability measures.

    •   Managers may sacrifice the firm's best long-term interests in order to meet the plan's short- or medium-run targets.

    •   Manager A may make all the right decisions, but fail to meet the plan because of events beyond his control. Manager B may make the wrong decisions, but be rescued by good luck. In other words, it may be difficult to separate performance and ability from results.

4. a. Sustainable growth rate = plowback ratio × ROE = $0.75 \times (1.40 \times 5\%) = 5.25\%$

    b. Internal growth rate = plowback ratio × ROE × $\dfrac{\text{equity}}{\text{assets}}$

    $$= 0.75 \times (1.40 \times 5\%) \times 0.60 = 3.15\%$$

5. Percentage of sales models assume that most variables vary in direct proportion to sales. In practice, however, the firm can increase sales without increasing fixed assets, by running plants at higher percentages of capacity, or by paying employees overtime. In this case, assets would rise less than proportionally to sales, but wages would rise more than proportionally (since overtime wage rates are higher than normal rates). Working capital may rise less than proportionally to sales since firms can exploit economies of scale in working capital management as sales increase.

    In general, percentage of sales models are better for long-term planning. Short-term plans must deal with specific and detailed cash needs over short horizons. They cannot ignore variations in the relationships among the balance sheet items. Long-term plans can abstract from these details and deal with the bigger picture using more general rules of thumb that tie the levels of these variables together.

6. If the firm reduces prices, sales revenue will increase less than proportionally to output, while costs and assets will increase roughly in proportion to output. Costs and assets will increase as a proportion of sales revenue.

7. Possible balancing items are dividends, borrowing, or equity issues. Firms tend to prefer to keep dividends steady (see Chapter 16), so in practice, this is not the best choice for balancing item. Similarly, equity issues are typically infrequent and for large amounts (see Chapter 15), so this too is not a good choice. In practice, then, borrowing is the most frequent balancing item. Usually, the borrowing source used as a balancing item is a bank loan.

8. Neither the growth rate of earnings nor the growth rate of sales translates generally into value maximizing policies for the firm; in this sense a focus on these variables is not an appropriate corporate goal. Nevertheless, targets for these growth rates might be convenient ways to signal the belief that, in a particular situation, increasing a variable like sales could be value enhancing. Moreover, focusing on a particular variable like sales growth might provide a guideline as to what aspect of corporate performance requires the most attention. These growth rates might be viewed as easily communicated proxies for factors that are more fundamental concerns of management.

9. In 2010, assets will increase by 20% of $3,000, or $600. Therefore debt and equity each must increase by 20%. Equity will increase to $2,400 and debt will increase to $1,200. Net income will increase to $600. The balancing item is dividends. If net income next year is $600 and equity increases by $400, then dividends must be $200.

10.

	15%	20%	25%
Growth in assets	$450.00	$600.00	$750.00
less: Retained earnings	287.50	300.00	312.50
External financing	$162.50	$300.00	$437.50

Net income = $500 × (1 + growth rate)

Retained earnings = Net income × 0.5

11. a. Internal growth rate = plowback ratio × ROE × $\dfrac{\text{equity}}{\text{assets}}$

$$= 0.5 \times \frac{500}{1,667} \times \frac{2}{3} = 0.10 = 10\%$$

Notice that:

ROE = net income in 2006 divided by shareholders' equity at year-end 2005

b. Sustainable growth rate = plowback ratio × ROE

$$= 0.5 \times \frac{500}{1,667} = 0.15 = 15\%$$

12. a. Net income in 2010 will increase by 15% from its current value of $500 to a new value of: $500 × 1.15 = $575

Sixty percent of earnings are paid out as dividends, while 40 percent of earnings are retained in the firm.

Assets increase in 2010 by:	0.15 × $3,000 = $450.00
less: Retained earnings in 2010:	$575 × (1 − 0.70) = 172.50
External financing in 2010	$277.50

b. Since dividend policy is fixed and no equity will be issued, debt must be the balancing item. Debt issued must be: $277.50

c. If debt issued in 2010 is limited to $100, and equity issues are ruled out, then the firm must finance its remaining asset requirements out of retained earnings. Retained earnings must be:

Increase in assets – debt issued = $(0.15 \times \$3,000) - \$100 = \$350$

Therefore, dividends must be:

Net income – retained earnings = $\$575 - \$350 = \$225$

13. a. Internal growth rate = plowback ratio $\times$ ROE $\times \dfrac{\text{equity}}{\text{assets}}$

$$= (1 - 0.70) \times \frac{500}{1,800} \times \frac{2}{3} = 0.0556 = 5.56\%$$

b. Sustainable growth rate = plowback ratio $\times$ ROE

$$= (1 - 0.70) \times \frac{500}{1,800} = 0.0833 = 8.33\%$$

14. Dividends fall by $36,000. Therefore, the requirement for external financing falls from $64,000 to $28,000. On the other hand, shareholders' equity will be increase by $36,000. The right-hand side of the balance sheet becomes (in thousands):

Long-term debt	$ 428
Shareholders' equity	672
Total	$1,100

15. a. The following first-stage pro forma statements show that higher revenue growth results in higher required external financing:

	Base case	20% growth	5% growth
Income Statement			
Revenue	$2,000	$2,400	$2,100
Cost of goods sold	1,800	2,160	1,890
EBIT	200	240	210
Interest expense	40	40	40
Earnings before taxes	160	200	170
State & federal tax	64	80	68
Net Income	96	120	102
Dividends	64	80	68
Retained Earnings	$ 32	$ 40	$ 34
Balance Sheet			
Assets			
Net working capital	$ 200	$ 240	$ 210
Fixed Assets	800	960	840
Total Assets	$1,000	$1,200	$1,050
Liabilities & shareholders' equity			
Long-term debt	$ 400	$ 400	$ 400
Shareholders' equity [a]	600	640	634
Total liabilities & shareholders' equity	$1,000	$1,040	$1,034
Required external financing [b]		$ 160	$ 16

b. **Second Stage Pro Forma**

Balance Sheet

Assets			
Net working capital	$ 200	$ 240	$ 210
Fixed Assets	800	960	840
Total Assets	$1,000	$1,200	$1,050
Liabilities & shareholders' equity			
Long-term debt [c]	$ 400	$ 560	$ 416
Shareholders' equity	600	640	634
Total liabilities & shareholders' equity	$1,000	$1,200	$1,050

Notes
a. Shareholders' equity increases by earnings retained in 2006
b. Required external financing = increase in net assets – retained earnings
c. Long-term debt, the balancing item, increases by required external financing

16. a. Net fixed assets grow by $200, which is 25% of the current value of $800. Therefore, in order for the ratio of revenues to total assets to remain constant, revenues also must grow by 25%.

Pro-forma Income Statement, 2010		Comment
Revenue	$2,250	25% higher
Fixed costs	56	unchanged
Variable costs	1,800	80% of revenue
Depreciation	80	10% of (2009 fixed assets)
Interest	24	$0.08 \times$ (2009 debt)
Taxable Income	290	
Taxes	116	40% of taxable income
Net Income	$ 174	
Dividends	$ 116	Payout ratio = 2/3
Retained Earnings	$ 58	

Balance Sheet, year-end 2007		
Assets		
Net working capital	$ 500	50% of fixed assets
Fixed assets	1,000	Increases by $200
Total assets	$1,500	
Liabilities & Shareholders' Equity		
Debt	$ 375	25% of total capital
Equity	1,125	
Total liabilities & Shareholders' equity	$1,500	

Notice that required external financing is:

Increase in assets – retained earnings = $300 – $58 = $242

$75 in new debt will be issued.
$167 in new equity must be issued.
Equity increases by $58 + $167 = $225

b. If debt is the balancing item, all external financing will come from new debt issues. Therefore, the right-hand side of the balance sheet will now be:

Debt	$ 542	Increases by $242
Equity	958	Increases by retained earnings
Total liabilities & Shareholders' equity	$1,500	

The debt ratio increases from 0.25 to: $\dfrac{542}{1,500} = 0.361$

17. a. $g = \text{plowback ratio} \times \text{ROE} = \dfrac{1{,}500}{2{,}000} \times \dfrac{2{,}000}{60{,}000} = 0.025 = 2.5\%$

   b. If $g = 0.025$, assets will grow by: $0.025 \times \$100{,}000 = \$2{,}500$

   If the debt/equity ratio is constant, then debt must grow by: $0.40 \times \$2{,}500 = \$1{,}000$

   Equity grows by \$1,500. Thus, the firm will issue \$1,000 in new debt.

   c. If no debt is issued, the maximum rate of growth is constrained by profits. If the firm retains all earnings (i.e., is willing to reduce dividends to zero), assets will grow by \$2,000, which provides a growth rate of 2%. If it maintains the dividend payout ratio of 0.75, then the maximum growth rate would be:

   $$\text{plowback ratio} \times \text{ROE} \times \dfrac{\text{equity}}{\text{assets}} = \dfrac{1{,}500}{2{,}000} \times \dfrac{2{,}000}{60{,}000} \times 0.6 = 0.015 = 1.5\%$$

18. a. $\dfrac{\text{equity}}{\text{assets}} = 1.0$

   plowback ratio = $1.0 - 0.4 = 0.6$

   asset turnover ratio = 0.8

   Target $g = 0.05 = 5\%$

   Since the firm is all-equity financed:

   $$\text{ROE} = \text{ROA} = \text{Asset turnover} \times \text{profit margin} = 0.8 \times 0.10 = 0.08 = 8\%$$

   Now calculate the sustainable growth rate:

   $$g = \text{plowback ratio} \times \text{ROE} = 0.6 \times 0.08 = 0.048 = 4.8\%$$

   The 5% target growth rate exceeds the sustainable growth rate.

   b. ROE must increase to $0.05/0.6 = 0.0833 = 8.33\%$

   ROE = asset turnover $\times$ profit margin

   $0.0833 = \text{asset turnover} \times 0.10 \Rightarrow \text{asset turnover} = 0.833$

   c. ROE = asset turnover $\times$ profit margin

   $0.0833 = 0.8 \times \text{profit margin} \Rightarrow \text{profit margin} = 0.104 = 10.4\%$

19. a. Internal growth rate = plowback ratio $\times$ ROE $\times \dfrac{\text{equity}}{\text{assets}}$

$$= 0.40 \times 0.25 \times 1 = 0.10 = 10\%$$

b. Retained earnings will be: $0.25 \times \$1,000,000 \times 0.40 = \$100,000$

New assets will be: $0.30 \times \$1$ million $= \$300,000$

External financing $= \$200,000$

c. If payout ratio $= 0$ so that plowback ratio $= 1$, then the internal growth rate increases to: $1 \times 0.25 \times 1 = 0.25 = 25\%$

d. If plowback ratio $= 1$, then retained earnings will be:

$$0.25 \times \$1,000,000 = \$250,000$$

External financing is now only: $\$300,000 - \$250,000 = \$50,000$

We conclude that reductions in the dividend payout ratio reduce requirements for external financing.

20. g = plowback ratio $\times$ ROE = plowback ratio $\times$ profit margin $\times$ asset turnover

$$= 0.60 \times 0.10 \times 0.6 = 0.036 = 3.6\%$$

21. Internal growth rate = plowback ratio $\times$ ROE $\times \dfrac{\text{equity}}{\text{assets}}$

$0.10 =$ plowback ratio $\times 0.18 \times 1.0$

Plowback ratio must be at least: $0.10/0.18 = 0.556$

Payout ratio can be at most: $1.0 - 0.556 = 0.444$

22. $\dfrac{\text{debt}}{\text{equity}} = \dfrac{1}{3} \Rightarrow \dfrac{\text{equity}}{\text{assets}} = \dfrac{3}{4}$

Internal growth rate = plowback ratio $\times$ ROE $\times \dfrac{\text{equity}}{\text{assets}}$

$0.10 =$ plowback ratio $\times 0.18 \times 0.75$

plowback ratio $= 0.10/(0.18 \times 0.75) = 0.741 = 74.1\%$

The maximum payout ratio falls to: $1 - 0.741 = 0.259 = 25.9\%$

23. Internal growth rate = plowback ratio $\times$ ROE $\times \dfrac{\text{equity}}{\text{assets}}$

Since the firm is all-equity financed, $\dfrac{\text{equity}}{\text{assets}} = 1$ and:

ROE = ROA = profit margin $\times$ asset turnover

Therefore:

g = plowback ratio $\times$ profit margin $\times$ asset turnover

$0.10 = 0.5 \times$ profit margin $\times 2.0 \Rightarrow$ profit margin $= 0.10 = 10\%$

24. If profit margin = 0.06 then:

$0.08 =$ plowback ratio $\times 0.06 \times 2 \Rightarrow$ plowback ratio $= 2/3$ and payout ratio $= 1/3$

25. Set plowback ratio equal to 1.0 so that:

g = plowback ratio $\times$ profit margin $\times$ asset turnover $= 1 \times 0.06 \times 2 = 0.12 = 12\%$

26. 2010 Income Statement, assuming 20% sales growth

Sales	$240,000
Costs	180,000
EBIT	60,000
Interest expense	10,000
Taxable income	50,000
Taxes at 35%	17,500
Net income	$ 32,500
Dividends	$ 13,000
Retained earnings	$ 19,500

If all assets grow by 20%, then total assets will increase from $200,000 to $240,000. The $40,000 increase is financed in part through the retained earnings of $19,500. The remaining $20,500 requires external financing.

27. Even if sales increase by 20%, the firm still has more than enough fixed assets to meet production. Only working capital will increase. Net working capital of the firm in 2003 was $30,000 ($40,000 of current assets minus $10,000 of accounts payable). The increase in net working capital will be $6,000, which is less than 2003 retained earnings. Thus required external financing is zero. The firm can use the surplus funds either to pay off debt, to buy back shares or to increase dividends, or to add to its cash balances.

28. If fixed assets are operating at only 75% of capacity, then fixed assets necessary to support current production levels would be only $0.75 \times \$160,000 = \$120,000$

Thus, at full capacity, the ratio of fixed assets to sales is: $\$120,000/\$200,000 = 0.6$

Since fixed assets are $160,000, sales can increase to $266,667 without requiring additional fixed assets. This means that sales can increase by $66,667 before additional fixed assets are needed.

The ratio of net working capital to sales is: $\$30,000/\$200,000 = 0.15$

The ratio of fixed assets to sales (at full capacity) is 0.60. Thus for sales levels above $266,667, the increase in assets corresponding to an increase in sales from the current level of $200,000 is:

$$\Delta NWC + \Delta Fixed\ assets = (0.15 \times \Delta Sales) + [0.60 \times (\Delta Sales - 66,667)]$$

If we set this expression equal to retained earnings ($19,500) we can obtain the maximum level to which sales can grow without requiring external financing:

$$(0.15 \times \Delta Sales) + [0.60 \times (\Delta Sales - 66,667)] = 19,500 \Rightarrow \Delta Sales = \$79,333$$

$$Final\ sales = Initial\ sales + \Delta Sales = \$200,000 + \$79,333 = \$279,333$$

29. If assets rise less than proportionally with sales, then the firm can enjoy greater sales growth before it needs to raise external funds.

30. [Note: You will find Excel spreadsheet solutions to Challenge Problem 30, at the Online Learning Center (http://www.mhhe.com/bmm6e)]

    a. The spreadsheet solution incorporates the following changes from the spreadsheet in Figure 18-2: the payout ratio in cell B9 is reduced to 0.6, and the growth rate in cell B3 is increased to 0.15. Required external financing increases to $104.4 in 2006 and $121.1 in 2007.

    b. Given the assumptions in part (a), total assets grow to $1,150.0 in 2009 and $1,322.5 in 2010. In order to maintain the debt-equity ratio at 2/3, we require that debt equal 40% of total assets, and equity equal 60% of total assets. Therefore, for 2009, debt and equity grow to $460 and $690, respectively. Since retained earnings equal $45.6 in 2009, new issues are:

       Debt: $460 – $400 = $60

       Equity: $690 – $600 – $45.6 = $44.4

       In 2010, debt and equity grow to $529.0 and $793.5, respectively, and retained earnings equal $52.4, so that new issues are:

       Debt: $529 – $460 = $69

       Equity: $793.5 – $690.0 – $52.4 = $51.1

    c. The formula in cell G20 is: 0.40*G17

       The formula in cell G21 is: 0.60*G17

Solution to Minicase for Chapter 18

You will find an Excel spreadsheet solution for this minicase at the Online Learning Center (http://www.mhhe.com/bmm6e).

Solutions to Chapter 19

Short-Term Financial Planning

1.
	Cash	Net Working Capital
a.	$2 million decrease	$2 million decrease
b.	$2,500 increase	Unchanged
c.	$5,000 decrease	Unchanged
d.	Unchanged	$1 million increase
e.	Unchanged	Unchanged
f.	$5 million increase	Unchanged

2. a. long-term financing, total capital requirement, marketable securities

   b. cash, cash, cash balance, marketable securities

3. a. Inventories of raw materials, work in process, and finished goods increase and cash decreases (use of cash).

   b. Accounts receivable increase (use of cash).

   c. Decrease in fixed assets (land), increase in cash (source of cash), and decrease in shareholders' equity when the loss on the land is recognized.

   d. Shareholders' equity decreases and cash decreases (use of cash).

   e. Retained earnings and cash decrease when the dividend is paid (use of cash).

   f. Long-term debt increases (source of cash), short-term debt decreases (use of cash).

4. Remember that:

   Cash conversion cycle = inventory period + receivables period – accounts payable period

   Notice from these answers that not all actions that shorten the cash conversion cycle are necessarily good for the firm, nor are all actions that lengthen the cash conversion cycle necessarily bad. The costs or benefits of the actions associated with changes in the cycle must also be considered.

   a. Lower inventory levels will reduce the inventory period and therefore reduce the cash conversion cycle.

   b. The accounts payable period will fall, which will lengthen the cash conversion cycle.

   c. The accounts receivable period will fall, which will shorten the cash conversion cycle.

   d. The accounts receivable period will rise (since customers pay their bills more slowly), which will lengthen the cash conversion cycle.

5. The firm can use its new system to maintain lower inventory levels. This will reduce the inventory period and therefore the cash conversion cycle, and will reduce net working capital as well.

6. $\text{Accounts receivable period} = \dfrac{(100+120)/2}{5,000/365} = 8.0 \text{ days}$

    $\text{Inventory period} = \dfrac{(500+600)/2}{4,200/365} = 47.8 \text{ days}$

    $\text{Accounts payable period} = \dfrac{(250+290)/2}{4,200/365} = 23.5 \text{ days}$

    Cash conversion cycle = 8.0 + 47.8 − 23.5 = 32.3 days

7. Cash conversion cycle = inventory period + receivables period − accounts payable period

    a. The discount should induce some customers to pay cash. Accounts receivable, the receivables period, and the cash conversion cycle will fall.

    b. Lower inventory turnover implies more days in inventory. The cash conversion cycle increases.

    c. If the firm produces goods more quickly, inventory levels corresponding to work in process will fall. Therefore, the inventory period and the cash conversion cycle fall.

    d. If the accounts payable period falls, the cash conversion cycle will increase.

    e. Because the goods are already ordered, inventory of finished product will fall relative to sales. Therefore the inventory period and the cash conversion cycle fall.

    f. Inventory increases imply a longer inventory period and longer cash conversion cycle.

8. a. The firm can use only 75% of the amount it borrows. So, if we let x equal the amount the firm borrows, then:

    $0.75\,x = 10,000 \Rightarrow x = 13,333$

    b. With the compensating balance, the effective interest rate is:

    $0.10/0.75 = 0.1333 = 13.33\%$

    The 12% loan without the compensating balance is a better deal.

    c. Now, the effective rate on the compensating balance is determined by finding the *net* interest paid by the firm. The firm borrows $13,333 and *pays* 10 percent interest on this amount, which is $1,333. It *receives* 4 percent interest on the $3,333 left with the bank; interest received is therefore $133 and the net interest payment is $1,200. The effective interest rate is thus: $1,200/$10,000 = 0.12 = 12\%$

    This is the same as the rate for the alternative loan. The firm will be indifferent between the two offers.

9. Assume that the loan calls for annual payment, so we don't have to be concerned with the consequences of compounding.

$$\text{Effective rate} = \frac{\text{interest paid}}{\text{funds available}} = \frac{0.08 \times \text{loan amount}}{0.9 \times \text{loan amount}} = \frac{0.08}{0.9} = 8.89\%$$

If the compensating balance is 20%, then: $\text{Effective rate} = \dfrac{0.08}{0.8} = 0.10 = 10\%$

10. The discount is 1.5%, but the firm collects one month earlier than it would otherwise. Suppose the stated price is $100. With the factor, the firm receives $98.50 immediately. Otherwise the firm extends a month of credit to its customers but receives $100. The implicit *monthly* interest rate (r) is defined by:

$$\$98.50 \times (1 + r) = \$100 \Rightarrow r = 0.01523$$

Therefore, the effective annual rate is determined as follows:

$$1 + r_{EAR} = (1 + r_{monthly})^{12} = (1.01523)^{12} = 1.1989 \Rightarrow r_{EAR} = 0.1989 = 19.89\%$$

If the average collection period is 1.5 months, the firm collects 1.5 months earlier than it would otherwise. Now, $r = 0.01523$ is the implicit rate for 1.5 months and the effective annual rate is determined as follows:

$$1 + r_{EAR} = (1 + r)^{(12/1.5)} = (1.01523)^8 = 1.1285 \Rightarrow r_{EAR} = 0.1285 = 12.85\%$$

11. a. If the loan is annual, then, for every $100 of stated loan amount, the borrower receives $94 and repays $100 in one year. The effective annual interest rate is:

$$\text{interest/loan amount} = \$6/\$94 = 0.0638 = 6.38\%$$

   b. If the loan is monthly, then the effective annual rate is:

$$\left(\frac{1}{1 - \dfrac{\text{annual interest rate}}{m}}\right)^m - 1 = \left(\frac{1}{1 - \dfrac{0.06}{12}}\right)^{12} - 1 = \left(\frac{1}{0.995}\right)^{12} - 1 = 0.0620 = 6.20\%$$

12. a. Consider a loan of $100. The interest over a one-year period is $6. The amount actually available is $75. Therefore, the effective annual rate is:

$$\$6/\$75 = 0.08 = 8\%$$

   b. The firm will pay interest of: $6\%/12 = 0.5\%$ per month. If the loan amount has a stated balance of $100, interest is $0.50 per month. The effective annual interest rate is:

$$\left(1 + \frac{\text{actual interest paid}}{\text{borrowed funds available}}\right)^m - 1 = \left(1 + \frac{\$0.50}{\$75}\right)^{12} - 1 = 0.0830 = 8.30\%$$

13. Month 3: $18,000 + (0.5 \times \$90,000) + (0.3 \times \$120,000) + (0.2 \times \$100,000) = \$119,000$

    Month 4: $14,000 + (0.5 \times \$70,000) + (0.3 \times \$90,000) + (0.2 \times \$120,000) = \$100,000$

14. A 30-day period is one-third of a calendar quarter. So one-third of the purchases will be paid in the *next* quarter, and two-thirds will be paid in the current quarter. If the payment delay is 60 days, then two-thirds of the purchases will be paid for in the next quarter and one-third will be paid in the current quarter.

15. The order is 0.75 times the following quarter's sales forecast:

Quarter	Order
1	$0.75 \times \$360 = \$270$
2	$0.75 \times \$336 = \$252$
3	$0.75 \times \$384 = \$288$
4	$0.75 \times \$384 = \$288$

16. Since the first quarter's sales forecast was $372, orders placed during the fourth quarter of the preceding year would have been: $0.75 \times \$372 = \$279$

Quarter	Payment*
1	$(1/3 \times \$279) + (2/3 \times \$270) = \$273$
2	$(1/3 \times \$270) + (2/3 \times \$252) = \$258$
3	$(1/3 \times \$252) + (2/3 \times \$288) = \$276$
4	$(1/3 \times \$288) + (2/3 \times \$288) = \$288$

*Payment = [(1/3) × previous period order] + [(2/3) × current period order]

17.

Quarter	Collections*
1	$(2/3 \times \$336) + (1/3 \times \$372) = \$348$
2	$(2/3 \times \$372) + (1/3 \times \$360) = \$368$
3	$(2/3 \times \$360) + (1/3 \times \$336) = \$352$
4	$(2/3 \times \$336) + (1/3 \times \$384) = \$352$

*Collections = [(2/3) × previous period sales] + [(1/3) × current period sales]

18.

	Quarter			
	First	Second	Third	Fourth
Sources of Cash				
Collections on accounts receivable	$348	$368	$352	$352
Uses of cash				
Payments of accounts payable	273	258	276	288
Labor & administrative expenses	65	65	65	65
Interest on long-term debt	40	40	40	40
Total uses of cash	378	363	381	393
Net cash inflow (equals sources minus uses)	−$30	+$5	−$29	−$41

19.

	Quarter			
	First	Second	Third	Fourth
Sources of Cash				
Cash at start of period	$40	$10	$15	−$14
Net cash inflow (from Problem #18)	−30	+ 5	−29	−41
Cash at end of period	10	15	−14	−55
Minimum operating cash balance	30	30	30	30
Cumulative financing required	$20	$15	$44	$85

20.

	Quarter			
	First	Second	Third	Fourth
A. Cash requirements				
Cash required for operations	$20.00	−$ 5.00	$29.00	$41.00
Interest on bank loan	0.00	0.40	0.31	0.89
Total cash required	$20.00	−$ 4.60	$29.31	$41.89
B. Cash raised in quarter				
Line of credit	$20.00	−$ 4.60	$29.31	$41.89
Total cash raised	$20.00	−$ 4.60	$29.31	$41.89
C. Repayments				
Of bank loan	0.00	4.60	0.00	0.00
D. Addition to cash balances	0.00	$ 0.00	$ 0.00	$ 0.00
E. Line of credit				
Beginning of quarter	$ 0.00	$20.00	$15.40	$44.71
End of quarter	$20.00	$15.40	$44.71	$86.60

21. Dynamic Mattress's new financing plan (figures in millions):

		Quarter		
	First	Second	Third	Fourth
A. Cash requirements				
Cash required for operations	$50.00	$15.00	−$26.00	−$35.00
Interest on bank loan	0.00	0.90	0.90	0.73
Interest on stretched payables	0.00	0.00	0.80	0.00
Total cash required	$50.00	$15.90	−$24.30	−$34.27
B. Cash raised in quarter				
Bank loan	$45.00	$ 0.00	$ 0.00	$ 0.00
Stretched payables	0.00	15.90	0.00	0.00
Securities sold	5.00	0.00	0.00	0.00
Total cash raised	$50.00	$15.90	$ 0.00	$ 0.00
C. Repayments				
Of stretched payables	0.00	0.00	15.90	0.00
Of bank loan	0.00	0.00	8.40	34.27
D. Addition to cash balances	$ 5.00	$ 0.00	$ 0.00	$ 0.00
E. Bank loan				
Beginning of quarter	$ 0.00	$45.00	$45.00	$36.60
End of quarter	$45.00	$45.00	$36.60	$ 2.33

22. Sources of cash

Sale of marketable securities	$ 2
Increased bank loans	1
Increased accounts payable	5
Cash from operations:	
Net income	6
Depreciation	2
Total sources	$16

Uses of cash

Increased inventory	$ 6
Increased accounts receivable	3
Invested in fixed assets	6
Dividend	1
Total uses	$16
Increase in cash balance	$ 0

23.

	February	March	April
Sources of cash			
Collections on current sales	$100	$110	$ 90
Collections on accounts receivable	90	100	110
Total sources of cash	$190	$210	$200
Uses of cash			
Payments of accounts payable	$ 30	$ 40	$ 30
Cash purchases	70	80	60
Labor & administrative expenses	30	30	30
Capital expenditures	100	0	0
Taxes, interest and dividends	10	10	10
Total uses of cash	$240	$160	$130
Net cash inflow	−$ 50	+$ 50	+$ 70
Cash at start of period	$100	$ 50	$100
+ Net cash inflow	−50	+50	+70
= Cash at end of period	$ 50	$100	$170
+ Minimum operating cash balance	$100	$100	$100
= Cumulative short-term financing required	$ 50	$ 0	−$ 70

Solution to Minicase for Chapter 19

[Note: You will find an Excel spreadsheet solution for this minicase at the Online Learning Center (www.mhhe.com/bmm6e)]

Capstan Auto has built up a high level of debt because its policy of granting free credit for six months has resulted in a large investment in working capital, specifically in accounts receivable. The firm seems to be using the bank loan as its balancing item, and financing its investment in working capital by borrowing ever greater amounts.

The following spreadsheet shows the effect of the firm's new credit policy, which began in 2013. Receivables in 2013:Q1 equal that quarter's sales. Thereafter, receivables equal current quarter sales plus last quarter sales, reflecting the six-month payment lag. The build-up of receivables shows up in the increase in net working capital.

The firm receives the cars at the *beginning* of each quarter and pays for them at the *end* of the quarter, which results in a match between inventory and payables. Changes in inventory and payables therefore cancel out in each quarter: Inventory at the end of each quarter equals the cost of the goods expected to be sold in the following quarter. Payables also equal this value since the firm pays for the cars imported at the start of the quarter (i.e., put into inventory at the end of the previous quarter) at the end of the current quarter.

The need for external finance in each quarter equals the investment in working capital minus the cash from the firm's operations (net income plus depreciation). The firm's policy has been to use the bank loan as its sole source of external finance. In each period the bank loan increases by the full amount of required external finance. The spreadsheet shows that by 2014:Q1, the bank loan has grown to $9.732 million.

If the firm's sales level off, then the build-up of working capital should also level off. The spreadsheet confirms this by examining the firm's cash flows and borrowing assuming that sales level off at 300 units a year. By 2014:Q4, sales have been at 300 for three consecutive quarters and, as a result, receivables have leveled off at $12,000. With no further build-up in working capital, the firm's required external finance is –$179 (which is simply the negative of cash flow from operations, i.e., net income + depreciation). This cash flow can be used to reduce the bank loan and, therefore, interest expense in 2013:Q1 is a bit lower:

interest expense in each quarter = 0.02 × loan balance at the end of the previous quarter

Therefore, in 2013:Q1, interest expense is a bit lower, the cash flow is a bit higher, and the firm can apply $182 to paying off the bank loan.

The firm is not necessarily in trouble. Its rapid build-up of debt reflects an investment in working capital, not negative cash flows from operations. However, by the end of 2014:Q1, the firm's ratio of debt to (debt + equity) has reached a troublesome level of:

$$9,732/(9,732 + 2,059) = 0.825$$

If the economy enters a recession, the firm might find itself overextended and unable to service the debt. In effect, the firm's payment policy results in a permanent investment in working capital. The firm probably ought to finance this investment with long-term sources of capital. While some long-term debt would be appropriate, the need right now is for the firm to contribute some additional equity capital. The bank should insist on additional equity financing before extending the line of credit.

Solutions to Chapter 20

Working Capital Management

1. a. The discount is: 1% of $1,000 = $10

    b. The customer gains an extra 40 days of credit.

    c. With the discount, the customer pays $990. Without the discount, the customer pays $1,000. The difference is: $10/$990 = 1.01%

    A rate of 1.01% per 40 days of extra credit is equivalent to an annual rate of:
    $$(1.0101)^{365/40} - 1 = 0.0960 = 9.60\%$$

2. open account
    commercial draft
    trade acceptance
    the customer's
    banker's acceptance

3. a. Perishable goods (bread) call for a shorter credit period.

    b. Rapid inventory turnover (higher turnover ratio) calls for a shorter credit period.

    c. The firm selling to customers with the more tangible and saleable assets will grant a longer credit period. This is the firm selling to electric utilities.

4. a. The service charge discourages late payment. The due lag decreases and, therefore, pay lag decreases.

    b. Companies might be forced to stretch payables. Due lag and, therefore, pay lag increase.

    c. Terms lag increases and, therefore, pay lag increases.

5. The current terms allow a 3% discount if the customer gives up an extra $40 - 20 = 20$ days of credit. The effective annual rate is:
    $$[1 + (3/97)]^{(365/20)} - 1 = 0.7435 = 74.35\%$$

    a. The implicit rate increases because the discount is higher:
    $$[1 + (4/96)]^{(365/20)} - 1 = 1.1064 = 110.64\%$$

b. The implicit rate increases because the extra days of credit 'bought' by forfeiting the discount decrease to: $40 - 30 = 10$ days

$$[1 + (3/97)]^{(365/10)} - 1 = 2.0397 = 203.97\%$$

c. The implicit rate increases because the extra days of credit "bought" by forfeiting the discount decreases to: $30 - 20 = 10$ days

$$[1 + (3/97)]^{(365/10)} - 1 = 2.0397 = 203.97\%$$

6. Ledger balance = starting balance − payments + deposits

Ledger balance = $250,000 − $20,000 − $60,000 + $45,000 = $215,000

The payment float is the outstanding total of not-yet-cleared checks written by the firm, which equals $60,000 in this case.

The net float is: $60,000 − $45,000 = $15,000

7. If you pay your bill by writing a check in the traditional manner, there will be a delay of several days before the check is presented to your bank, and the bank debits your account. During this period, the money stays in your account and you may earn interest on the funds. In contrast, if you use the Internet to order your bank to send out a check on your behalf, the bank can debit your account immediately, at which point you will stop earning interest on the funds. The bank, however, still has access to the funds until the check it sends out actually clears. Therefore, the bank is willing to provide you this service "for free." In addition, it is cheaper for the bank to process electronic order payments than paper payments, which is another source of savings that induce them to offer the service for no extra charge.

8. a. Payment float = $20,000 × 6 = $120,000
      Availability float = $22,000 × 3 = $ 66,000
      Net float = $ 54,000

   b. If availability float were reduced by one day, then interest could be earned on $22,000. Annual interest earnings would be: $0.06 × \$22,000 = \$1,320$

9. a. The lock-box reduces collection float by:
         400 payments per day × $2,000 per payment × 2 days = $1,600,000

      Daily interest saved = $0.00015 × \$1,600,000 = \$240$

      The bank charge each day is: 400 payments per day × $0.40 per payment = $160

      The lock-box is worthwhile; interest earnings exceed the bank charges.

   b. Break-even occurs when interest earned equals the bank fees:
         $0.00015 × [400 × \$2,000 × \text{Days saved}] = \$160 \Rightarrow \text{Days saved} = 1.33$

10. concentration banking
    wire transfer
    a lock-box system

11. a. Two-thirds of customers pay within 15 days. The other one-third of customers pay by day 30. Therefore, the accounts receivable period is:

    $$(2/3 \times 15) + (1/3 \times 30) = 20 \text{ days}$$

    b. Investment in A/R = accounts receivable period $\times$ daily sales

    $$= 20 \times \frac{\$20 \text{ million}}{365} = \$1.096 \text{ million}$$

    c. With greater incentive to pay early, more customers will pay within 15 days instead of 30 days. Therefore, the accounts receivable period is likely to decrease.

12. a. PV of a cash-on-delivery sale = $50 – $40 = $10 per carton

    Under the present cash-on-delivery policy, unit sales equal 1,000 cartons per month:

    $$\$10 \text{ per carton} \times 1,000 \text{ cartons} = \$10,000$$

    If credit is extended, sales increase, but present value per carton decreases to:

    $$\text{PV of revenue} - \text{Cost} = \frac{\$50}{1.01} - \$40 = \$9.505 \text{ per carton}$$

    $$\$9.505 \text{ per carton} \times 1,060 \text{ cartons} = \$10,075$$

    The higher sales more than make up for the time value cost of the credit extended.

    b. If the interest rate is 1.5%, PV per carton decreases to:

    $$\text{PV of revenue} - \text{Cost} = \frac{\$50}{1.015} - \$40 = \$9.261 \text{ per carton}$$

    $$\$9.261 \text{ per carton} \times 1,060 \text{ cartons} = \$9,817$$

    At the higher interest rate, the higher sales no longer are enough to make up for the cost of the credit extended.

    c. The PV of the old customers remains unaffected. The PV of the new customers is positive: The additional sales gained by extending credit is 60 cartons. The profit margin (in present value terms) is:

    $$\frac{\$50}{1.015} - \$40 = \$9.261 \text{ per carton}$$

13. PV(COST) = 96

    PV(REV) = 101/1.01 = 100

    a.   The expected profit from a sale is:
$$[0.93 \times (\$100 - \$96)] - (0.07 \times \$96) = -\$3$$

The firm should *not* extend credit.

    b.   At the break-even probability, expected profit equals zero:
$$[p \times (\$100 - \$96)] - [(1 - p) \times \$96] = 0 \Rightarrow p = 0.96$$

So if the firm is to break even, 96% of its customers must pay their bills.

    c.   A paying customer now represents a *perpetuity* of profits equal to:
$$\$100 - \$96 = \$4 \text{ per month}$$

The present value is: $\$4/0.01 = \$400$

So the present value of a sale, given a 7% default rate, is:
$$(0.93 \times \$400) - (0.07 \times \$96) = \$365.28$$

It clearly pays to extend credit.

    d. $(p \times \$400) - [(1 - p) \times \$96] = 0 \Rightarrow p = 0.194 = 19.4\%$

So the probability of payment must be greater than 19.4% to justify extending credit.

---

14. a.   The expected profit for a sale is:
$$[0.95 \times (\$1,200 - \$1,050)] - (0.05 \times \$1,050) = \$90$$

    b.   The break-even probability of collection is found by solving for p as follows:
$$[p \times (\$1,200 - \$1,050)] - [(1 - p) \times \$1,050] = 0 \Rightarrow p = 1,050/1,200 = 0.875$$

15. From the discussion in the text regarding financial ratios (see Chapter 4), important ratios to consider are:

- Cash flow/Total debt
- Net income/Total assets
- Total debt/Total assets
- Working capital/Total assets
- Current assets/Current liabilities

16. The cost is $50.

$$PV \text{ (revenues)} = \frac{\$60}{(1.08)^{1/2}} = \$57.74$$

The expected profit for the order is therefore:

$$[0.75 \times (57.74 - 50)] - (0.25 \times 50) = -\$6.70 \text{ per iron}$$

You should reject the order.

17. The more stringent policy should be adopted because profit will increase, as shown in the following table. For every $100 of current sales:

	Current Policy	More Stringent Policy
Sales	100.0	95.0
Less bad debts*	6.0	3.8
Less cost of goods**	80.0	76.0
Profits	14.0	15.2

*6% of sales under current policy; 4% under proposed policy.
**80% of sales

18. a. Allowing for the possibility of default, the present value of a sale under current credit terms is:

$$\left[0.75 \times \left(\frac{15}{1.01} - 10 \right) \right] - (0.25 \times 10) = 1.14$$

Under a cash-on-delivery policy, sales would be 40% lower, but defaults and the time value cost of extended credit would be eliminated. Present value (assuming sales volume equal to 60% of current levels) would be:

$$0.6 \times (15 - 10) = 3$$

The switch to a COD policy seems to make sense.

b. If customers who pay bills on time generate six additional repeat sales, then each successful sale is repeated an additional six times; in contrast, a defaulting sale occurs only once. The PV of a credit sale becomes (note that the 6-month annuity factor for 1% per month is 5.7955):

$$\left[0.75 \times \left(\frac{15}{1.01} - 10 \right) \right] + \left[0.75 \times \left(\frac{15}{1.01} - 10 \right) \right]$$

$$\times \text{annuity factor}(1\%, 6 \text{ months}) - (0.25 \times 10) = \$22.23$$

The present value of a cash-on-delivery policy given the lower sales volume is:

$$0.60 \times [(15 - 10) + (15 - 10) \times \text{Annuity factor}(1\%, 6 \text{ months})] = \$20.39$$

In this case, repeat sales make the extension of credit a preferable strategy.

19. Profits from cash sales are currently: $100 \times (\$101 - \$80) = \$2,100$

    a. If one month (30 days) free credit is granted, the present value of revenue per unit decreases to: $\$101/1.01 = \$100$

    Assuming that both old and new customers take advantage of the free credit, the present value of profits will increase to: $110 \times (\$100 - \$80) = \$2,200$

    Allowing trade credit therefore is beneficial.

    b. Now assume that 5% of all customers will default on their bills. The expected value of (discounted) profits becomes:

$$\text{Units sold} \times [p \times PV(REV - COST) - (1 - p) \times PV(COST)] =$$

$$\$110 \times [0.95 \times (\$100 - \$80) - (0.05 \times \$80)] = \$1,650$$

    This is less than current profit of $2,100, which means that trade credit should not be allowed.

    c. If only *new* customers pose default risk, you need to look at the incremental profit from the new customers the firm will attract by relaxing credit policy minus the value of the free credit that the firm extends to its current customers. The free credit costs the firm $1 per current customer, since the present value of a sale falls from $101 to $100.

    Value of new customers $= 10 \times [0.95 \times (\$100 - \$80) - (0.05 \times \$80)] = \$150$

    Cost of free credit to current customers $= 100 \times \$1 = \$100$

    Net benefit from advancing credit $= \$150 - \$100 = \$50$

    Now it appears worthwhile to allow trade credit.

20.   a. Collection float decreases by: $15,000 per day $\times$ 2 days saved $= \$30,000$

    b. Daily interest saving $= 0.0002 \times \$30,000 = \$6$

    c. Monthly savings $= 30 \times \$6 = \$180$
    This is the maximum fee Sherman's should pay.

21.   a. The lock box will collect an average of: $300,000/30 = \$10,000$ per day

    The money will be available three days earlier; this will increase the cash available to JAC by $30,000. Thus, JAC will be better off accepting the compensating balance offer: $25,000 is tied up in the compensating balance, but the lock-box frees up $30,000.

    b. Let x equal the average check size for break-even. Then the number of checks written per month is $(300,000/x)$ and the monthly cost of the lockbox is:

$$(300,000/x) \times 0.10$$

The alternative is the compensating balance of $25,000; its monthly cost is the lost interest, which is equal to:

$$\$25,000 \times (0.06/12)$$

These costs are equal if:

$$(\$300,000/x) \times 0.10 = \$25,000 \times (0.06/12) \Rightarrow x = \$240$$

If the average check size is greater than $240, then paying per check is less costly; if the average check size is less than $240, then the compensating balance arrangement is less costly.

c. In part (a), we compared balances with balances: how many dollars are made available to JAC compared to the number of dollars required to be kept in the bank. In part (b), one cost is compared to another. The interest forgone by holding the compensating balances is compared to the cost of processing checks, and so here we need to know the interest rate.

22. Total compensating balances increase by $100,000. However, collection float decreases by $1 million. Opening the new account increases funds on which the firm can earn interest by $900,000. The firm should open the account.

23. With an increase in the rate of interest, the opportunity cost of holding cash increases. This decreases cash balances relative to sales.

24. PV(REV) = $1,200
     PV(COST) = $1,000

Slow payers have a 70% probability of paying their bills. The expected profit from a sale to a slow payer is therefore:

$$[0.70 \times (\$1,200 - \$1,000)] - (0.30 \times \$1,000) = -\$160$$

The expected savings from the credit check equals the probability of uncovering a slow payer times the expected loss saved by denying credit to the slow payer:

$$0.10 \times \$160 = \$16$$

The credit check costs $5, so Cast Iron should undertake the credit check.

25. The possibility of collecting a portion of the amount owed to the firm reduces the expected loss from advancing credit to slow payers and reduces the incentive to pay for a credit check. Even with a relatively high probability of default, the prospect of collecting a portion of the bad debt may mean that you would choose to advance credit to these customers.

26. Let n equal the average collection period, in days. Then, for every $100 in sales:

$$PV(REV) = \frac{\$100}{(1.15)^{n/365}}$$

Costs = 85 percent of $100 = $85

Classification	Collection Period	PV(REV)
1	45	$100/(1.15)^{(45/365)} = $98.29
2	42	$100/(1.15)^{(42/365)} = $98.40
3	50	$100/(1.15)^{(50/365)} = $98.10
4	85	$100/(1.15)^{(85/365)} = $96.80

Classification	Probability	$[p \times PV(REV - COST)] - [(1 - p) \times COST]$
1	1.00	$1.00 \times (\$98.29 - \$85) = \$13.29$
2	0.98	$[0.98 \times (\$98.40 - \$85)] - (0.02 \times \$85) = \$11.43$
3	0.90	$[0.90 \times (\$98.10 - \$85)] - (0.10 \times \$85) = \$3.29$
4	0.80	$[0.80 \times (\$96.80 - \$85)] - (0.20 \times \$85) = -\$7.56$

If customers can be classified without cost, then Velcro should sell only to groups 1, 2, and 3. The exception would be if non-defaulting group 4 accounts subsequently become regular and reliable customers (i.e., become members of group 1, 2, or 3). In that case, extending credit to *new* group 4 customers would be profitable.

27. a. For every $100 in current sales, Galenic has $5.00 profit (ignoring bad debts); this implies costs of $95.00. If the bad debt ratio is 1%, then, per $100 sales, the bad debts will be $1 and actual profit will be $4.00, a net profit margin of 4%.

   b. Sales will fall to 91.6% of their previous level ($9,160/$10,000), or to $91.60 per $100 of original sales. With a cost-to-revenue ratio of 95%, total costs (ignoring bad debts) will be:

   $$0.95 \times \$91.60 = \$87.02$$

   Bad debts will be: $(\$60/\$9,160) \times \$91.60 = \$0.60$

   Under the new scoring system, profit per $100 of original sales will be:

   $$\$91.60 - \$87.02 - \$0.60 = \$3.98$$

   Profit will be slightly less than under the current policy. Although the profit *margin* is higher, sales are lower and total profit decreases slightly. Therefore, the new scoring system reduces Galenic's profit by denying credit to this group.

   Another way to see this is to compute the expected profit on the 'worse than 80' group: probability of default = 40/840 = 1/21

Therefore, the expected profit for $100 of sales is:

$$[p \times PV(REV - COST)] - [(1 - p) \times PV(COST)] = \left[\frac{20}{21} \times (100 - 95)\right] - \left[\frac{1}{21} \times 95\right] = 0.24$$

This result is small, but positive. Therefore, denying credit to this group would reduce expected profit by a small amount.

c. There are many reasons why the estimated and actual default rates may differ. For example, the credit scoring system is based on historical data and does not allow for changing customer behavior; also, the estimation process ignores data from loan applications that have been rejected, which may lead to biases in the credit scoring system.

d. If one of the variables in the proposed scoring system is whether the customer has an existing account with Galenic, the credit scoring system is likely to be biased because it will ignore the potential profit from new customers who might generate repeat orders.

Solution to Minicase for Chapter 20

1.   Relevant credit information:

i.   Earnings record is only fair.

ii.   Expectation that MS will pay its bills slowly.

iii.   The firm has a $5 million line of credit, but it is facing a pending renegotiation of its $15 million term loan.

iv.   Some of MS's financial ratios are as follows:

$$\text{Long-term debt ratio} = \frac{40.8}{40.8 + 65.1} = 0.385$$

$$\frac{\text{market equity}}{\text{total book debt}} = \frac{58}{40.8 + 22.8} = 0.912$$

$$\frac{\text{retained earnings}}{\text{total assets}} = \frac{55.1}{147.7} = 0.373$$

$$\frac{\text{net working capital}}{\text{total assets}} = \frac{48.7 - 41.8}{147.7} = 0.047$$

$$\text{Current ratio} = \frac{48.7}{41.8} = 1.165$$

$$\text{Quick ratio} = \frac{5 + 16.2}{41.8} = 0.507$$

$$\text{Asset turnover} = \frac{\text{Sales}}{\text{total assets}} = \frac{149.8}{(147.7 + 160.9)/2} = 0.971$$

$$\text{Inventory turnover} = \frac{131}{(27.5 + 32.5)/2} = 4.367$$

$$\frac{\text{EBIT}}{\text{average total assets}} = \frac{9}{(147.7 + 160.9)/2} = 0.0583 = 5.83\%$$

$$\text{Net profit margin} = \frac{\text{EBIT} - \text{tax}}{\text{Sales}} = \frac{9 - 1.4}{149.8} = 0.0507 = 5.07\%$$

$$\text{Return on equity} = \frac{2.5}{(65.1 + 74.4)/2} = 0.0358 = 3.58\%$$

In particular, the liquidity ratios for the firm are low. Also, both asset turnover and profit margin are below average. This lends some support to the decision to refuse credit.

The Z-score for MS is calculated as follows:

$$Z = \left(3.3 \times \frac{\text{EBIT}}{\text{total assets}}\right) + \left(1.0 \times \frac{\text{sales}}{\text{total assets}}\right) + \left(0.6 \times \frac{\text{market equity}}{\text{book debt}}\right) +$$

$$\left(1.4 \times \frac{\text{retained earnings}}{\text{total assets}}\right) + \left(1.2 \times \frac{\text{working capital}}{\text{total assets}}\right)$$

$$= (3.3 \times 0.0583) + (1.0 \times 0.971) + (0.6 \times 0.912) + (1.4 \times 0.373) + (1.2 \times 0.047) = 2.289$$

This Z-score is worse than the cut-off described in the text, indicating significant bankruptcy risk, and also would argue against extending credit.

2. **Breakeven probability of default**

At a purchase price of $10,000 the sale of each encapsulator will bring in $500 in profit, assuming that MS forgoes the discount. If it takes the discount, which seems unlikely, the net price would fall to $9,800 and the profit would fall to $300.

Assume first that, if MS pays, it does so on the due date, exactly 60 days after the sale. Then, at an 8% interest rate, the net present value of profit per unit is:

NPV per unit = PV(sales price) – cost of goods

$$\text{NPV per unit} = = \frac{\$10,000}{(1.08)^{60/365}} - \$9,500 = \$9,874 - \$9,500 = \$374$$

Therefore, the break-even probability is determined as follows:

$$(p \times 374) - [(1-p) \times 9,500] = 0 \Rightarrow p = 0.96$$

The sale has a positive NPV if the probability of collection exceeds 96 percent.

If MS pays 30 days slow (i.e., in 90 days), then the present value of the sale is less than $9,874 and, consequently, the break-even probability is even higher.

3. **Repeat orders**

Given MS's marginal, at best, credit rating and the break-even probability near 1.0, MS would not be given credit if this is a one-time sale. However, MEC believes that this sale will in all probability lead to more profitable sales in the future. Therefore, MEC will be willing to grant credit even when the probability of collection is considerably below 96 percent.

Solutions for Chapter 21

Mergers, Acquisitions and Corporate Control

1. a. Merging to achieve economies of scale makes economic sense.

   b. Merging to reduce risk by diversification does not make economic sense. Shareholders can diversify for themselves.

   c. Merging to redeploy cash might make economic sense, but note that there are other ways to redeploy excess cash besides using it to purchase another firm.

   d. Merging to increase earnings per share does not make economic sense.

2. The firms can benefit from operational efficiencies. Heating will be busier in the winter, Air Conditioning in the summer. By merging, the firms can even out the workload over the year and use their resources at full capacity.

3. a. True.

   b. False.

   c. True.

   d. True.

   e. Largely false. While there are some gains from mergers, they do not seem to be 'substantial.'

   f. False. In a tender offer, the acquirer 'goes over the heads' of management directly to the shareholders.

   g. False. This is not true when the acquired firm is paid for with stock.

4. a. LBO: Company or business bought out by private investors, largely debt-financed.

   b. Poison pill: Shareholders are issued rights to buy shares if bidder acquires large stake in the firm.

   c. Tender offer: Offer to buy shares directly from stockholders.

   d. Shark repellent: Changes in corporate charter designed to deter unwelcome takeover.

   e. Proxy contest: Attempt to gain control of a firm by winning the votes of its stockholders.

5. a. True

   b. True

   c. True

6. Pre-merger data:

Acquiring: Value = 10,000,000 × $40 = $400,000,000

Takeover Target: Value = 5,000,000 × $20 = $100,000,000

Gain from merger = $25,000,000

The merger gain per share of Takeover Target is: $25 million/5 million shares = $5

Thus, Acquiring can pay up to $25 per share for Target, $5 above the current price. If Acquiring pays this amount, the NPV of the merger to Acquiring will be zero.

7. Acquiring: Value = $400 million

P/E = 12

Earnings = $400 million/12 = $33.33 million

Target: Value = $100 million

P/E = 8

Earnings = $100 million/8 = $12.50 million

Merged: Value = $400 + $100 + $25 = $525 million

Current earnings = $33.33 + $12.50 = $45.83 million

P/E = $525/$45.83 = 11.46

The P/E of the merged firm is less than that of Acquiring.

8. a. The present value of the $500,000 annual savings is: $500,000/0.08 = $6.25 million

This is the gain from the merger.

b. The cost of the offer is: $14 million – $10 million = $4 million

c. NPV = $6.25 million – $4 million = $2.25 million

9. a. The merged company will have a total value of:

$20 million + $10 million + $6.25 million (from cost savings) = $36.25 million

Since the Pogo shareholders own half of the firm, their stock is now worth $18.125 million.

b. The cost of the stock alternative is $8.125 million. This is the increase in the value of the stock held by Pogo shareholders.

c. NPV = –$1.875 million. This equals the decrease in the value of the stock held by Velcro's original shareholders. It also equals gains from the merger, $6.25 million, minus the cost of the stock purchase, $8.125 million.

10. a. At a price of $25 per share, Immense will have to pay $25 million to Sleepy. The current value of Sleepy is $20 million and Immense believes it can increase the value by $5 million. So Immense would have to pay the full value of the target firm under the improved management; therefore, the deal would be a zero-NPV proposition for Immense. The deal is just barely acceptable for shareholders of Immense, and clearly attractive for Sleepy's shareholders. Therefore, it can be accomplished on a friendly basis.

   b. If Sleepy tries to get $28 a share, the deal will have negative NPV to Immense shareholders. There could not be a friendly takeover on this basis.

11.

	P/E	Shares	Price	EPS*	Earnings**
Castles in the Sand (CS)	10	2 million	$40	$4.00	$8.0 million
Firm Foundation (FF)	8	1 million	$20	$2.50	$2.5 million

   * EPS = Price divided by P/E ratio
   ** Earnings = EPS × Shares

   a. New shares issued = 0.5 million

   Total shares = 2.0 million + 0.5 million = 2.5 million

   Total earnings = $8 million + $2.5 million = $10.5 million

   EPS = $10.5 million/2.5 million = $4.20

   b. Value = (2 million × $40) + (1 million × $20) = $100 million

   Shares = 2.5 million

   Price = $100 million/2.5 million = $40 per share

   Thus CS shareholders' wealth is unchanged. FF shareholders have stock worth:

   $40 × 0.5 million = $20 million

   The value of FF is also unchanged.

   P/E of merged firm = $100 million/$10.5 million = 9.52

   The P/E of the merged firm is between the P/Es of the two original firms.

   c. If the P/E of CS remains at 10, the merged firm will sell for: $4.20 × 10 = $42

   The firm is thus worth: $42 × 2.5 million = $105 million

   Notice that the combined market value of the old firms was only $100 million.

   d. Gain to CS: $2/share × 2 million shares = $4 million

   Gain to FF: Value of new shares – Original value of firm =

   (0.5 million × $42) – $20 million = $1 million

   The total gain is thus $5 million, which is the increase in the combined market value of the firms.

12. SCC value = 3,000 × $50.00 = $150,000
     SDP value = 2,000 × $17.50 = $ 35,000
     Merger gain   = $ 15,000

   a. Cost of merger to SCC = ($20 − $17.50) × 2,000 = $5,000

   NPV = gain − cost = $15,000 − $5,000 = $10,000

   b. SCC will sell for its original price plus the per share NPV of the merger:

   $50 + ($10,000/3,000) = $53.33 which represents a 6.66% gain.

   The price of SDP will increase from $17.50 to the tender price of $20, a percentage gain of: $2.50/$17.50 = 0.1429 = 14.29%

   c. Shares issued to acquire SDP = 0.40 × 2,000 = 800 shares

   Value of merged firm: $150,000   (SCC)
                            + 35,000   (SDP)
                            + 15,000   (Merger gain)
                            $200,000

   Shares outstanding = 3,000 + 800 = 3,800

   Price = $200,000/3,800 = $52.63

   Notice that SCC sells for a lower post-merger price than in part (b), despite the fact that the terms of the merger *seemed* equivalent.

   d. NPV = Price gain per share × original shares outstanding.

   = $2.63 × 3,000 = $7,890

   This is less than the $10,000 NPV from part (a).

   Because SDP shareholders receive stock in SCC, and the price of SCC shares rises to reflect the NPV of the merger, SDP shareholders capture an extra part of the merger gains from SCC shareholders.

13. a. First note that, because there are no real gains from the merger, earnings and market value are equal to the respective sums of the values for each firm independently:

   Total market value = $4,000,000 + $5,000,000 = $9,000,000

   Total earnings = $200,000 + $500,000 = $700,000

   Because total earnings are $700,000 and earnings per share is $2.67, shares outstanding must be: $700,000/$2.67 = 262,172

   Price per share = $9,000,000/262,172 = $34.33

   Price-earnings ratio = $34.33/$2.67 = 12.86

b. World Enterprises originally had 100,000 shares outstanding. It must have issued $262{,}172 - 100{,}000 = 162{,}172$ new shares to take over Wheelrim and Axle. Because Wheelrim had 200,000 shares outstanding, we conclude that 162,172 World Enterprise shares were exchanged for 200,000 Wheelrim shares. Thus, 0.81 shares of World Enterprises were exchanged for each share of Wheelrim.

c. The cost of the merger is the difference between the value of the World Enterprises shares given to the Wheelrim shareholders and the value of Wheelrim. World Enterprise gave stock worth $\$34.33 \times 162{,}172 = \$5{,}567{,}365$ for a company worth \$5,000,000. The cost is thus \$567,365.

d. The World Enterprise shares outstanding before the merger decline in value by the cost of the merger (since there were no economic gains to offset the cost). The shares fall in value by \$567,365. The price of the original 100,000 shares falls to \$34.33 per share from an original value of \$40.

14. a. We can use the stock valuation formula from Chapter 6 to value the stream of dividends. The first step is to determine the discount rate for the common stock of Plastitoys (Company B, the acquired company). Use the current stock price, forecasted dividend, and forecasted growth rate to solve for r in the following equation:

$$P_0 = \frac{DIV_1}{r - g}$$

If the forecast dividend per share = DIV_1 = \$0.80 then:

$$\$20 = \frac{\$0.80}{r - 0.06} \Rightarrow r = 0.10$$

Under new management, the growth rate would increase to 8 percent, and Company B would be worth:

$$P_0 = \frac{\$0.80}{0.10 - 0.08} = \$40$$

The value of the combined firm (Company AB) is the sum of the value of the acquiring firm (Leisure Products, Company A), and the post-merger value of Plastitoys (Company B):

$$PV_{AB} = (1{,}000{,}000 \times \$90) + (600{,}000 \times \$40) = \$114{,}000{,}000$$

We now calculate the gain from the acquisition as:

$$Gain = PV_{AB} - (PV_A + PV_B)$$
$$= \$114{,}000{,}000 - (\$90{,}000{,}000 + \$12{,}000{,}000) = \$12{,}000{,}000$$

b. Because this is a cash acquisition:

$$Cost = Cash\ paid - PV_B = (\$25 \times 600{,}000) - \$12{,}000{,}000 = \$3{,}000{,}000$$

c. Because this merger is financed with stock, the cost depends on the value of the stock given to the shareholders of Plastitoys. In order to acquire Plastitoys, Leisure Products will have to offer: 600,000/3 = 200,000 shares

Therefore, after the merger, there will be 1,200,000 shares outstanding, and the value of the merged firm will be $114,000,000 (see part a).

Price per share = $114,000,000/1,200,000 = $95

Therefore:

$$\text{Cost} = \text{Value of shares offered to firm B} - PV_B$$

$$= (\$95 \times 200,000) - \$12,000,000 = \$7,000,000$$

d. If the acquisition is for cash, the cost of the merger is unaffected by the change in the forecasted growth rate. The price paid for Plastitoys is still $15,000,000 and its current value is still $12,000,000. The cost remains at $3,000,000.

If the acquisition is for stock, however, the value of the stock given to the shareholders of Plastitoys will be lower than under the original growth forecast. Therefore, the cost to Leisure Products will be lower.

If the value of Plastitoys is unaffected by the merger, then:

$$PV_{AB} = (\$90 \times 1,000,000) + (\$20 \times 600,000) = \$102,000,000$$

The new share price will be:

$$\$102,000,000/1,200,000 = \$85.00$$

Therefore, the cost of the merger is:

$$\text{Cost} = (\$85 \times 200,000) - (\$20 \times 600,000) = \$5,000,000$$

This is $2 million less than the original estimate.

Solution to Minicase for Chapter 21

The market values of the two firms in March, before McPhee's price increased in response to a possible takeover were:

McPhee: £4.90 × 5 million = £ 24.5 million

Fenton: £8.00 × 10 million = £ 80.0 million

Combined value: £104.5 million

We are told that the London stock market as a whole has been largely unchanged during this period, so we can assume that changes in the prices of McPhee and Fenton shares between March and June 11 are due to news about the potential merger.

After the takeover bid was announced, the combined market value of the two firms becomes:

McPhee: £6.32 × 5 million = £ 31.6 million

Fenton: £7.90 × 10 million = £ 79.0 million

Combined value: £110.6 million

Thus, the market agrees with Fenton that there are gains to be had from a merger and new management. Still, the market is not as optimistic as Fenton. The combined value of the shares increases by £6.1 million, which is less than Fenton's estimate of cost savings worth £10 million.

The gain of the merger based on the market's assessment is therefore £6.1 million. However, in light of the drop in the market value of Fenton stock, the cost must be greater than this amount. In fact, the cost to Fenton is the increase in the value of McPhee shares resulting from the announcement of the takeover bid – this is the premium paid to the McPhee shareholders. McPhee shares increase in value by £7.1 million, so the NPV of the merger to Fenton is:

Economic gain – costs = £6.1 – £7.1 = –£1 million

This is the amount by which the stock value declines.

It would not be wise for Fenton to sweeten its offer. The verdict of the market is that it already is paying more for McPhee than the company will be worth. Any increase in the offer would most likely further reduce the value of Fenton shares.

Solutions to Chapter 22

International Financial Management

1. a. You can buy: 100/1.4621 = 68.395 euros for $100
       You can buy: $100 \times 1.4621 = 146.21$ dollars for 100 euros

    b. You can buy: $100 \times 1.1322 = 113.22$ Swiss francs for $100

       You can buy: $100/1.1322 = 88.32$ dollars for 100 Swiss francs

    c. If the British pound depreciates, then $1 will buy more British pounds, so the direct exchange rate ($/£) will decrease and the indirect exchange rate (£/$) will increase.

    d. One U.S. dollar can buy .9870 Canadian dollars. Therefore, one U.S. dollar is worth less than one Canadian dollar.

2. a. 111.715 ¥/$

    b. 108.173 yen = 1 dollar

    c. The yen is selling at a forward premium on the dollar. You get fewer yen for each dollar in the forward market.

    d. $\dfrac{111.715 - 108.173}{108.173} = 0.0327 = 3.27\%$

    e. $\dfrac{1 + r_{¥}}{1 + r_{\$}} = \dfrac{f_{¥/\$}}{s_{¥/\$}}$

       $\dfrac{1 + r_{¥}}{1.041} = \dfrac{108.173}{111.715} \Rightarrow r_{¥} = 0.007994 = 0.80\%$

    f. 108.173 yen = 1 dollar

    g. $\dfrac{1 + i_{¥}}{1 + i_{\$}} = \dfrac{f_{¥/\$}}{s_{¥/\$}} = \dfrac{108.173}{111.715} = 0.9683$

3. a. The interest rate differential equals the forward premium or discount, i.e., for currency x:

$$\frac{1+r_x}{1+r_\$} = \frac{f_{x/\$}}{s_{x/\$}}$$

b. The expectations theory of forward rates, or the expectations theory of exchange rates, predicts that the forward rate equals the expected future spot exchange rate. Equivalently, the percentage difference between the forward rate and today's spot rate is equal to the expected percentage change in the spot rate:

$$\frac{f_{x/\$}}{s_{x/\$}} = \frac{E(s_{x/\$})}{s_{x/\$}}$$

c. Prices of goods in different countries are equal when translated to a common currency. It follows that the expected inflation differential equals the expected percentage change in the spot rate:

$$\frac{1+i_x}{1+i_\$} = \frac{E(s_{x/\$})}{s_{x/\$}}$$

d. Expected real interest rates in different countries are equal:

$$\frac{1+r_x}{E(1+i_x)} = \frac{1+r_\$}{E(1+i_\$)}$$

4. The following items are needed to do capital budgeting calculations in your own currency:
   - Forecasts of the foreign inflation rate to produce cash-flow forecasts
   - Forecasts of future exchange rates to convert cash flows into domestic currency
   - Domestic interest rates to discount domestic currency cash flows

5. If international capital markets are competitive, the real cost of funds in Japan must be the same as the real cost of funds elsewhere. That is, the low Japanese yen interest rate is likely to reflect the relatively low expected rate of inflation in Japan and the expected appreciation of the Japanese yen. Note that the parity relationships imply that the difference in interest rates is equal to the expected change in the spot exchange rate and also equal to the expected difference in inflation rates. If the funds are to be used outside Japan, Ms. Stone should consider whether to hedge against changes in the exchange rate, and how much this hedging will cost.

6. a. Buy euros forward. This locks in the dollar value of the euros that the importer will pay in six months.

7. If the dollar depreciates, then, in order to maintain a fixed yen price, Sanyo will need to raise the dollar price. This action can cause Sanyo to lose business in the U.S. It can hedge this exchange rate risk by selling dollars forward, so that any loss in U.S. profits due to dollar depreciation will be offset by gains on the forward sale of the dollar.

    Alternatively, Sanyo can fix the dollar price of its products. This means that its U.S. sales are independent of the exchange rate. But then the yen value of the dollar revenues that it realizes in the U.S. will decrease if the dollar depreciates. To reduce this exchange rate risk, Sanyo can sell dollars forward, meaning that its future dollar revenues can be exchanged for yen at the forward exchange rate.

8. The firm can borrow the present value of 1 million Australian dollars, sell those Australian dollars for U.S. dollars in the spot market, and invest the proceeds in an 8-year U.S. dollar loan. In 8 years, it can repay the Australian loan with the anticipated Australian dollar payment.

9.

	1 month	12 months
Dollar interest rate (annually compounded)	3.5%	4.10%
Lira interest rate (annually compounded)	16%	16.2% [b]
Forward lira per dollar [a]	1.1835 [c]	1.3090

Notes:

a. Spot Lira per dollar = 1.1723

b. To find this value we use the interest rate parity relationship. Denote the annual peso interest rate as r_x. Then:

$$\frac{1+r_x}{1+r_\$} = \frac{f_{x/\$}}{s_{x/\$}} \Rightarrow r_x = \left[\frac{f_{x/\$}}{s_{x/\$}} \times (1+r_\$)\right] - 1$$

$$r_x = \left[\frac{1.309}{1.1723} \times 1.041\right] - 1 = .162 = 16.2\%$$

c. Again, we can use interest rate parity, this time for a one-month horizon. Parity implies that:

$$f_{x/\$} = s_{x/\$} \times \frac{1+r_x}{1+r_\$} = 1.1723 \times \left(\frac{1.16}{1.035}\right)^{1/12} = 1.1835$$

We need to take the 1/12 power in the above equation because the interest rates in the table are expressed as effective annual (compounded) rates. We need to put the interest rates on a monthly basis to compute the one-month forward exchange rate.

10. Let $s_£$ represent the spot rate ($\$/£$) in one year. The rate of return to a U.S. investor is given by:

$$1 + r_\$ = (1 + r_£) \times (s_£/2)$$

If the pound appreciates (meaning that $s_£ > 2$), then the dollar-denominated return is higher. Since $(1 + r_£) = 1.04$ then:

$$1 + r_\$ = 1.04 \times (s_£/2)$$

	$s_£$	$r_\$$
a.	2	4.0%
b.	2.20	14%
c.	1.80	−6%

11. We can utilize the interest rate parity theorem:

$$\frac{1+r_£}{1+r_\$} = \frac{f_{£/\$}}{s_{£/\$}}$$

The indirect exchange rates are:

$$s_{£/\$} = 1/1.9906 = £\,0.5024/\$$$

$$f_{£/\$} = 1/1.9857 = £\,0.5036/\$$$

Remembering that we are using 3-month interest rates expressed as annual rates, we have:

$$\frac{(1+r_£)^{1/4}}{(1+0.035)^{1/4}} = \frac{0.5036}{0.5024} \Rightarrow r_£ = 0.0277 = 2.77\%$$

If the sterling interest rate were higher than this, you could earn an immediate arbitrage profit by buying sterling, investing in a 3-month sterling deposit and selling the proceeds forward.

12. a. The Canadian dollar is at a forward discount. It takes more Canadian dollars to buy one U.S dollar in the forward market than in the spot market.

    b. $\dfrac{0.9870 - 0.9884}{0.9884} = 0.00142$ or a 0.142% discount

    c. Using the expectations theory of exchange rates, the forecast is:
    $1 (US) = 0.9884 Canadian dollars.

    d. $100,000/0.9884 = \$101,173.60$ (US)

13. The interest rate in the U.S. is 5%. Borrowing or lending in the U.K. and covering interest rate risk with futures or forwards offers a rate of return of:

$$r_\$ = \left[(1 + r_£) \times \left(\frac{f_{\$/£}}{s_{\$/£}}\right)\right] - 1 = \left[1.05 \times \frac{1.84}{1.87}\right] - 1 = 0.0332 = 3.32\%$$

It appears advantageous to borrow in the U.S. where the rate is lower, and to lend in the U.K. where the rate is higher. In other words, the interest rate parity relationship is violated.

An arbitrage strategy to take advantage of this violation involves simultaneous lending and borrowing with the covering of exchange rate risk:

Action Now	CF in $	Action at period-end	CF in $
Lend £1.0 in U.K.	−$1.87	Loan repaid; Exchange proceeds for dollars	$1.05 \times E_1$
Borrow in U.S.	$1.87	Repay loan	-1.87×1.03
Sell forward £ 1.05 for $1.84/£ (i.e., sell forward proceeds from the U.K loan)	$0.00	Unwind	$1.05 \times (1.84 - E_1)$
TOTAL	$0.00		$0.0059

This strategy thus provides a *riskless* payoff of $0.0059 (for every pound loaned in the U.K.) with an initial cash outflow of *zero*. It is a pure arbitrage opportunity. With no money down, you can earn riskless profits; clearly, you (and other investors) would pursue this strategy to the fullest extent possible. As a result, we would expect the price pressure from this arbitrage activity to restore the interest-rate parity relationship.

14. According to purchasing power parity, the Canadian dollar should be depreciating relative to the U.S. dollar. The purchasing power of Canadian dollars is falling faster than that of U.S. dollars. Therefore, the number of U.S. dollars that can be obtained for one Canadian dollar should be falling.

15. 936.050 Koren won per dollar

    111.715 yen per dollar

    Since 111.715 yen have the same value as 936.05 Won, each won should be worth: 111.715/936.05 = .119347 yen

    So the bank would quote an exchange rate of ¥.119347/Korean Won. If it did not, you could earn riskless profits.

    Suppose that the exchange rate were ¥.11/Korean Won. Then an investor could:

    (1) Convert $1 into ¥111.715
    (2) Convert the ¥111.715 into: 111.715/.11 = 1015.59 Won
    (3) Convert the Korean Won into: 1015.59/936.05 = $1.09

    The investor therefore immediately and risklessly converts $1 into $1.09.

16. The forecasted leos cash flows are converted into dollars at the spot rate that is forecast for each date. The current spot rate is 2 leos per dollar, but the leo is expected to depreciate at 2% per year.

Year	0	1	2	3	4	5
Leo cash flow, millions	−7.600	2.000	2.500	3.000	3.500	4.000
Forecast exchange rate	2.000	2.040	2.081	2.122	2.165	2.208
$ cash flow, millions	−3.800	0.980	1.201	1.414	1.617	1.812

At a discount rate of 15%, the net present value of the dollar cash flows is $0.72 million.

[NOTE: As we point out in the text, we think it is poor practice to combine the profits from the Narnian operation with the profits that are expected from guessing the direction of currency movements. The exchange rate forecasts used in the problem are inconsistent with the interest rate and inflation rate forecasts. It makes more sense to first consider whether the project is worthwhile, and then to determine whether the firm should hedge against, or bet on, exchange rate changes.]

17.

	Dollar value of euro revenue given exchange rate		Additional income from forward contract given exchange rate		Total profit (or loss) given exchange rate	
Revenue in euros (million)	1.35	1.55	1.35	1.55	1.35	1.55
1 (Receive order)	1.35	1.55	+0.08	−0.12	+1.43	+1.43
0 (Lose order)	0.00	0.00	+0.08	−0.12	+0.08	−0.12

Note: profit on the forward contract = forward rate − ultimate spot exchange rate

$$= 1.43 - \text{spot rate}$$

Selling the euros forward results in a hedged position only if the export order is received and the firm receives euro-denominated cash flows. In this case, the profit on the forward sale offsets the fluctuation in the dollar value of the euro revenue. However, if the order is not received, euro revenue will be zero and the forward sale of euros *introduces* foreign exchange exposure.

18. a. Revenue is in Trinidadian dollars, whereas the U.S. firm is concerned with the U.S. dollar value of revenue. Therefore, the value of the revenues in U.S. dollars depends on the exchange rate at the time the goods are sold.

b. If the U.S. firm borrows in Trinidad and converts the borrowed funds to dollars, the future revenue in Trinidadian dollars can be used to pay off the Trinidadian debt. Therefore, the loan offsets the exposure created by foreign-currency denominated cash inflows.

c. Now costs as well as revenues are foreign currency denominated. The firm's foreign exchange exposure is based on its net profits rather than its gross revenue. Therefore, its exposure is mitigated.

19.   a.   Most revenues are in dollars while a large fraction of cost is in Swiss francs. If the Swiss franc appreciates, then net cash flow will decline when expressed in a common currency (either dollars or Swiss francs). The stock price will fall.

      b.   Nestle's net cash flow as measured in a non-Swiss currency, such as U.S. dollars, will be largely unaffected by the appreciation of the Swiss franc since neither costs nor revenues are denominated in Swiss francs. However, the value of the cash flow stream (which is in non-Swiss currencies) will fall as measured in Swiss francs. Therefore, the dollar value of Nestle stock might be unaffected, but the Swiss franc value of the stock might fall.

      c.   Costs are in Swiss francs. The Swiss franc value of revenues is hedged. So the Swiss franc value of Union Bank should be unaffected by the appreciation.

20.   <u>Do calculations in U.S. dollars:</u>

Period:	1	2	3
Real cash flow (thousands of pesos)	250,000	250,000	250,000
Nominal cash flow (thousands of pesos)	260,000	270,400	281,216
Forecast exchange rate *	11.2291	11.5531	11.8863
Nominal cash flow ($ million)	23.154	23.405	23.659
PV of cash flows	20.673	18.658	16.840

* From purchasing power parity:

$$\text{expected spot rate} = \text{current spot rate} \times \left(\frac{1+r_p}{1+r_\$}\right)^T = 10.9143 \times \left(\frac{1.07}{1.04}\right)^T$$

** Discount rate = interest rate + risk premium = $0.04 + 0.08 = 0.12 = 12.0\%$

Project cost (in dollars) = 500 million/10.9143 = $45.812 million

NPV = –$45.812 + $20.673 + $18.658 + $16.840 = $10.356 million

21. a. The exchange rate exposure for Cookham Industries is shown in the graph below:

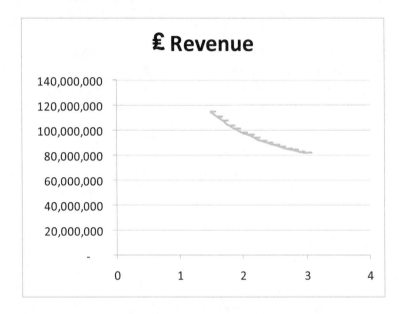

Cookham's British pound revenue varies from a high of £114,625,000 if the exchange rate is $1.50/£, to a low of £81,250,000 if the exchange rate rises to $3/£.

b. Given the demand function (Quantity sold = 1,000,000 – 100 × Price), Cookham's expected dollar revenue is $207,931,250 has shown in the Excel table below:

Cookham Industries
Current Exchange Rate =   2

Exchange Rate	Dollar Price	Quantity Sold	$ Revenue
1.5	175	982,500	171,937,500
1.6	180	982,000	176,760,000
1.7	185	981,500	181,577,500
1.8	190	981,000	186,390,000
1.9	195	980,500	191,197,500
2	200	980,000	196,000,000
2.1	205	979,500	200,797,500
2.2	210	979,000	205,590,000
2.3	215	978,500	210,377,500
2.4	220	978,000	215,160,000
2.5	225	977,500	219,937,500
2.6	230	977,000	224,710,000
2.7	235	976,500	229,477,500
2.8	240	976,000	234,240,000
2.9	245	975,500	238,997,500
3	250	975,000	243,750,000

| | | Expected $ Rev | 207,931,250 |

Selling forward Cookham's expected dollar revenue is not an effective hedge as the exposure is simply reversed.

Cookham Industries
Current Exchange Rate =   2

Exchange Rate	Dollar Price	Quantity Sold	$ Revenue	£ Revenue	£ Gain(Loss) Forward Hedge	Forward Hedge £ Revenue
1.5	175	982,500	171,937,500	114,625,000	(34,655,208)	79,969,792
1.6	180	982,000	176,760,000	110,475,000	(25,991,406)	84,483,594
1.7	185	981,500	181,577,500	106,810,294	(18,346,875)	88,463,419
1.8	190	981,000	186,390,000	103,550,000	(11,551,736)	91,998,264
1.9	195	980,500	191,197,500	100,630,263	(5,471,875)	95,158,388
2	200	980,000	196,000,000	98,000,000	-	98,000,000
2.1	205	979,500	200,797,500	95,617,857	4,950,744	100,568,601
2.2	210	979,000	205,590,000	93,450,000	9,451,420	102,901,420
2.3	215	978,500	210,377,500	91,468,478	13,560,734	105,029,212
2.4	220	978,000	215,160,000	89,650,000	17,327,604	106,977,604
2.5	225	977,500	219,937,500	87,975,000	20,793,125	108,768,125
2.6	230	977,000	224,710,000	86,426,923	23,992,067	110,418,990
2.7	235	976,500	229,477,500	84,991,667	26,954,051	111,945,718
2.8	240	976,000	234,240,000	83,657,143	29,704,464	113,361,607
2.9	245	975,500	238,997,500	82,412,931	32,265,194	114,678,125
3	250	975,000	243,750,000	81,250,000	34,655,208	115,905,208
		Expected $ Rev	207,931,250			
		Exposure £		(16,750,000)		(18,030,208)

c. A hedge ratio based on the change in revenue and exchange rates provides a perfect hedge. See the Excel table below:

Cookham Industries
Current Exchange Rate =   2

Exchange Rate	Dollar Price	Quantity Sold	$ Revenue	£ Revenue	£ Gain(Loss) Forward Hedge	Forward Hedge £ Revenue	Hedge Ratio	£ Gain(Loss) Hedge	£ Revenue
1.5	175	982,500	171,937,500	114,625,000	(34,655,208)	79,969,792	100,125,000	(16,687,500)	97,937,500
1.6	180	982,000	176,760,000	110,475,000	(25,991,406)	84,483,594	100,125,000	(12,515,625)	97,959,375
1.7	185	981,500	181,577,500	106,810,294	(18,346,875)	88,463,419	100,125,000	(8,834,559)	97,975,735
1.8	190	981,000	186,390,000	103,550,000	(11,551,736)	91,998,264	100,125,000	(5,562,500)	97,987,500
1.9	195	980,500	191,197,500	100,630,263	(5,471,875)	95,158,388	100,125,000	(2,634,868)	97,995,395
2	200	980,000	196,000,000	98,000,000	-	98,000,000	100,125,000	-	98,000,000
2.1	205	979,500	200,797,500	95,617,857	4,950,744	100,568,601	100,125,000	2,383,929	98,001,786
2.2	210	979,000	205,590,000	93,450,000	9,451,420	102,901,420	100,125,000	4,551,136	98,001,136
2.3	215	978,500	210,377,500	91,468,478	13,560,734	105,029,212	100,125,000	6,529,891	97,998,370
2.4	220	978,000	215,160,000	89,650,000	17,327,604	106,977,604	100,125,000	8,343,750	97,993,750
2.5	225	977,500	219,937,500	87,975,000	20,793,125	108,768,125	100,125,000	10,012,500	97,987,500
2.6	230	977,000	224,710,000	86,426,923	23,992,067	110,418,990	100,125,000	11,552,885	97,979,808
2.7	235	976,500	229,477,500	84,991,667	26,954,051	111,945,718	100,125,000	12,979,167	97,970,833
2.8	240	976,000	234,240,000	83,657,143	29,704,464	113,361,607	100,125,000	14,303,571	97,960,714
2.9	245	975,500	238,997,500	82,412,931	32,265,194	114,678,125	100,125,000	15,536,638	97,949,569
3	250	975,000	243,750,000	81,250,000	34,655,208	115,905,208	100,125,000	16,687,500	97,937,500
		Expected $ Rev	207,931,250						
		Exposure £		(16,750,000)		(18,030,208)			(62,500)

This hedge ratio performs better than that in part b because fewer dollars are sold forward when the exchange rate moves against Cookham.

Solution to Minicase for Chapter 22

The points you should make are:

a. When judging the cost of forward cover, the relevant comparison is between the forward rate and the *expected* spot rate. Since the forward rate is *on average* close to the subsequent spot rate, the cost of insurance is low.

b. The firm could buy spot yen today but would then receive the low yen rate of interest for 1 year rather than the higher dollar rate. Interest rate parity states that the two methods of hedging (buying yen forward or buying spot and investing in yen deposits) have similar cost.

c. The yen interest rate is likely to be low because investors expect the yen to appreciate against the dollar. The firm can expect the benefit of borrowing at the low interest rate to be offset by the extra cost of buying yen to pay the interest and principal. Also, borrowing yen would add currency risk and it would be odd to do this at the same time as buying yen and putting them on deposit.

Solutions to Chapter 23

Options

1. Payoff and profit if stock price on expiration date = $720:

	Cost	Payoff	Profit
Call option, X = 620	123.1	100	1.32–
Put option, X = 620	19.9	0	9.91–
Call option, X = 720	55.5	0	–55.5
Put option, X = 720	52	0	–52
Call option, X = 820	17.9	0	–17.9
Put option, X = 820	115.2	100	–15.2

2. a. Payoff and profit if stock price on expiration date = $780:

	Cost	Payoff	Profit
Call option, X = 620	123.1	160	9.63
Put option, X = 620	19.9	0	9.91–
Call option, X = 720	55.5	60	4.5
Put option, X = 720	52	0	–52
Call option, X = 820	17.9	0	–17.9
Put option, X = 820	115.2	40	–75.2

   b. Payoff and profit if stock price on expiration date = $680:

	Cost	Payoff	Profit
Call option, X = 620	123.1	60	1.36–
Put option, X = 620	19.9	0	9.91–
Call option, X = 720	55.5	0	–55.5
Put option, X = 720	52	40	–12
Call option, X = 820	17.9	0	–17.9
Put option, X = 820	115.2	140	24.8

3. a. The price of the March 2008 call with exercise price of $720 is $55.50. The price of the January 2009 call with exercise price of $720 is $121.30.

   b. The January 2009 calls cost more than the March 2008 calls because there is more uncertainty about the stock price in January 2009 than there is about the stock price in March 2008, and uncertainty surrounding the stock price makes options more valuable.

c. This is true of put options as well. The March 2008 put with exercise price of $720 has a price of $52.00, while the January 2009 put with exercise price of $720 has a price of $121.70. The reason this is true for puts is the same reason that it is true for calls; i.e., there is greater uncertainty about the stock price in January 2009 than there is about stock price in March 2008, and uncertainty surrounding the stock price makes the put options more valuable.

4. call; exercise; put; exercise

5. Figure 23-7(a) represents a call seller; Figure 23-7(b) represents a call buyer.

6. Consider options with exercise price of $100. Call the stock price at the expiration date S.

	Payoff to option position at expiration	
	$S < 100$	$S \geq 100$
Call option buyer	0	$S - 100$
Put option seller	$S - 100$	0

While it is true that both call buyers and put sellers hope that the stock price increases, the positions are not equivalent.

7. a. The value of the portfolio is equal to the exercise price of the put option, $100 (i.e., you would exercise the option to sell the share of stock for the $100 exercise price).

   b. The value of the portfolio is equal to the value of the stock (i.e., you would throw away the put and either keep the share of stock or sell it at the market price).

8. Consider options with exercise price of $100. Call the stock price at the expiration date S.

   a.

	Value of asset at option expiration	
	$S < 100$	$S \geq 100$
Buy a call	0	$S - 100$
Invest PV(100)	100	100
Total	100	S

   b.

	Value of asset at option expiration	
	$S < 100$	$S \geq 100$
Buy a share	S	S
Buy a put	$100 - S$	0
Total	100	S

c.

	Value of asset at option expiration	
	S < 100	S ≥ 100
Buy a share	S	S
Buy a put	100 – S	0
Sell a call	0	100 – S
Total	100	100

d.

	Value of asset at option expiration	
	S < 100	S ≥ 100
Buy a call	0	S – 100
Buy a put	100 – S	0
Total	100 – S	S – 100

9. a. The package of investments that would provide the set of payoffs depicted in Figure 23-8 is: buy a March 2008 call with exercise price $720 and buy a March 2008 put with exercise price $720.

 b. Table 23-2 shows that, in December this package would have cost:

 $55.5 + $52 = $107.50

 c. Table 23-2 indicates that, in December 2007, the price of Google stock was $720. An investor who believed that the price of Google would vary considerably between December 2007 and March 2008 might invest in this package. The greater the change in price from $720, the greater the payoff to the straddle position.

10. The lower bound is the call option's value if it expired immediately: either zero, or the stock price less the exercise price, whichever is greater. The upper bound is the stock price.

11. a. Zero

 b. Stock price less the present value of the exercise price.

12. Let X denote the exercise price:

	Payoff to option position at expiration			
	$S < 620$	$620 < S < 720$	$720 < S < 820$	$S \geq 820$
Buy call (X = 620)	0	$S - 620$	$S - 620$	$S - 620$
Sell 2 calls (X = 720)	0	0	$-2(S - 720)$	$-2(S - 720)$
Buy call (X = 200)	0	0	0	$S - 820$
Total	0	$S - 620$	$820 - S$	0

Notice that, if S is between 620 and 820 at option expiration, the total payoff to the portfolio is positive. Otherwise the total payoff is zero. This portfolio has only nonnegative payoffs. But it has zero cost if the price of the X = 720 call is equal to the average of the prices of the other two calls. This situation cannot persist. At a cost of zero, all investors will attempt to buy an unlimited amount of this portfolio. We conclude that the price of the X = 720 call must be *less than* the average of the prices of the other two calls. In this case, the cost of establishing the portfolio is positive, which is consistent with the nonnegative payoffs to the portfolio.

13. a. Decreases

    b. Increases

    c. Decreases (The present value of the exercise price decreases.)

    d. Increases

    e. Decreases

    f. Decreases

14. If you hold call options, then you will be tempted to choose the high-risk proposal. This increases the expected payoff and therefore the value of your options. (Notice that the options introduce a potential conflict of interest between managers and shareholders. The options can lead managers to *prefer* projects with high volatility.)

15. a. call

    b. put

    c. put (You can think of the ability to sell the machine as analogous to a put option with 'exercise price' equal to the price of the machine in the secondhand market.)

16. a. The project gives the firm a call option to pursue (buy) a project [the project is potential expansion of the existing switching project] in the future if that project turns out to be valuable.

    b. The real option is the ability to sell the equipment. This is a put option that would not be available if the firm were to choose the more specialized equipment.

17. a. This is a 5-year call option on oil. The exercise price is $15 per barrel, the price at which the crude can be developed.

    b. This is a put option to abandon the restaurant for an exercise price of $5 million. The restaurant's current value is given by the perpetuity value ($700,000/r), which is the value of the 'underlying asset.'

18. The price support system gives farmers the right to sell their crops to the government. This is a put option with exercise price equal to the support price.

19. a. If the portfolio value exceeds the threshold, the manager's bonus is proportional to the difference between the portfolio value and the threshold. If the stock price is below the threshold, the manager gets nothing. This is just like the payoff to a call option on the portfolio with exercise price equal to the threshold. The call would also provide a payment only if the portfolio value exceeds a threshold value equal to the exercise price.

    b. Such contracts could induce managers to increase portfolio risk since that would increase the value of the implicit call option.

20. a. Rank and File has an option to put (sell) the stock to the underwriter.

    b. The value of the option depends on the volatility of the stock value, the length of the period for which the underwriter guarantees the issue, the interest rate, the price at which the underwriter is obligated to buy the stock, and the market value of the stock in the absence of the underwriter's guarantee.

21. a. Because the depositor receives a zero rate of return if the market declines and a proportion of any rise in the market index, the depositor has a payoff that is effectively the same as that on a call option on the index. One way for the bank to hedge its position is to purchase call options on the market index. That way, the options implicitly sold are hedged by the options purchased.

    b. In this case, the depositor has in effect purchased a put option from the bank. To hedge, the bank should purchase puts to offset the exposure of the puts implicitly sold.

22. The FDIC pays out an amount equal to deposits minus bank assets if assets are insufficient to cover all deposits. This is the payoff to a put option on the bank assets with exercise price equal to the deposits owed to bank customers.

23. The projects would give the U.S. the ability to 'buy' energy for the fixed cost of the synthetic fuels. This is a call option with exercise price equal to the cost of synthetic fuel. Greater uncertainty in oil prices would increase the value of the option, and should make investors willing to spend more to develop such technologies.

24. a. Buy a call option for $3.
   Exercise the call to purchase stock.
   Pay the $20 exercise price.
   Sell the share for $25.
   Riskless profit = $25 − ($3 + $20) = $2

   As investors rush to pursue this strategy, they will drive up the call price until the profit opportunity disappears.

   b. Buy a share and a put option for a total outlay of: $25 + $4 = $29
   Immediately exercise the put to sell the share for $30.
   Riskless profit = $30 − $29 = $1

25. At an 8 percent yield to maturity, a 10-year, 6 percent coupon bond ordinarily would sell for:

   [$60 × annuity factor(8%, 10 years)] + $1,000/(1.08)^{10} =

   $$\$60\times\left[\frac{1}{0.08}-\frac{1}{0.08\times(1.08)^{10}}\right]+\frac{\$1,000}{1.08^{10}}=\$865.80$$

   Therefore, the bondholder's call option is worth: $1,050 − $865.80 = $184.20
   The bond is also worth more than the shares it can be converted into. This is because the bond has a 'floor' value equal to its value as a 'straight' 6% coupon bond. Even if the stock price declines significantly, the bond will not sell for less than the straight bond value. This extra protection makes the bond worth more than the shares it can be converted into.

26. a. The package of investments that would provide the set of payoffs depicted in Figure 23-9 is: buy one March 2008 call with exercise price $620, sell two March 2008 calls with exercise price $720, and buy one March 2008 call with exercise price $820. (Payoffs for a butterfly spread are also shown in the table for the solution to Problem 12.)

   b. Table 23-2 shows that, in December 2007, this butterfly spread (with a March 2006 expiration date, for example) would have cost:

   $123.10 − (2 × $55.50) + $17.90 = $30.00

c. In contrast to the straddle described in Problem 9, an investor who takes a position in a butterfly spread expects price to remain relatively unchanged between December 2007 and March 2008. The closer the price of Google stock remains to its December 2007 price of $720, the greater the payoff to the butterfly position.

27. a. If the stock price is $1,440, then the call will be worth: $1,440 – $720 = $720

   If the stock price is $360, then the call will be worthless.

   b.

	Payoff at option expiration	
	S = 360	S = 1,440
3 calls (X = 720)	0	2160
Value of 2 shares	720	2880
Repay loan	–720	–720
Total	0	2160

   c. The net outlay required to buy two shares and borrow the PV of $720 is:

   $$(2 \times \$720) - (\$720/1.0159) = \$731.27$$

   d. The three calls must also sell for $731.27, since the payoff to the calls is identical to the payoff to the shares-plus-borrowing position. Therefore, each call option sells for: $731.27/3 = $243.76

   e. The call option in this problem is worth more than the value derived in the example in the chapter. This is because the higher volatility assumed in this example increases the value of the call.

28. Return to the example in the chapter. If the interest rate is zero, then your promise to pay $2,160 at option expiration would bring in $2,160 today. The net outlay for Strategy B (buy 4 shares and borrow PV of $2,160) would then be: $(4 \times \$720) - \$2,160 = \$720$

   Each option would be worth: $720/7 = $102.86

   The call is worth more when the interest rate is higher (i.e., 1.59%).

29. Value of the call option using Excel Spreadsheet Solution is $8.77.

INPUTS		OUTPUTS		FORMULA FOR OUTPUT IN COLUMN E
Standard deviation (annual)	0.4000	PV(Ex. Price)	48.077	B6/(1+B4)^B3
Maturity (in years)	1.000	d1	0.298	(LN(B5/E2)+(0.5*B2^2)*B3)/(B2*SQRT(B3))
Risk-free rate (effective annual rate)	0.04	d2	–0.102	E3-B2*SQRT(B3)
Stock Price	50	N(d1)	0.617	NORMSDIST(E3)
Exercise price	50	N(d2)	0.459	NORMSDIST(E4)
		B/S call value	8.772	B5*E5 – E2*E6
		B/S put value	6.849	E2*(1–E6) – B5*(1–E5)

30. Solution to each of parts a through e below:

    a.

INPUTS		OUTPUTS		FORMULA FOR OUTPUT IN COLUMN E
Standard deviation (annual)	0.4000	PV(Ex. Price)	46.228	B6/(1+B4)^B3
Maturity (in years)	2.000	d1	0.422	(LN(B5/E2)+(0.5*B2^2)*B3)/(B2*SQRT(B3))
Risk-free rate (effective annual rate)	0.04	d2	–0.144	E3–B2*SQRT(B3)
Stock Price	50	N(d1)	0.663	NORMSDIST(E3)
Exercise price	50	N(d2)	0.443	NORMSDIST(E4)
		B/S call value	12.701	B5*E5 – E2*E6
		B/S put value	8.929	E2*(1–E6) – B5*(1–E5)

The value of the call rises with an increase in the time to expiration.

    b.

INPUTS		OUTPUTS		FORMULA FOR OUTPUT IN COLUMN E
Standard deviation (annual)	0.5000	PV(Ex. Price)	48.077	B6/(1+B4)^B3
Maturity (in years)	1.000	d1	0.328	(LN(B5/E2)+(0.5*B2^2)*B3)/(B2*SQRT(B3))
Risk-free rate (effective annual rate)	0.04	d2	–0.172	E3–B2*SQRT(B3)
Stock Price	50	N(d1)	0.629	NORMSDIST(E3)
Exercise price	50	N(d2)	0.432	NORMSDIST(E4)
		B/S call value	10.671	B5*E5 – E2*E6
		B/S put value	8.748	E2*(1–E6) – B5*(1–E5)

The value of the call rises with an increase in volatility (standard deviation).

c.

INPUTS		OUTPUTS		FORMULA FOR OUTPUT IN COLUMN E
Standard deviation (annual)	0.4000	PV(Ex. Price)	57.692	B6/(1+B4)^B3
Maturity (in years)	1.000	d1	−0.158	(LN(B5/E2)+(0.5*B2^2)*B3)/(B2*SQRT(B3))
Risk-free rate (effective annual rate)	0.04	d2	−0.558	E3–B2*SQRT(B3)
Stock Price	50	N(d1)	0.437	NORMSDIST(E3)
Exercise price	60	N(d2)	0.289	NORMSDIST(E4)
		B/S call value	5.222	B5*E5 – E2*E6
		B/S put value	12.914	E2*(1–E6) – B5*(1–E5)

The value of the call falls with an increase in the exercise price.

d.

INPUTS		OUTPUTS		FORMULA FOR OUTPUT IN COLUMN E
Standard deviation (annual)	0.4000	PV(Ex. Price)	48.077	B6/(1+B4)^B3
Maturity (in years)	1.000	d1	0.754	(LN(B5/E2)+(0.5*B2^2)*B3)/(B2*SQRT(B3))
Risk-free rate (effective annual rate)	0.04	d2	0.354	E3–B2*SQRT(B3)
Stock Price	60	N(d1)	0.775	NORMSDIST(E3)
Exercise price	50	N(d2)	0.638	NORMSDIST(E4)
		B/S call value	15.786	B5*E5 – E2*E6
		B/S put value	3.862	E2*(1–E6) – B5*(1–E5)

The value of the call rises with an increase in the stock price.

e.

INPUTS		OUTPUTS		FORMULA FOR OUTPUT IN COLUMN E
Standard deviation (annual)	0.4000	PV(Ex. Price)	47.170	B6/(1+B4)^B3
Maturity (in years)	1.000	d1	0.346	(LN(B5/E2)+(0.5*B2^2)*B3)/(B2*SQRT(B3))
Risk-free rate (effective annual rate)	0.06	d2	−0.054	E3–B2*SQRT(B3)
Stock Price	50	N(d1)	0.635	NORMSDIST(E3)
Exercise price	50	N(d2)	0.478	NORMSDIST(E4)
		B/S call value	9.197	B5*E5 – E2*E6
		B/S put value	6.367	E2*(1–E6) – B5*(1–E5)

The value of the call rises with an increase in the interest rate.

31. a. The implied volatility for the option in Problem 29 is 43.82%.

INPUTS		OUTPUTS		FORMULA FOR OUTPUT IN COLUMN E
Standard deviation (annual)	0.4382	PV(Ex. Price)	48.077	B6/(1+B4)^B3
Maturity (in years)	1.000	d1	0.309	(LN(B5/E2)+(0.5*B2^2)*B3)/(B2*SQRT(B3))
Risk-free rate (effective annual rate)	0.04	d2	−0.130	E3–B2*SQRT(B3)
Stock Price	50	N(d1)	0.621	NORMSDIST(E3)
Exercise price	50	N(d2)	0.448	NORMSDIST(E4)
		B/S call value	9.500	B5*E5 – E2*E6
		B/S put value	7.577	E2*(1–E6) – B5*(1–E5)

b. The implied volatility for the option in Problem 29 falls to 41.19% if the call option price is only $9. The value of a call option falls if expected volatility is lower.

INPUTS		OUTPUTS		FORMULA FOR OUTPUT IN COLUMN E
Standard deviation (annual)	0.4119	PV(Ex. Price)	48.077	B6/(1+B4)^B3
Maturity (in years)	1.000	d1	0.301	(LN(B5/E2)+(0.5*B2^2)*B3)/(B2*SQRT(B3))
Risk-free rate (effective annual rate)	0.04	d2	−0.111	E3–B2*SQRT(B3)
Stock Price	50	N(d1)	0.618	NORMSDIST(E3)
Exercise price	50	N(d2)	0.456	NORMSDIST(E4)
		B/S call value	9.000	B5*E5 – E2*E6
		B/S put value	7.076	E2*(1–E6) – B5*(1–E5)

Solutions to Chapter 24

Risk Management

1. Insurance is a part of risk management that is similar in many ways to hedging. Both activities are designed to eliminate the firm's exposure to a particular source of risk. Hedging and insurance have several advantages. They can reduce the probability of encountering financial distress, or in extreme cases, bankruptcy. They make the firm's performance less vulnerable to events not under the firm's control, and therefore enable managers and investors to better evaluate performance. By reducing the impact of such random events, they also facilitate planning.

    Hedging and insurance make most sense when the source of uncertainty has a significant impact on the firm's performance. It is not worth the time or effort to protect against events that cannot materially affect the firm.

2. a. She should sell futures. If interest rates rise and bond prices fall, her gain on the futures will offset the loss on the bonds.

   b. He should sell futures. If interest rates rise and bond prices fall, the firm's profits on the futures will offset the lower price the firm will receive for its bonds.

3. Scan *The Wall Street Journal* and you will see a wide array of futures on agricultural commodities, as well as other raw materials. Purchasers of any of these commodities can hedge cost risk by buying futures contracts, and producers can hedge revenue risk by selling futures contracts.

4. The object of hedging is to eliminate risk. If you eliminate uncertainty, you eliminate the happy surprises as well as the unhappy ones. If the farmer wishes to lock in the value of the wheat, then it is inconsistent to argue later that he is subject to the risk of losing the opportunity to sell wheat at a price higher than $9.40. Farmers who are in a position to benefit from increases in wheat prices are at least implicitly speculating on wheat prices, not hedging.

5. The contract size is 5000 bushels, so the farmer who *sells* a wheat futures contract realizes the following cash flows on each contract:

	Futures price	Change in futures price	Cash flow per contract (5,000 × decrease in futures price)
Day 1	$9.83	0.00	0
Day 2	$9.89	+0.06	−300
Day 3	$9.70	−0.19	+950
Day 4	$9.50	−0.20	+1,000
Day 5	$9.60	+0.10	−500
Total		−0.23	+1,150

The sum of the mark to market cash flows equals the total decrease in the futures price times 5000. This is the same payment that would be required if the contract were not marked to market. Only the timing of the cash flows is affected by marking to market.

6. One advantage of holding futures is the greater liquidity (ease of purchasing and selling positions) than is typical in the spot market. Another is the fact that you do not need to buy the commodity. You simply put up the margin on the contract until the maturity date of the contract. This saves the opportunity cost of capital on those funds for the length of the contract. A third advantage is that, if you hold futures instead of the underlying commodity, you will not incur storage, insurance, or spoilage costs on the commodity.

The disadvantage of the futures position is that you do not receive the benefits that might accrue from holding the underlying asset. For example, holding stock rather than stock index futures allows the investor to receive the dividends on the stocks. Holding copper inventories rather than copper futures allows a producer to avoid inventory shortage costs.

7.

		Gold Price		
		$800	$860	$920
a.	Revenues	$800,000	$860,000	$920,000
	Futures contract gain	80000	20,000	−40,000
b.	Total revenues	$880,000	$880,000	$880,000
c.	Revenues	$800,000	$860,000	$920,000
	+ Put option payoff	60,000	0	0
	−Put option costs	6,000	6,000	6,000
	Total revenues	$866,000	$866,000	$926,000

8.

		Gold Price		
		$800	$860	$920
a.	Cost of gold	$800,000	$860,000	$920,000
	+ Cost of call	10,000	10,000	10,000
	− Call option payoff	0	0	60,000
	Net outlay	$810,000	$870,000	$990,000
b.	Cost of gold	$400,000	$430,000	$460,000
	+ Cost of call	20,000	20,000	20,000
	− Call option payoff	0	0	80,000
	Net outlay	$420,000	$450,000	$560,000

The more expensive calls (with the lower exercise price) provide a better outcome (a lower net outlay) when the price of gold is high, but a worse outcome when the price of gold is low.

9.   Suppose you lend $100 today, for one year, at 4% and borrow $100 today for two years at 5%. Your net cash flow today is zero. In one year, you will receive $104, and you will owe: $100 \times (1.05)^2 = \$110.25$ for payment one more year hence.

This is effectively a one-year borrowing agreement at rate:

($110.25/$104) − 1 = 0.060 = 6.0%

This is the forward rate for year 2. Since you can create a 'synthetic loan' at the forward rate, which is less than the bank's offer, you should reject the offer.

10.   One way to protect the position is to sell 10 million yen forward. This locks in the dollar value of the yen you will receive if you get the contract. However, if you do not receive the contract, you will have inadvertently ended up speculating against the yen. Suppose the forward price for delivery in 3 months is ¥105/$, and you agree to sell forward 10 million yen or $95,238. Consider the possible outcomes if the spot rate three months from now will be either ¥100/$ or ¥110/$:

	¥100/$	¥110/$
If you win contract:		
Dollar value of contract	$100,000	$90,909
Profit on forward contract	−4,762	4,329
Total	$ 95,238	$95,238
If you lose contract:		
Dollar value of contract	$ 0	$ 0
Profit on forward contract	−4,762	4,329
Total	−$ 4,762	$ 4,329

If you win the contract, the forward contract locks in the dollar value of the contract at the forward exchange rate. However, if you lose the contract, then your short position in yen will result in losses if the yen appreciates and gains if the yen depreciates. This is a speculative position.

Another approach is to buy put options on yen. If you buy options to sell 10 million yen at an exercise price of ¥105/$, then, if you win the contract, you are guaranteed an exchange rate no worse than ¥105/$ if the yen depreciates, but you can benefit from appreciation in the yen. This *appears* to be superior to the forward hedge, but remember that the options hedge requires that you purchase the put. This hedge can be costly.

11. Assume that the futures price for oil is $20 per barrel. Petrochemical will take a long position to hedge its cost of buying oil. Onnex will take a short position to hedge its revenue from selling oil.

	Oil Price (dollars per barrel)		
Cost for Petrochemical	$80	$90	$100
Cost of 1,000 barrels	$80,000	$90,000	$100,000
− Cash flow on long futures position	−10,000	0	10,000
Net cost	$90,000	$90,000	$ 90,000

	Oil Price (dollars per barrel)		
Revenue for Onnex	$80	$90	$100
Revenue from 1,000 barrels	$80,000	$90,000	$100,000
+ Cash flow on short futures position	10,000	0	−10,000
Net revenues	$90,000	$90,000	$ 90,000

The advantage of futures is the ability to lock in a riskless position without paying any money. The advantage of the option hedge is that you benefit if prices move in one direction without losing if they move in the other direction. However, this asymmetry comes at a price: the cost of the option.

12. You receive the gold at the maturity date, and you pay the futures price *on that date*. Your total payments, including the net proceeds from marking to market, equal the futures price on the day that you enter the futures contract.

The futures price is higher than the current spot price for gold. This reflects the fact that the futures contract ensures your receipt of the gold without tying up your money now. The difference between the spot price and the futures price reflects compensation for the time value of money. Another way to put it is that the spot price must be lower than the futures price in order to compensate investors who buy and store gold for the opportunity cost of their funds until the futures maturity date.

13. The car manufacturers could have bought dollars forward for a specified number of euros (or equivalently, sold euro contracts). This would serve to hedge total profits because, when profits in the U.S. market decrease due to appreciation in the euro, the company would realize greater profits on its futures or forward contracts.

    On the other hand, it is less clear that such hedging would improve the competitive position of the manufacturers. Once the contracts are in place, each firm should still evaluate the car sale as an *incremental* transaction that is independent of any proceeds from the forward position. Is the dollar price charged on each incremental sale enough to cover the incremental costs incurred in euros? If not, the firm may decide to raise the dollar price regardless of any profits on futures contracts. So, while the hedge can stabilize the value of overall profits in the face of currency risk, it is less likely to affect the competitive position of the firm.

14. A currency swap is an agreement to exchange a series of payments in one currency for a specified series of payments in another currency. For example, a U.S. firm that will be buying £1 million of supplies per year from a British producer might enter into a currency swap in which it pays $1.5 million per year and receives £1 million pounds in return. This arrangement locks in the dollar cost of the parts purchased from the U.K. supplier.

    An interest rate swap is an exchange of a series of fixed payments for a series of payments linked to market interest rates. For example, a bank that pays its depositors an interest rate that rises and falls with the level of general market rates might enter a swap to exchange a fixed payment of $60,000 per year for a floating payment equal to the T-bill rate times $1 million. (For example, if the T-bill rate is 4 percent, then the floating rate payment would be $40,000.) This arrangement locks in the amount of the bank's expenses: the receipt of floating rate payments offsets the payments to depositors, so the bank is left with only the fixed payments on the swap agreement.

15. Notice that, while Firm A pays a higher interest rate in both markets (presumably because it presents greater default risk), it has a *relative* disadvantage when borrowing in the U.S., where its cost of funds is 2% higher than Firm B's. In comparison, Firm A gets relatively better terms in euro countries, where its cost of funds is only 1% higher than Firm B's. Instead of borrowing in the desired currency, each firm should borrow in the currency for which it has a comparative advantage. Then the firms can swap cash flows back into the desired currency. Suppose that A sets a goal of reducing its dollar interest rate to 7.5%, which is 0.5% lower than its rate on a dollar loan. Any additional savings from the swap will accrue to Firm B. Here is how the swap might work.

Step 1: Firm B borrows $1,000 at a 6% rate in the U.S. (where it has a comparative advantage) and is obligated to pay $60 per year for four years and $1,060 in the fifth year.

Step 2: Firm A calculates that the present value of Firm B's debt payments, using its own target 7.5% interest rate, is $939.31. Therefore, Firm A borrows this amount of money in Switzerland, where it has its comparative advantage. Firm A borrows 939.31 euros. At a 6% interest rate, Firm A must pay:

$$0.06 \times 939.31 = 56.36 \text{ euros per year for four years}$$

And then, in the fifth year, Firm A must pay: $56.36 + 939.31 = 995.67$ euros

Step 3: The two firms enter a swap arrangement to exchange cash flows equal to the other's principal and interest payments. So Firm A pays $60 to Firm B and receives 56.36 euros per year for four years. In year 5, Firm A pays $1,060 in return for 995.67 euros.

Firm A's net cash flows are as follows: It initially receives $939.31 by exchanging the proceeds from its euro borrowing into dollars. It uses the income from the swap to pay its euro bonds, and pays $60 per year for four years and $1,060 in year 5 on the swap. The effective interest rate (yield to maturity) on this loan is 7.5%, which is better than Firm A could have done in the U.S. (To determine the yield, think of Firm A as effectively issuing a five-year 6% coupon bond for a price of $939.31.)

Firm B receives $1,000 initially, which it exchanges for 1,000 euros. Its net cash outflows in the following years are 56.36 euros per year for five years and an additional payment of 939.31 euros in the fifth year. This corresponds to a yield to maturity of 4.53%, which is a better rate than it could have obtained by borrowing in euros directly. (This is the yield to maturity on a bond sold with a coupon rate of 6%, face value 939.31, at a price of 1,000.)

Each party receives a better rate than would have been available by borrowing directly in the preferred currency.